THE OTHER SIDE OF THE NIGHT

Also by Daniel Allen Butler

"Unsinkable"—The Full Story
of RMS Titanic

The Lusitania: *The Life, Loss, and Legacy*
of an Ocean Legend

Warrior Queens—the Queen Mary *and*
Queen Elizabeth *in World War Two*

The Age of Cunard: A Transatlantic History, 1939–2003

Distant Victory: The Battle of Jutland
and the Allied Triumph in the First World War

The First Jihad: The Battle for Khartoum
and the Dawn of Militant Islam

THE OTHER SIDE OF THE NIGHT

The *Carpathia*, the *Californian*,
and the Night the
Titanic Was Lost

By
DANIEL ALLEN BUTLER

CASEMATE
Philadelphia & Newbury

Published in the United States of America in 2009 by
CASEMATE
1016 Warrior Road, Drexel Hill, PA 19026

and in Great Britain by
CASEMATE
17 Cheap Street, Newbury RG20 5DD

Copyright 2009 © Daniel Allen Butler

ISBN 978-1-935149-02-6

Cataloging-in-publication data is available from the Library of Congress
and the British Library.

10 9 8 7 6 5 4 3 2 1

Printed and bound in the United States of America.

For a complete list of Casemate titles please contact:

CASEMATE PUBLISHERS
Telephone (610) 853-9131, Fax (610) 853-9146
E-mail: casemate@casematepublishing.com

CASEMATE PUBLISHERS
Telephone (01635) 231091, Fax (01635) 41619
E-mail: casemate-uk@casematepublishing.co.uk

CONTENTS

To
the Memory of

Walter Lord

Friend and mentor,
who first showed us all that
"Night to Remember"
so many years ago . . .

FOR THOSE IN PERIL ON THE SEA...

Eternal Father, strong to save,

Whose arm hath bound the restless wave,

Who biddest the mighty ocean deep

Its own appointed limits keep;

Oh, hear us when we cry to Thee,

For those in peril on the sea!

O Christ! Whose voice the waters heard

And hushed their raging at Thy Word,

Who walked on the foaming deep,

And calm amidst its rage didst sleep,

Oh, hear us when we cry to Thee,

For those in peril on the sea!

Most Holy Spirit! Who didst brood

Upon the chaos dark and rude,

And bid its angry tumult cease,

And give, for wild confusion, peace;

Oh, hear us when we cry to Thee,

For those in peril on the sea!

O Trinity of love and power!

Our family shield in danger's hour;

From rock and tempest, fire and foe,

Protect us wheresoever we go;

Thus evermore shall rise to Thee

Glad hymns of praise from land and sea.

—*"Eternal Father, Strong to Save"*
written by William Whiting, 1860

THE OTHER SIDE OF THE NIGHT

And those who have survived will now quietly begin
to forget the dead: they won't remember
who was who or which was which.
It is all over.

—Jean Anouilh, *Antigone* (1946)

Who died? Who did the murder? Tell us now.

—Sophocles, *Antigone* (500 BC)

Chapter 1

THE CRUELEST OCEAN

At the dawn of the Age of Exploration, as the darkness of the Middle Ages began to recede, the most important sea route in the world was the one that began in the waters surrounding western Europe, ran south down the coast of Africa to round the Cape of Good Hope, and gave out into the broad expanse of the Indian Ocean. It was this route that allowed Portuguese and Dutch traders, using navigational secrets that they jealously guarded from the eyes of their Spanish and English competitors, to bring the flavors and textures of the mysterious and exotic Far East to a cold and drab European continent: spices, silks, ivory, jade, jewels, fruit trees, and tea.

But though the trade route to the East would remain a source of immense wealth for another three hundred years, once Christopher Columbus stumbled upon the New World in 1492 it slowly began to give pride of place to another passage. In the decades that followed Columbus' voyages, the Spanish and Portuguese began to systematically plunder the cultures and empires of Central and South America, and for the next two centuries a steady procession of galleons passed back and forth between Europe and the Americas. Those sailing east were laden with treasure, while those sailing west were filled with explorers, missionaries, adventurers, and eventually settlers. Full-bellied, with steep-sided hulls and high forecastles and poopdecks, these ships were slow, cumbersome, and at best only indifferent sailers, often vulnerable to the ferocious storms that ripped up and down the

American coasts. Nevertheless, the sheer volume of booty they carried back to Lisbon and Cadiz caused the westward passages across the Atlantic to usurp the primacy of the route around the southern tip of Africa, which fell into an eclipse from which it would never escape, as the fortunes made in trading spices in India were soon surpassed by the fortunes gathered from the looted treasures of the Incas, Mayas, Toltecs, and Aztecs.

In the 17th and 18th centuries, as the Spanish and Portuguese empires began their decline and the number of galleons sailing across the Atlantic diminished in proportion, their place being taken primarily by British ships. These were called East Indiamen—they were stout, bluff, and highly seaworthy—and they carried a commerce in trade goods rather than plunder between the Old World and the New. As the beginning of the 19th century approached, the jewel in the maritime crown of shipping lanes was the route that spanned the Atlantic from Great Britain to North America.

What made it so valuable was the simple fact that Britain's economy was the fastest-growing in the world, while Canada and the American colonies were its largest markets. Britain supplied most of North America's demands for industry as well as meeting its requirements for precision manufactures, along with specialized materials and luxuries that were as yet beyond the Americans' and Canadians' ability to produce. Russian oak from the Baltic states, British railroad rolling stock, Austrian crystal, German optics, French wines and fabrics, Irish laces, all were carried to the United States in British ships. On their return crossings, those same ships would have cargo holds full of raw cotton from the American South, Canadian and American ores, pine and fir from the Pacific Northwest and Canada, and countless tons of grain. As more sophisticated and diverse commerce developed, ships began to be more specialized, their size, hull forms, and sail plans adapted to specific roles, be they carrying cotton or tobacco, tea or coffee beans, passengers to Europe or immigrants to the United States—or, given over to darker tasks, rum-running and slaving.

Yet no matter what form of trade or commerce a ship might be undertaking as it made its way across the Atlantic, it was never an easy or safe passage. In particular, the North Atlantic soon came to be regarded as the cruelest ocean. Capricious and chimerical, the North Atlantic could transform herself from a vista of gently rolling swells passing beneath an azure sky to a maelstrom of towering waves driven by howling winds under glowering leaden clouds, and then to a smooth, tranquil calm under impossibly bright stars, all in a matter of hours. Her tricks were many, her weapons legion: the North Atlantic could conjure up impenetrable fog to confuse and bewilder helmsmen, driving rain that blinded helm and lookout alike, wind-driven sleet that could abrade the paint from a ship's hull or tear a topman from the rigging, hurricane-force winds, seas sixty . . . eighty . . . a hundred feet high—and always at her disposal she had one of her most subtle devices: ice.

The mot of Samuel Johnson, that an ocean voyage was much like being thrown into jail with the added opportunity of being drowned, has been repeated often enough that it has become something of a weak joke. Yet in Johnson's day it was a profound, if acerbic, observation, made all the more so by its undeniable truth. Passage across the Atlantic meant being confined to cramped, dimly lit and poorly ventilated quarters, for weeks, sometimes months, on end, while being fed a monotonous diet of barely edible food. Nor was the chance of being drowned inconsiderable, for throughout most of the 18th century nearly one in every five ships which set sail from London or Bristol, New York, Boston, Halifax, Southampton or Liverpool never arrived at its intended port.

Records exist to bear this out. Historians estimate that in the past 400 years, over a thousand ships have been lost just along the North Carolina coastline alone, a treacherous stretch of water known as "The Graveyard of the Atlantic." Farther up the Atlantic, off the coast of New England, records show that in the years between 1790 and 1850, three out of every five American sailors working those waters would eventually lose their lives to drowning. It is a matter of official note that, from 1840 to 1893, 7,523 people perished as 125 passenger ships were lost on the North Atlantic. Often the circumstances were such that a ship setting out on what would prove to be her final voyage would simply sail into oblivion. Running afoul of ice, winds, waves, or the ever-present threat of a fire on board, unless by some fortunate chance another passing vessel was nearby to render assistance, a ship which found itself in distress was doomed.

For the most part, the missing ships were merchant vessels mainly carrying cargo, along with a handful of passengers, and were crewed by some fifty to sixty sailors. Records of the losses, though not thorough by modern standards, are plentiful but obscure: more attention was paid to the vanished cargoes than to the lives lost, as those keeping the records were mostly insurers who, while not entirely indifferent to the fate of the crews aboard lost ships, had financial losses as their first priority. As for any passengers aboard a ship gone missing, their fate was accepted as simply one of the risks taken when crossing the open ocean. One of the hidden barbs in Samuel Johnson's comment was the implication that an ocean voyage was something that no sane person ever willingly undertook, and that even when necessary there was something vaguely disreputable about it.

That attitude began shifting as Western Europe and North America moved into the 19th century. As the Industrial Revolution took hold on both continents, business became more international, compelling more and more industrialists, businessmen, and merchants to hazard the trip across the North Atlantic for commercial purposes. At the same time the social changes being wrought in the nations of Western Europe, particularly in Great Britain, transforming agrarian communities into industrial societies, created a surplus population which began emigrating from Europe to Canada and the United States, a migration which would gradually shape the character of both continents.

Suddenly there was a new industry on the North Atlantic, whole shipping lines springing up devoted to carrying passengers as well as cargo. Names that would become household words in a few decades' time appeared in the newspapers, advertising crossings to and from Liverpool, Cobh (later Queenstown), London, Hamburg, Bremen, New York, Boston, Philadelphia, and Halifax—names like Cunard, White Star, Collins, Inman, Hamburg-Amerika, Norddeutscher-Lloyd, and Holland-America. People began moving across the ocean in unprecedented numbers, until hundreds, then eventually thousands, of passengers were being carried by individual ships at one time. But while the nature of business on the North Atlantic had changed, the ocean itself hadn't, and when one of these passenger-laden ships went missing, the loss of life was no longer negligible. In fact, it could be horrific.

One of first recorded passenger ships to disappear was the square-rigged packet *Lady of the Lake,* bound from England to Quebec in 1833, when she was lost in mid-Atlantic with 215 passengers and crew aboard. It was believed that she struck an iceberg. A similar fate overtook the *Ocean Queen*, which disappeared somewhere in mid-ocean with ninety souls aboard her in 1834. Two years later the packet *Driver* with 372 people aboard sailed from Boston and was never seen again. Another tragedy came in 1840, when the 222-ton *Rosalie*, built in 1838, vanished in the Sargasso Sea. In September 1853, the emigrant ship *Annie Jane* foundered somewhere west of Scotland, taking all 348 passengers and crew with her, leaving not a trace.

Sometimes there were tantalizing hints as to the fates of missing ships. In August 1840 the steamship *President*, ostensibly the pride of the American merchant fleet, made a somewhat unimpressive debut as she took more than sixteen days to cross from New York to Liverpool on her maiden voyage. Despite the extravagant claims of speed made by her owners, the *President*'s crossing was fully three days longer than the rival Cunard Line's new *Acadia*, also on her maiden voyage. But the *President* soon became a popular ship and usually sailed with a full or nearly full passenger list. The only persistent criticism of her was that her coal consumption was considered by some of her officers to be excessive, and on one occasion she had to turn back to New York to avoid running out of coal in mid-Atlantic.

On March 11, 1841, the *President* left New York with 136 passengers and crew aboard, and almost immediately was caught in a fierce gale. An American packet, the *Orpheus*, saw her two days later, "rising on top of a tremendous sea, pitching and laboring very heavily." She was never seen again. There were only a few clues to her fate, mostly scattered reports of wreckage found floating on the sea, but eventually the conclusion was inevitable—the *President* had sunk, taking everyone aboard with her.

Rigged as she was like any other steamer of the day with a full set of masts and yards, she should have been able to ride out almost any storm under sail, even if she were deprived of the power of her engines. What is most likely was that she encountered a rogue wave—

at the time a little-known phenomenon—one of those enormous walls of water that suddenly rears up before or alongside a ship, breaking over it with thousands of tons of water, sufficient to reduce even the stoutest wooden hull to flinders in moments. It was only one of many weapons the North Atlantic had at her disposal to teach respect to those who failed to show her sufficient deference.

Whatever the exact cause, the disappearance of the *President* was like a brooding spectre that hovered over the Atlantic for a long time. The disaster badly frightened those travelers who had to make a transatlantic crossing, and they switched their bookings from steamers to sailing packets in droves, although it was never explained how the fact that the *President* was a steamship had contributed to her disappearance. Yet, a year later, the number of passengers making the crossing on steamships was barely half of what it had been before the *President* was lost. There was more to come.

Not all ships that were lost simply sailed into oblivion. On September 27, 1854, the speedy *Arctic*, the finest ship in Collins' fleet, six days out of Liverpool and about sixty miles south of Cape Race, Newfoundland, was caught in a heavy fog and rammed by the small French steamer *Vesta*. At first the damage to the *Arctic* seemed slight, but it soon became obvious that the flooding was rising faster than the ship's pumps could cope. The *Arctic*'s captain, James Luce, steered his ship toward Newfoundland, hoping to run her into shallow water and save her.

But while she was still some twenty miles short of her goal, the rising water quenched the fires in the *Arctic*'s boilers and she lost all power. With the ship's situation now hopeless, her captain ordered the passengers into lifeboats. In what was one of the saddest chapters of the history of the American merchant marine, the *Arctic*'s crew, abandoning all pretense of discipline, commandeered the boats—in some cases physically throwing passengers out—and rowed away, leaving those still on board to their fate. Shortly afterward the ship sank, taking with her almost 400 lives, leaving only forty-five survivors.

Tragedy would again strike the Collins Line two years later. In late January 1856, Cunard's brand-new *Persia* was ready to set out on her maiden voyage from Liverpool to New York. By purest chance, the then-fastest ship on the Atlantic run, the Collins Line's *Pacific*, had left

Liverpool just three days before with forty-five passengers and 141 crew aboard. Although the captain of the *Persia* was firm in his protests that there would be no "race" to New York between his ship and the *Pacific*, the public certainly anticipated such a contest. There was much belching of smoke and furious churning of paddlewheels when the *Persia* pulled away from the dock that morning, but unknown to those watching her depart, there would be no record crossing for the *Persia* on this voyage. Five days out of Liverpool, making well over eleven knots, she ran headlong into a field of ice. Her bow was damaged—sixteen feet of her hull plating had its rivets sheered off—and her starboard paddlewheel and its housing were crushed and crumpled. Her speed reduced by more than half, down by the head, nevertheless the *Persia* pressed on to New York, her iron hull having withstood an impact that would have shivered a wooden-hulled vessel.

When the *Persia* limped into New York on February 9, there was no sign of the *Pacific*—she had literally vanished without a trace. As more and more ships made port in New York and Boston and reported the extent of the icefield that the *Persia* had encountered, it became clear what had most likely happened to the *Pacific*. Running at eleven knots or better, she had driven into the ice, and the impact which the *Persia*'s iron hull had been able to absorb had overpowered the wooden keel and frames of the *Pacific*, sending her to the bottom with everyone aboard her. It would be more than a century before her wreck was found—in the same waters where the *Persia* had rammed the ice floe.

Disaster would twice overtake the Inman Line as well. In 1854, the *City of Glasgow*, a beautiful Clyde-built ship, disappeared in the North Atlantic with 480 passengers and crew aboard her. Sixteen years later, somewhere between New York and Liverpool, the *City of Boston*, with 177 passengers and crew, vanished forever. It's believed that she was a victim of a fire onboard; certainly fire caused the loss of Hamburg-Amerika's *Austria* in 1858, costing 471 lives.

Collision was a hazard as well, as ships would get lost in fog, storm, and mist, and blunder into each other. Almost 400 people drowned when Hamburg-Amerika's *Cimbria* was accidentally rammed and sunk. In 1891 the Anchor Line's *Utopia* sank after colliding with a collier, and 562 aboard her were lost. Norddeutscher-Lloyd's *Elbe* was the victim of a collision in 1895, at the cost of 332 passengers and crew; in 1898 the French Line's *La Bourgogne* was rammed by a merchantman and quickly sank, taking 549 lives with her.

Naval ships were by no means immune from the North Atlantic's furies either. HMS *Atalanta* had begun her career with the Royal Navy as HMS *Juno* in 1844. After service in the Pacific she became in turn a storeship, a barracks, and the headquarters of the Portsmouth Dockyard police before being converted into a training ship in 1878 and renamed. Sailing to Bermuda in January 1888, *Atalanta* arrived there on the 29th, and set sail for home on the 31st with 250 young cadets and thirty-one officers and ratings aboard. She never arrived at Portsmouth, nor was any trace of her or any clue to her fate ever found. Her disappearance was considered a national catastrophe in Britain.

What marked each of these tragedies–along with countless others—was the inability of the ship in distress to summon aid from any other ship that was out of immediate sight or sound. The problem was, in a nutshell, communications—or rather a lack of them. The simple truth was that once a ship sailed out of sight of land, it was as remote and inaccessible to the rest of the world as if it were on the far side of the moon. Yet, ships die hard, and save for those rare occurrences when the sea would literally rear up and smash apart some hapless vessel, hammering its remains to the bottom, there was almost always time for a ship struggling to survive to summon assistance, to signal her distress—but only if there was another ship near enough to see or hear. But unless some means was devised that allowed a ship at sea to signal "over the horizon" to other ships or even the shore, the fate of any vessel finding itself alone and in distress was inevitable.

The solution would be provided at the beginning of the 20th century by a young Italian engineer, Guglielmo Marconi. Born in Bologna, Italy, on April 25, 1874, he was the second son of Giuseppe Marconi, an Italian country gentleman, and Annie Jameson, the daughter of a member of the Irish gentry who had been born and raised in Daphne Castle in County Wexford, Ireland. Demonstrating a powerful intellect even as a youth, Marconi was privately educated at schools in Bologna, Florence, and Leghorn, where he showed a keen interest in physical sciences—particularly electricity—in early adolescence. Constructing his own laboratory at his father's country estate at Pontecchio, he began experimenting in 1895, building on the work of Hertz, Preece, Lodge, Maxwell, Righi, and other scientists who had specialized in electrical studies.

Working carefully and methodically, that same year he was able to construct a device that produced controlled, modulated electric sparks which were translated into electrical signals that could be picked up by a receiving device over a distance of one and a half miles without the use of wires. The system was practical, reliable, and in one fell swoop, Marconi became the inventor of "wireless" telegraphy. The potential applications for such a system were immediately obvious to Marconi, and he attempted to interest the Italian government in his invention, only to be rebuffed. So he did exactly what any other young inventor who had created some new technological marvel did during the 1890s—he took it to London.

Communications was one of the Victorians' great fascinations. Postal deliveries six times a day in the cities, telegraph lines running to every town and most villages, great underwater cables cris-crossing the oceans—these were among the hallmarks of the high tide of the British Empire. With colonies, protectorates, territories, mandates, embassies, and consulates girdling the globe, not to mention an equally vast collection of business enterprises, the Victorians' obsession with communications was an understandable consequence of the need to manage the far-flung marches of the Empire. When young Marconi arrived in London in 1896, he immediately took his apparatus to the Engineer-in-Chief of the Post Office, Mr. (later Sir) William Preece. Preece, who was the antithesis of the stereotypical myopic civil servant appointed only on the basis of whom rather than what he knew, immediately saw the value as well as the potential of wireless, and set the process in motion by which later that year Marconi was granted the world's first patent for a system of wireless telegraphy.

A series of successful demonstrations followed in London, on Salisbury Plain, and across the Bristol Channel, all of which received considerable attention in the British press. Marconi saw to this, for in addition to being an engineering genius he had a shrewd business mind, and understood that good press coverage all but guaranteed the success of his next venture. That came in July 1897 when he formed The Wireless Telegraph & Signal Company, which three years later was renamed Marconi's Wireless Telegraph Company Limited. So successful was he in promoting his invention, and so successful was his wireless system in operation, that within a few years "Marconi" became synonymous with "wireless" and the two were often used interchangeably.

In 1898, both the Royal Navy and the United States Navy began installing experimental wireless sets aboard some of their warships, demonstrating that wireless communication at sea was a practical proposition, and the following year Marconi established regular wireless communication between France and England across the English Channel, setting up permanent stations on the Isle of Wight, at Bournemouth, and later at in Dorset. In 1900 he took out his famous patent No. 7777 for "tuned" or "syntonic telegraphy"; that is, wireless circuits that could be "tuned" to send and receive on a specific, regulated frequency rather than across the entire electro-magnetic spectrum. This single development would prove to be the foundation of the radio, television, and computer industries of the 20th century and beyond.

As his experiments continued, Marconi expanded his devices' capabilities. Marconi International Marine was formed in April 1900 to develop shipboard wireless sets for merchant vessels and passenger ships, the first installations being undertaken the following year. In December 1901, he staged a demonstration that proved wireless waves were unaffected by the curvature of the Earth, transmitting the first transatlantic wireless signals between Poldhu, Cornwall—near Land's End, the uttermost southwestern corner of England—and St. John's, Newfoundland, a distance of 2,100 miles. Exactly a year later he transmitted the first complete messages to Poldhu from stations at Glace Bay, Nova Scotia, and later Cape Cod, Massachusetts, tests that resulted in the establishment of the first transatlantic commercial wireless service in 1907.

Almost immediately there was competition. There was France's Compagnie Generale Telegraphique, which had played a major role in laying the first transatlantic telegraph cables in the 1880s; the

American Marconi Company, wholly independent of the various British Marconi corporations, which was formed in 1899 and began supplying most of the American merchant marine; while the largest competitor was the giant German electrical firm Telefunken, formed in 1903 from the merger of divisions of two rival firms, AEG and Braun-Siemens, which supplied wireless equipment used by the German government, the German Army, and the German Navy, and which also had a monopoly on the sets installed in German merchant ships.

The rivalry between British Marconi and American Marconi was intense but good-natured, the only real source of friction between the two firms being the British use of International Morse Code, while American Marconi insisted on using American Morse. The difference was much like that between British spoken English and American spoken English—close but not always compatible. The French, of course, simply made a point of being French, and their operators only contacted the wireless stations of other nationalities when it was absolutely necessary.

Marconi's rivalry with Telefunken, on the other hand, was barely civil. While an enduring complaint about wireless of that era was the deliberate interference often caused by operators of one company with the signals of another, the worst and most frequent offenders were the German Telefunken operators, who, as an assertion of the alleged superiority of German wireless, often seemed to take an almost childish delight in interfering with Marconi messages.

For the wireless system to work it required trained personnel to operate it. Marconi Marine operators received their instruction at the Marconi School in Liverpool (called by its students the Tin Tabernacle), where they learned much more than simply the dot-dash rudiments of Morse. The school had several sets of working wireless apparatuses that were used for instruction, including a half-kilowatt set which had a range of about 100 miles, which was used for basic instruction, as well as several of the standard one and a half-kilowatt sets that were used on most Marconi-equipped ocean liners and a powerful five-kilowatt set. The school accommodated sixty pupils and the average term of instruction spanned ten months. Courses in electricity, magnetism, radio-wave propagation, troubleshooting of equipment, and the new regulations, such that they were, of the International Radiotelegraphy Convention, were all included.

The Convention was very clear about how wireless operators were supposed to conduct themselves, and quite explicit about the priority of certain types of transmissions. The courses in radio wave propagation explained to the operators the effect of the ionosphere on wireless transmission and why both transmission and reception were clearer and longer ranged at night than during the day. Of course, this benefit in range and clarity often meant that the majority of a wireless operator's work was done during hours when most of the rest of the world was asleep.

The young men who graduated from the "Tin Tabernacle" quickly found themselves employed on ships all over the world. They were a distinctive type of youth, always intelligent, often high-strung, energetic and intense, yet time and again they would prove remarkably cool and calm in an emergency, carrying out their duties even when their own lives seemed to be in danger. Their position aboard the ships on which they served was somewhat peculiar: although they would be required to sign the ship's articles and were subject to the orders and discipline of the ship's captain and officers, they weren't actually part of the crew. The company which owned the particular vessel in question would contract with Marconi Marine for their services, so that they remained Marconi employees no matter to which ship of what shipping line they were posted aboard.

At that time there was no requirement for a 24-hour wireless watch to be maintained by any ships, save warships, so the wireless operators usually worked a schedule set for them by their ship's captain. On large ships, such as the fast German liners or Cunard's soon-to-be-launched *Lusitania* and *Mauretania*, there would be two wireless operators who alternated shifts, twelve hours on, twelve off, seven days a week. Smaller vessels warranted only one operator, who usually pulled duty in fifteen- to eighteen-hour stretches.

It was not hard work in the conventional sense, but the long hours of enforced immobility and intense concentration as the operator sat at his table, headphones on, key at hand, were exhausting. The pay did little to compensate for this: a senior operator only made £8 ($40) a month, a junior operator only £5 ($25). It was the knowledge that they were part of a small, select fraternity, sitting on the leading edge of a new, revolutionary technology that few people understood and even fewer could operate, capable of snatching messages seemingly out of the thin air with their ungainly looking apparatus, that kept most operators at their stations.

The skill of the early wireless operators was nothing short of amazing. Spending long hours, sitting almost motionless, only their hands moving as they worked the key of their apparatus; or sitting listening through their bulky headphones as they sought to pluck the signals from other stations out of the ether. It was all far more difficult than is popularly supposed. Instead of the carefully modulated buzzes, beeps, or tones that today are most commonly associated with Morse Code, the sounds made by open spark transmitters of the day were more like bursts and crashes of controlled static, which resembled nothing so much as the interference distant lightning will create on a radio. And yet these bursts and crashes, and the various signals into which they would evolve, would save thousands of lives in the decades to come.

From the very beginning of his work Marconi had made it clear that his primary goal was to perfect wireless communication in order to bring an end to the isolation of ships at sea. An accident to the East Goodwin lightship, moored off the Goodwin Sands at the Dover Straits in the English Channel, offered the first proof of his success. On the evening of April 28, 1899, wrapped in a thick fog, she was rammed by the freighter *R.F. Matthews*. The lightship had been equipped with one of Marconi's first shipboard apparatuses, and within minutes a message had been sent to the wireless station at the South Foreland lighthouse: "Help, we have just been run into by the steamer 'R.F. Matthews' ... Our bows are damaged."

A lifeboat was quickly dispatched to the lightship but fortunately the damage was relatively minor and the crew was in no danger. Yet the incident made it clear to even the most casual observer that communications between ships, and between ships and the shore, were now not only possible but practical. In the words of historian Warren Tute, in his book *Atlantic Conquest*, "Wireless telegraphy was to deprive the sea of its ancient terror of silence." The ultimate proof of that came ten years later.

On January 22, 1909, the White Star Line's R.M.S. *Republic* left New York bound for Naples, Italy with 525 passengers and 297 crew aboard. Just before six o'clock the next morning she found herself surrounded by thick fog 175 miles from the Ambrose Lighthouse. Her skipper, Captain William Sealby, reduced speed to barely steerageway and began sounding the ship's steam whistle at short intervals. It was a situation fraught with danger, for in heavy fog, doing anything could lead to disaster—including doing nothing. It was a circumstance that had led to catastrophe for many other ships—and was about to do so again.

Unknown to Sealby, the Lloyd-Italiano steamer *Florida*, inbound for New York from Naples, was not far from his ship, thoroughly lost. The fog swallowed up the *Republic*'s whistle, and though she was ablaze with light from bow to stern, the fog was so heavy that the glow was diffused and muffled at only a few hundred yards off. At 5:51 a.m., the *Florida* suddenly loomed out of the darkness on the *Republic*'s port side and drove her bow deep into the White Star liner, almost squarely amidships. The *Republic*'s engine room immediately started flooding, and before long it became clear to her chief engineer that the pumps, while slowing the inrush of water, would be unable to stop it. When the water rose high enough to reach the boilers, the *Republic* would lose all power and quickly sink. Captain Sealby swiftly mustered the passengers and crew, and began preparing to abandon ship.

Had the collision taken place a decade earlier, the situation would have been exceedingly grim for the *Republic*, as the only ship known to be nearby was the *Florida*, now drifting unseen somewhere in the fog, the extent of her own damage then unknown. But circumstances were different in this case: the *Republic* was fitted with an early version of the 1½-kilowatt Marconi wireless, and Sealby instructed the Marconi operator, 25-year-old Jack Binns, to send out a call for assistance—the international distress signal "CQD." Binns quickly made contact with a sister ship, White Star's *Baltic*, which was 200 miles away but coming hard, as well as the U.S. Coast Guard's Nantucket wireless station. Soon that station was relaying the *Republic*'s signals as power began to fade on the sinking ship, and over the next thirty-six hours Binns remained at his post, as a half-dozen ships, including the Cunard Line's *Lucania*, the French Line's *La Tourraine*, the Inman Line's *New York*, and a U.S. Coast Guard Cutter, the *Gresham*, began converging on the sinking *Republic*.

Meanwhile the *Florida* had drifted back out of the fog and lay a few hundred yards off the *Republic*'s port side. Her captain had the ship sounded and found that her collision bulkhead was holding firm, so Captain Sealby proposed that the *Republic*'s passengers and crew be taken aboard the Italian ship. A daring transfer of passengers and crew began, using the *Republic*'s lifeboats, working in relays against rising swells and rain, shuttling back and forth between the sinking liner and the *Florida*. It would take almost twelve hours to get everyone but a handful of the *Republic*'s officers and crew off the sinking ship. Now the problem was that the *Florida* was dangerously overloaded, and it was only when the *Baltic* appeared on the scene and took off the excess passengers that the danger was finally past for the small Italian steamer.

The fog began to lift, and Captain Sealby, along with the forty-six crewmen who remained aboard, began preparing the *Republic* to be taken in tow, in the hope that she could be run into shallow water and saved. She was slowly settling stern-first, and though some progress was made toward Nantucket, at a little before 8:30 p.m. on the 26th, the *Republic* began sinking rapidly. Within minutes she was gone, Captain Sealby and his crew being swept off the ship as she went under.

Miraculously, only four lives had been lost in the entire incident, all victims of the collision itself. It created a stir on both sides of the Atlantic, where both Captain Sealby and Jack Binns were rightly hailed as heroes. Binns in particular was singled out: he had spent almost thirty-six hours at his wireless key, without relief, without sleep, with little to eat or drink except an occasional cup of coffee, exposed to the wind and rain the entire time, for the collision had torn away two of the wireless office's walls. His success in reaching ships hundreds of miles away that otherwise would never have known of the *Republic*'s plight, but were able to come to her assistance, drew attention to the lifesaving potential of wireless as nothing else could have done.

The dramatic image of the *Baltic*'s dash through storm and fog in

In quick succession the twin German shipping lines, Hamburg-Amerika and Norrdeutscher-Lloyd, introduced a series of very fast, very luxurious liners that quickly began skimming the cream of the North Atlantic passenger trade, and were making enormous inroads on the volume of immigrant traffic being carried to the New World as well. The first of these ships was the mean-looking, imposing, unmistakably German *Kaiser Wilhelm der Grosse*. In the words of John Malcolm Brinnin, she ushered in "a period of steamship history when the landscapes of Valhalla enscrolled on the walls and ceilings of grand saloons would all but collapse under their own weight, as well as a period when Teutonic efficiency united with matchless engine power would give Germany all the honors on the northern seas. And when the wits of the first decade of the [Twentieth] Century began to say something was 'hideously' or 'divinely' 'North German Lloyd' they meant, according to one American contemporary, 'two of everything but the kitchen range, then gilded.'" Her pretentiousness slowed her not a whit, for the *Kaiser Wilhelm der Grosse* immediately took the Blue Ribband (the honor for speed champion), romping across the North Atlantic on her maiden voyage in early 1897 at nearly 22 knots.

Not content in merely besting the British steamship lines, whose transatlantic ascendancy had heretofore been unchallenged, the Germans embarrassed them by next introducing the *Deutschland*, which belonged to the Hamburg-Amerika Line, crossing the "Big Pond" at a speed of nearly 23 knots. Long, low, with a sleek four-funneled superstructure, the *Deutschland* looked the very part of the Atlantic greyhound. Yet her pre-eminence was to last less than a year as, adding insult to injury, the new *Kronprinz Wilhelm* set a new record at 23½ knots. The year after that the *Kaiser Wilhelm II* proved a shade faster still. This Teutonic monopoly on the Blue Ribband was more than Great Britain could stand—a head to head showdown was approaching between these upstart Germans and the established maritime prowess of the British.

Almost overnight, it seemed, Cunard's entire fleet seemed dated and obsolescent, a collection of dowdy, frumpy old ladies whose staid conservatism, which had once seemed to be part of their appeal, was now seen as quaint and homely—and hopelessly passé. Even the vaunted claim, "The Cunard has never lost a life," which had been invoked with suitable gravity for more than half a century any time a newcomer to the North Atlantic appeared to challenge the line, now lost its potency. Safety was no longer enough, as passengers wanted speed and luxury just as much, if not even more. That the Germans were each carrying roughly twice as many passengers as Cunard was bad enough, but because of the sensation these new ships were creating for Norddeutscher-Lloyd and Hamburg-Amerika, along with the accompanying publicity, they were attracting still more passengers. Even if a traveler wasn't able to make his or her crossing on one of the German speedsters, the cachet of sailing on one their stablemates was still attractive. And because Cunard, like the German lines, relied heavily on the immigrant trade to make its profits, any decline in the number of fare-paying passengers carried serious financial consequences.

Cunard's response to the German challengers would soon appear, first in the form of the *Caronia* and *Carmania*—the "Pretty Sisters,"—and ultimately in the awesome shapes of the *Lusitania* and *Mauretania*, ships that would be triumphs of speed and luxury on such a scale that the German shipping lines would never recover their brief pre-eminence on the North Atlantic. But those magnificent ships were still to come when construction began on a handful of modern, if somewhat modest, Cunard liners. The first step taken toward refurbishing the fleet was an order placed for three liners, two to be built by C.S. Swan & Hunter and one by the John Brown shipyard. The first two would be the *Ivernia* and *Saxonia*, followed two years later by a ship that would be neither the largest nor the fastest ship in the line's service, but would ultimately become one of the most famous in the whole history of Cunard: the *Carpathia*.

Built in the Swan Hunter yard, the *Ivernia* was launched in late 1899, and entered service in April 1900. At close to 14,000 gross tons, she was the largest ship yet built for Cunard, but she would hold that honor for little more than a month, as the next ship to enter service, the *Saxonia*, was even larger. Built by the John Brown shipyard on Clydeside, in Scotland, the *Saxonia* was launched on December 16, 1899, with a gross tonnage of over 14,200 tons. By mid-May 1900 her fitting out was complete, and she set out on her maiden voyage from Liverpool to Boston on May 22. She was equipped with a pair of quadruple expansion engines, which turned two propellers. Not yet ready to challenge the Germans head-to-head, Cunard's priority with the three sisters was size, not speed, and the *Saxonia*'s machinery gave her a service speed of 15 knots.

The appearance of the *Ivernia* and *Saxonia* was distinctive, if not particularly handsome. They had long, black hulls with a graceful sheer, straight up-and-down cutter bows, and attractive counter sterns reminiscent of the popular *Campania* and *Lucania*; but there the resemblance ended. Rather than the multi-tiered superstructure sported by their predecessors, surmounted by clusters of vent cowls and topped by a pair of powerful-looking funnels, the superstructures in these new ships were long and low, creating the visual impression that they had been somehow flattened out and spread the length of the hull. Atop it all would be perched a single tall, almost spindly funnel; spaced equidistant along the length of the ships were four masts. As awkward as this arrangement may sound, as a whole the proportions worked together to create a look that was modern and purposeful, if not exactly handsome.

This class of ships had been designed from the outset to make money for Cunard by carrying both passengers and cargo. The four masts were no affectation added for appearance—they acted as kingposts for the booms that were used when loading or unloading cargo. The cargo spaces were quite large, and as a consequence the passenger accommodations were not as extensive as might have been expected of the largest ships in the Cunard fleet. Accommodations were for two hundred Second Class passengers and fifteen hundred Third Class—there were no First Class cabins at all. Their dual roles as cargo *and* passenger ships were confirmation, if any were needed, of Cunard's straitened circumstances: the line could no longer depend for its revenues on ships built exclusively for passengers, but as in its early days the company was once again looking to freighting as a way to help it stay solvent. In the first few years of the 20th century Cunard needed to earn every pound it possibly could.

The third ship of this trio, the *Carpathia,* joined the *Ivernia* and *Saxonia* in 1903. Her keel had been laid down on September 10, 1901 at the Wallsend shipyard Swan & Hunter, and she was launched on August 6, 1902. An interesting sidelight to her construction was that while the *Carpathia* was taking shape in one of the yard's gantries, at the other end of the shipyard archaeologists had begun excavating the recently-discovered eastern end of Hadrian's Wall, the ancient Roman boundary between Britannia and Caledonia (Britain and Scotland)—a fascinating juxtaposition of the ancient world and the modern. As the *Carpathia* was just barely larger than 14,000 tons, the *Saxonia* remained the largest ship in Cunard service until the *Caronia* made her appearance in 1905.

In her role as a cargo carrier, the *Carpathia* was a bit more specialized than her two sisters. Designed to carry refrigerated food, in particular meat, she had been built with three large refrigerated holds, as well as one for her own provisions. Her powerplant was identical to that of the *Ivernia* and *Saxonia*, a pair of ten-cylinder quadruple expansion engines turning two propellers, which gave her a top speed during her sea trials of just over 15 knots.

Like her two sisters, the *Carpathia* was originally designed to carry just Second and Third Class passengers. Despite the absence of First Class berthing, the standard of the accommodations was remarkably high: rather than imitate the gilt-and-marble extravagance of the German ships, Cunard placed a premium on quiet comfort. Even in Third Class there were features normally found only in higher classes on other companies' ships—they included a smoking room (the usual practice was for Third Class smokers to make do with taking their nicotine on the open deck, quite an impossible feat in anything but clear weather), a bar, a ladies' sitting room and a dining saloon spacious enough to serve 300 people at one sitting—quite large as a standard for any class of passengers at the time. Second Class had similar amenities, somewhat more opulent in decor, of course, and it also had a library.

While the term "steerage" was still used more-or-less interchangeably with "Third Class," the circumstances that greeted Third Class passengers in the first decade of the 20th century were a far cry from the "dank 'tween decks" of sixty years before. The culmination of the trend begun by William Inman a half-century earlier, the accommodations aboard the *Carpathia* were typical of a new consciousness of the value of Third Class passengers to the Cunard Line.

William Inman, a Liverpool shipowner who formed the line which bore his family name, had revolutionized the immigrant trade in the mid-19th century. While the rest of the steamship industry focused their efforts on luring First Class travelers aboard their ships, Inman recognized the potential market that emigrants represented, especially the Irish, and decided that the time had come to take advantage of the opportunity. Rather than compelling them to cross the Irish Sea to embark at Liverpool or Bristol, he began embarking them at Queenstown (now Cobh), which sat on a small harbor on the south Irish coast.

Charmingly, Inman's wife took on a very active role the business, creating the ships' interiors as well as drawing up their sailing schedules. She also made it her business to look after the welfare of Inman passengers: on one occasion she disguised herself as an emigrant on the passage from Liverpool to Queenstown in order to experience firsthand what life was like for the steerage passengers. For as little as £5 ($25), an Inman ship would carry an emigrant from Liverpool to Philadelphia. The fare included three meals a day: arrowroot with sugar and milk, oatmeal porridge and molasses at breakfast; a mix of salt beef and fresh beef at dinner; tea and gruel for supper. Bland and monotonous it may have been, but a genuine improvement over the offerings of other lines, where emigrants had often been expected to provide their own food and prepare it during the voyage. Little wonder, then, that impoverished Irish families soon flocked to the Inman offices in Dublin and Queenstown. Other steamship lines, including Cunard, were quick to copy Inman's success, and within a generation Queenstown had been transformed into one of the busiest emigration ports in Europe.

A great many myths have built up around the flood of immigrants that flowed to the shores of the New World at the end of the 19th century and the beginning of the 20th, aided by a spate of romanticized reporting, photographs, and artwork from the period. All too often the steerage passengers were portrayed as "tired, poor . . . huddled masses"—babushka- and shawl-clad mothers gripping the hands of small, wide-eyed children, or wide-eyed young men in ill-fitting clothing clutching their few belongings in loosely tied bundles, all hoping to find their fortunes in such exotic locales as New York, Pittsburgh, or Chicago.

The truth was, as with so many subjects of the journalism of that day, a good deal more mundane. Despite the increasing numbers of central and southern Europeans emigrating to America, the majority of those leaving the Old World for the New were still Anglo-Saxon. Many were Germans, whose Fatherland was undergoing a bewilderingly rapid transformation from an agrarian society to an industrial juggernaut, with all the attendant social dislocations. Many others were Britons, often skilled or semi-skilled workers, sometimes craftsmen, occasionally members of the professions, forced by lack of work in England or Scotland to seek employment in America, as Great Britain began edging toward her slow industrial and economical decline. To these people a ship was transportation, its sole purpose to take them from Liverpool (or Southampton or Cherbourg or Queenstown) to Halifax, Boston, or New York. Passengers like these were not influenced by such luxuries as Grand Staircases, electric elevators, or swimming baths, the baubles dangled before potential First Class passengers to attract their patronage. Their interests lay in clean quarters and decent food. In this respect the Cunard Line served them admirably.

Third Class berthing on a ship like the *Carpathia* was spread out along the lower three decks of the ship, the superstructure being the exclusive preserve of Second Class. The quarters would be divided into sections for single men, single women, married couples, and families. There was a near-Puritanical streak at work in the layout of these sections, peculiar to the morals and morality of the day, which made sure single men and women wouldn't have cabins anywhere near each other. Single men were usually berthed forward, single women aft, with married couples and families distributed between the two areas. The cabins themselves were spacious, spotless, and if a bit austere, were by all reports comfortable enough. The unmarried men or women would share a room with three to five other passengers of the same sex, while married couples and families had rooms to themselves.

The Third Class galley provided a fare that, while not spectacular, offered good food and plenty of it; in some cases, especially with those from the more impoverished Balkan countries or Irish counties, the steerage passengers ate better aboard ship than they ever had at home.

All in all, they received a good deal more than most expected when they paid for their passage, especially when fares could be as low as £7 for a Third Class berth: a clean bed, fresh linens, and soap each morning, and three meals a day.

Her completion delayed by a strike at Swan & Hunter, the *Carpathia* finally passed her sea trials in April 1903, and left Liverpool on her maiden voyage on May 5, stopping first at Queenstown on her way to New York. Cunard created a schedule for the *Carpathia* which put her on the run between either Liverpool and New York, or Liverpool and Boston, during the summer months, while between November and May, she carried immigrants (mainly Italian and Hungarian) from Trieste and Fiume in the Adriatic to America. Though this schedule had been designed first and foremost to serve the immigrant trade, which was Cunard's bread-and-butter in these years, it wasn't long before the Mediterranean crossings began to enjoy a vogue among wealthy Americans on holiday. Soon Gibraltar, Genoa, and Naples (and sometimes Messina and Palermo) were added to the itinerary as ports of call.

Inevitably, in an effort to capitalize on this new found popularity for the Mediterranean, Cunard sent the *Carpathia* back to Swan & Hunter in 1905, there to be refitted with entirely new accommodations. Cabins and public rooms for 100 First Class passengers were provided. Second Class accommodation remained at 200, while by converting some of the cargo space and making a minor reduction in cabin sizes, Third Class berthing was increased to 2,250 passengers. While she could still work her passage by carrying cargo, the *Carpathia* was now very much a passenger liner, and in a low-key way, one of Cunard's most popular.

While there would always be that segment of the traveling public which clamored for the thrill—and sometimes discomfort—of a six-day passage on Cunard's new Blue Ribband speedsters, *Lusitania* and *Mauretania*, there were just as many who enjoyed the leisurely pace of a ten day crossing to Liverpool or fourteen days to Trieste aboard the *Carpathia*. By 1909 she had been placed on the Mediterranean run permanently, only returning to Liverpool at the end of each year for a refit. In January 1912, the *Carpathia* was given a new captain, the man with whom her name would forever be linked, even long after he had gone on to far greater and more glamorous commands.

Arthur Henry Rostron was born in Astley Bridge, near Bolton, Lancashire, to James and Nancy Rostron in 1869. Educated at the Bolton School from 1882 to 1883, and then at the Astley Bridge High School, the young Rostron decided that he wanted to pursue a career at sea, and so joined the cadet school HMS *Conway*, in Liverpool, at the age of thirteen. After two years of training there, he was apprenticed to a Liverpool shipping firm bearing the imposing name of the Waverley Line of Messrs. Williamson, Milligan, and Co. Sailing first on an iron-hulled clipper ship, *Cedric the Saxon*, Rostron spent the next six years at sea, sailing to all parts of the world including the Americas, India, and Australia, gaining invaluable experience in practical seamanship while he studied for his various Mates' examinations. By 1887 he was serving as Second Mate aboard the barque *Red Gauntlet*. Rostron would later remember that while he was aboard her he had his closest brush with death at sea, when the *Red Gauntlet* toppled over on her beam ends (literally lying on her side) during a storm off the south coast of New Zealand; the ship managed to recover and Rostron lived.

In December 1894, at the relatively young age of twenty-five, he reached a major milestone in his professional career when he passed the examination for his Extra Master's certificate. He promptly joined the Cunard Line in January 1895 and was given a position as fourth officer on the ocean liner RMS *Umbria*. Possession of both a Master's and an Extra Master's certificate was crucial to the ambitions of any young man aspiring to the command of a ship in the British Merchant Marine. These certificates were first issued by the Board of Trade in 1845, and were made compulsory for all captains and watch-standing officers after 1850.

A Master's certificate—"ticket" was the popular parlance—meant that the holder was fully qualified to stand watches and make decisions about the speed, safety, and navigation of a ship without having to consult with and obtain the approval of a senior officer. Earning a Master's ticket not only required several years of experience at sea, it also meant sitting for a grueling Board of Trade examination in which the applicant would be tested on his knowledge of shiphandling, lading, navigation, and safety at sea. An applicant had to be 21 years of age to be eligible to sit for the examination, and if he passed, his ticket would be endorsed for either sail or steam.

The written examination was daunting. The candidate would be expected to determine latitude by the altitude of the Polar star at any time; determine latitude by the meridian altitude of the moon; find the magnetic bearing of any fixed object when at sea or at anchor; to construct deviation curves; explain the effect of a ship's iron or steel hull on the compasses, as well as correct for it; show a practical knowledge of the use of charts in navigation, including course corrections required by currents; and how to use and correct depth soundings. If the candidate was sitting for a sailing master's examination, he would be required to demonstrate his knowledge of making and taking in sail, whether in moderate and stormy weather. All applicants would have to show that they were familiar with the rules of the road at sea for both steamers and sailing vessels, including their regulation lights and fog and sound signals; and be able to describe the signals of distress, the signals to be made by ships wanting a pilot, and the liabilities and penalties incurred by the misuse of these signals. In particular he would have to show that he understood the use of rockets if his ship was in distress.

An oral examination would follow, where the candidate would be expected to show that he had a thorough and practical knowledge of an incredible range of subjects, beginning with the law as it applied to hiring, discharging, and managing a crew; the law regarding load-line marks, as well as how to complete the appropriate reports in respect to lading; and the entries to be made in the ship's official log. Other questions would cover how to prevent and check an outbreak of scurvy on board ship; invoices, bills of lading, dealing with Lloyd's of London agents; the prevailing winds and currents of any part of the globe, as well as the trade routes and tides. Finally, he would have to be prepared to answer any other relevant questions which the Examiner might ask.

While all of this may seem a bit tedious, or even mundane, nothing could better demonstrate the bewildering range of responsibilities which a ship's master faced on each and every sailing. The examination for an Extra Master's ticket was even more demanding, as it would cover both steamships *and* sailing vessels, regardless of what the applicant's previous experience might be. But possession of an Extra Master's certificate literally was a "ticket" for an ambitious merchant marine officer, for it was an unchallengeable endorsement of competence, and as such allowed its holder to grasp the rungs of the ladder of promotion which could lead to one day being given command of one of the most famous vessels in the world.

In the years after Rostron joined Cunard, he rose steadily, if unspectacularly, up the company ladder. This was not a reflection on Rostron's abilities, for Cunard captains were expected to be conscientious and circumspect—but never spectacular. It was with as much truth as wit that Mark Twain had once summed up Cunard's attitude when he observed, "The Cunard people would not take Noah as first mate until they had worked him through the lower grades and tried him for ten years or such matter. . . . It takes them about ten or fifteen years to manufacture a captain; but when they have him manufactured to suit at last they have full confidence in him. The only order they give a captain is this, brief and to the point: 'Your ship is loaded, take her; speed is nothing; follow your own road, deliver her safe, bring her back safe—safety is all that is required." Arthur Rostron's career demonstrated the truth of Twain's remarks; in fact, it would eventually demonstrate the wisdom of Cunard's methods.

He served on various vessels, including *Campania, Etruria, Ivernia, Pannonia, Saxonia, Servia,* and *Ultonia,* the only break in his service coming in 1905 when, as an officer of the Royal Naval Reserve, Rostron was obliged to temporarily serve in the British Navy during the Russo-Japanese War. He worked his way up the ranks until September 1907, when he was named as First Officer of the shiny new *Lusitania,* then the largest and, it was hoped, fastest ship yet to be built. He held this post all through her sea-trials, which were the most extensive ever conducted for a passenger liner up to that time. It was with some surprise then that he received the news, the day before the *Lusitania* departed Liverpool on her maiden voyage, that he was being taken off her bridge; but the surprise was a pleasant one, for Rostron was informed that he was being given his first command, the cargo ship *Brescia.* Then in quick succession, he commanded the *Ivernia, Pavonia, Pannonia,* and *Saxonia.*

There is a temptation among some maritime historians to anticipate events and overplay the regard in which Arthur Rostron was held within Cunard before April 1912. What is unquestionable, however, is that he was a conscientious officer who was respected by his peers and crews alike. He was known throughout the company as "the Electric Spark" for his decisiveness and boundless, infectious energy. He was also noted for his piety; he neither smoked nor drank, was never heard to use profanity, and in a day and age when recourse to the Almighty was not regarded as quaint or a sign of weak-mindedness, was known to turn to prayer for guidance.

He took command of the *Carpathia* on January 18, 1912, and took her to New York for the first time a week later. For the next four months the *Carpathia* plied her regular service between New York and Fiume. While on her westbound crossings the *Carpathia* would usually be heavy with immigrants in Third Class but relatively few passengers in First or Second Class, while on her eastbound passages she was usually carrying Americans on holiday, calling at the ports of Europe or visiting the Mediterranean, so that much of Third Class would be sitting empty. Consequently it was hardly surprising when, on April 11, 1912, the *Carpathia* pulled away from Cunard's Pier 54, into the Hudson River and out of New York harbor with 125 First Class passengers aboard, 65 in Second Class, and 550 Third Class passengers rattling about in a space designed for four times that number.

Captain Rostron was once heard to comment that all Cunard ships had three sides—port, starboard, and social, and that the captain must be the master of all of them. The years of the Edwardian Era were when ships' captains came to the fore: while their social standing had been rising for decades, they were now approaching the pinnacle of their power and fame. A popular captain who gained a reputation for being a good host, an entertaining storyteller, and a discerning social arbiter quickly attracted a loyal coterie of passengers, almost invariably wealthy and socially prominent, who would follow him from ship to ship, or if he preferred to stay with one vessel, as did many Cunard captains, they would travel exclusively on that ship. Both for the money they spent and the attention they attracted, these recurring entourages were worth their weight in gold to Cunard.

Not all captains enjoyed the social side of their responsibilities, however. Captain William Turner, who was the first captain of both the *Lusitania* and the *Mauretania*, cordially detested most passengers, regarding them as overblown bores and busybodies, and he vastly preferred the company of his officers and the surroundings of his bridge to that of the Captain's Table in the First Class Dining Saloon. Because Turner's skills as a mariner made him too valuable to lose, Cunard created the position of Staff Captain, a "second" captain, qualified in every way as a ship's master, who would relieve Turner of some of the burden of the administrative details of the ship's operations, as well as take over the duty of entertaining the passengers. Apparently it was a successful solution all around, for the position of Staff Captain became a permanent fixture on Cunard's larger ships, even though most Captains found presiding over their own table at dinner to be one of the more pleasant aspects of their job.

The *Carpathia*, however, was not large enough to warrant a Staff Captain, and in any event, Arthur Rostron seemed to enjoy the social side of command as much as any ship's master. Only rarely would a member of the British, Italian or Austrian aristocracy appear on the *Carpathia*'s passenger lists—for the most part their ilk preferred the glamour of the *Lusitania* or *Mauretania*, White Star's *Olympic*, or the fast German liners. Consequently, the men who, along with their wives, occupied the captain's table on the *Carpathia* would be men from the world of business, manufacturing or trades, men with whom Rostron could easily relate, who had attained their affluence and social station through intelligence, hard work, and perseverance.

On the voyage in April 1912, the first two days out of New York were utterly uneventful, as was expected, and the passengers and crew of the *Carpathia* settled into a comfortable routine as the ship made her steady progress eastward. The weather was brisk, not particularly warm for April, but not unbearably cold. It would get warmer as the *Carpathia* made her way southward past the Azores and on through Gibraltar into the Med. Captain Rostron knew that the previous winter had been rather mild in the Arctic, and as a result the amount of ice which was drifting down into the North Atlantic was considerably heavier than usual. However, that was not a worry for him or the *Carpathia*, as her course would take her more than eighty miles south of the westbound routes, where the ice might be more of a hazard.

Sunday morning, April 14, was a little different than the previous

two days. For the crew, after breakfast was over, there came a faithfully followed Sunday ritual of a passenger ship at sea: the Captain's
Inspection. It was an impressive sight with Captain Rostron leading
the way, followed by the Department Heads—Chief Officer, Chief
Engineer Johnston, Chief Steward Hughes, Purser Brown—all in their
best uniforms. From top deck to bottom, bow to stern, and through
all the public rooms, they visited every accessible part of the ship. The
inevitable small deficiencies were found—a spotted carpet in one of
the lounges, a small spill of oil in one of the engineering spaces, a
crewman's bunk or locker not quite properly squared away. It is as
ironclad an unwritten law in the merchant marine as it is in the military that there is no such thing as a perfect inspection. However, of
serious deficiencies there were none.

Next came the Boat Drill. As outlined by the Board of Trade, Boat
Drill only required a ship's officers to supervise a picked crew, mustered beforehand, to uncover a designated lifeboat on each side of the
ship, swing it out over the ship's side, and climb aboard. Some officers
would require the crewmen to examine the oars, mast, sail, and rigging that were stowed in each boat, and account for the required kegs
of water and tins of biscuit. Others weren't so demanding. Once this
was accomplished, the crewmen would climb out of the boat, swing it
back inboard, pull the cover back on and return to work. On the
Carpathia, as on almost every other liner on the North Atlantic, only
the crew had assigned boat stations, and these were merely assignments telling the crewmen which boats they were supposed to assist in
loading and lowering. As for the passengers, there were no lifeboat
assignments of any kind.

At noon, on Sunday as on every day, the captain and his officers
gathered on the starboard bridge wing, each with a sextant in hand.
They would take a series of sun sightings to work out the ship's precise position, which would then be recorded in the ship's log, along
with the distance covered in the previous twenty-four hours. Like most
of her contemporaries, the *Carpathia* held a sweepstakes for the passengers to wager on the day's run. Once the noon sun-sightings were
taken and the distance known, the ship's siren blew and those passengers who had placed wagers would gather in the First Class Lounge to
await the results. On the larger express liners, the winnings in the

sweepstakes could amount to several hundred pounds (or dollars) but that of the *Carpathia* was, of course, far more modest. Still, it was always exciting, particularly for a passage which promised to have very little if anything in the way of other excitement.

In the wireless office, which was located in the after superstructure, above the Second Class smoking room, young Harold Cottam was being kept quite busy. Just 21 years old, Cottam had been the youngest graduate ever of the Marconi School, having completed the course at the age of 17. He had to wait almost three years before having the chance to go to sea, as regulations forbid any operator younger than 21 to be posted to a ship, though sometimes the officials would look the other way when a particularly talented but under-age applicant came forward; in the meantime he worked mainly as a shore operator in Liverpool. Then came his first posting at sea, aboard the White Star Line's *Medic*, on the Australian run. After four months on the *Medic*, he joined the *Carpathia* in February, and quickly became comfortable aboard her, for Rostron was a good skipper who had a better grasp of the realities of wireless than many of his contemporaries.

Wireless, while becoming more reliable with every passing year, was still a far-from-perfected technology in 1912. Ranges were still limited, the performance of some sets was marginal, and there was a shortage of skilled operators; but the rapidly growing number of conventions and etiquette were adding a much needed measure of discipline to wireless communications. What was most noticeably lacking was standardization—there were a half dozen types of equipment; two different Morse codes, American and International; no regulations concerning the hours wireless watch was to be kept; and no definite order in the ships' crew organizations as to where the wireless operator belonged. This was due, of course, to the fact that the wireless operators did not actually work for the shipping line that owned their particular vessel, but were actually employees of British Marconi.

Another problem was the sheer volume of work which sometimes beset the operators. Passengers seemed to take an almost childish delight in sending messages to friends and families from the middle of the Atlantic Ocean. As a result, a good deal of any Marconi man's time was taken up with private messages that had nothing to do with the ship itself, mostly of the "Having a wonderful time, wish you were here" variety. These messages had to be handled, since the passengers were paying for the service, but they tended to cause the work to get piled up, and occasionally interfered with traffic important to the safe navigation of the ship. This could present a problem on a smaller vessel like the *Carpathia*, which only had one operator, who typically worked a fifteen- to eighteen-hour shift, taking his meals at his desk, other breaks coming irregularly and infrequently. Adding to the problem was that there were no set, uniform procedures for handling messages unless they were specifically addressed to a ship's captain. Otherwise, Cottam, like his colleagues throughout the merchant fleet, took care of any incoming messages as best he could.

This Sunday was no exception. In addition to the usual spate of passengers' messages, there was an unusual number of reports of ice being sent by ships on the northern track. Cottam listened intently, copying down anything that might prove useful for the *Carpathia*, periodically taking the messages up to the bridge when there seemed to be a lull in the traffic. Cottam, like most of his fellow Marconi men, knew little of navigation, so he used his discretion in regard to what went to the bridge and what did not, but he wisely preferred to err on the side of caution.

At about 7:00 p.m. that evening, Cottam heard directly from his friend Jack Phillips, who was the senior operator on board the new White Star liner *Titanic*. Phillips was sending a ship-to-ship message from one of the *Titanic*'s First Class passengers to a Mrs. Marshall aboard the *Carpathia*. The *Titanic* had been silent for most of the afternoon—Cottam suspected it was equipment problems—and Phillips didn't seem inclined toward much small talk, as fellow operators would sometimes engage in, so Cottam sat back and listened as Phillips sent message after message to the Marconi station at Cape Race. Phillips would send a message, wait for one minute to give operators on other ships a chance to start sending messages of their own, and if none began, would tap out another. It was during these breaks that Cottam picked up ice warnings sent from the liner *Mesaba* and the cargo ship *Californian*.

It was just before 10:00 p.m. that Cottam gathered up his collection of accumulated messages and went forward to the bridge, where he found Captain Rostron, First Officer Dean, and Second Officer Bissett preparing for the change of watch. Rostron took the messages and thanked Cottam, who then returned to the wireless office. Quickly reading the messages, Rostron paid particular attention to the ice warnings, noting that all of the positions given were well to the north of the *Carpathia*'s course. Turning to Bissett, he remarked with a smile, "Wonderful thing, wireless, isn't it?"

He would soon find out just how wonderful it was.

Chapter 3

THE *CALIFORNIAN* AND
STANLEY LORD

Though the cachet of the North Atlantic run accrued to the big passenger lines—the power and glamor of Cunard, White Star, or Germany's Norddeutscher-Lloyd and Hamburg-Amerika, the handsome ships of the Canadian Pacific Railroad, the homeliness of Holland America, or the elegance of the French Line—most of the real work of the shipping world was done by the multitude of ships that sailed under the flags of the smaller, less glamorous shipping companies that for more than a hundred years, from the middle of the 19th century to the middle of the 20th, ran regular services across the North Atlantic. These were ships that would never compete for the Blue Ribband, never be acclaimed for their opulence or their excesses (although some of them were quite luxurious in their own right), or vie for the title of "the largest ship in the world." Nonetheless, the role they played and the need they filled sustained the lifeline of commerce and trade which was so vital to the two continents which they connected.

In the summer of 1901 one of these small, undistinguished ships was ordered by the Leyland Line, a company which prospered in carrying cargo rather than passengers. Leyland commissioned the Caledon Shipbuilding and Engineering Company Ltd., of Dundee, Scotland, to construct the new vessel. Laid down with the builder's hull number 159, the new ship was something of a point of pride for Caledon Shipbuilding, and a milestone in the firm's effort to grow into

37

a genuine competitor to the large Clydeside shipyards, as she was the largest ship yet ordered from the yard.

The new vessel would have a displacement of 6,223 gross registered tons, with a length of 447 feet, a beam of 52 feet and a designed draft of 30 feet. She would be powered by a single reciprocating engine, turning a single screw, with a designed speed of 13½ knots. While typical of hundreds of British merchant ships that traversed the world's sealanes, these were not particularly impressive figures when compared to the later behemoths that would take to the North Atlantic, or even by the standards of the day. (The largest ship in the world in 1901 was White Star's *Celtic* with a length of 700 feet, and a displacement of 21,035 tons.)

In appearance, too, No. 159 would be much like a thousand other freighters already crisscrossing the North Atlantic, her aesthetics dictated by function. Beginning at her old-fashioned up-and-down stem, she was built with a steep-sided, almost sheerless hull, her flush weather-deck running unbroken from bow to stern. Her superstructure sat squarely amidships, taking up barely a quarter of her length. Atop it sat a quartet of spindly ventilators, above them looming a single funnel, painted in the salmon-pink and black of the Leyland Line. There were four masts, which also doubled as kingposts for handling cargo. Altogether an unremarkable ship, Hull No. 159 would be almost stereotypical of the ocean-going freighter of the early 20th century.

The stereotype would extend to more than just her size, configuration, and purpose. As designed, she would require a crew of roughly fifty stokers, trimmers, assistant engineers, and deckhands. With more than half the space within her hull given over to cargo, and nearly a third taken up by her boilers and engine room, there would be precious little space in which her crewmen would live. The crew was "comfortably housed below the shelter deck forward," as the builders euphemistically described what was nothing more than the traditional forecastle, or "fo'c's'le."

There lurks beneath that somewhat romantic sounding bit of nautical tradition one of the darkest yet best concealed secrets of the British Empire. A realm flung to the four corners of the world, the Empire was maintained by the sinews of Great Britain's sealanes and the ships which plied them; it was carried on the backs of British merchant seamen. In return they were fed, clothed, quartered, and payed to such a pitiful standard that such conditions would never have been tolerated in the foulest tenement slums of smoky, soot-covered, industrial Sheffield, Manchester, Birmingham, or Glasgow.

Poorly lit, inadequately ventilated, badly heated, the crew's quarters would consist of cramped rooms where four, six, sometimes eight men would bunk. The prevailing impression was one of almost continuous dampness—often in rough or stormy weather, despite the best efforts to secure it, the forecastle would be awash, the crewmen donning sodden clothing at the beginning of their watches, and returning to damp bunks at the end, with little chance to ever get completely dry before the ship made port. Their diet was dull and monotonous, a mess of bully beef, porridge, beans, and tea. Lime or lemon juice was mandatory, of course, to prevent scurvy (despite its association with the long-past days of sail, scurvy remains a threat to the health of sailors even in the 21st century), but this was about the only concession the shipping lines made to the men's health. Alcohol was forbidden below decks, but this was a prohibition honored more in the breach than in the observance, as seeking solace in rum or gin was sometimes the only recourse many of the men had to endure their work and their lot; inevitably, alcoholism was rife among seamen in those decades.

So was tuberculosis, although it would not be recognized for the threat it was in the merchant marine until well into the 1930s. When the 17th-century philosopher Thomas Hobbes described life in the Middle Ages as "nasty, brutish, and short," he might equally well have been speaking of the lot of British merchant seamen for much of the 19th and 20th centuries. There was little that the men could do to improve their situation, for there were always more unemployed deckhands and men from the "black gang" of the engine rooms than there were berths: once a man had a job, he would tolerate almost anything to assure that he kept it.

The explanation for such a dreadful state of affairs could be summed up in one word: greed. The shipowners, already wealthy, simply accrued more wealth by forcing shipping rates as high as they could while keeping wages as low as possible. When J.P. Morgan was forming International Mercantile Marine, he began cutting shipping fares to the bone to compel his competitors to allow themselves to be absorbed by IMM; he was able to do so in part by reducing seamen's wages. However, once the cartel was formed, shipping rates rose again, but wages remained the same for the crews.

Wages were what might be expected. While deckhands—the skilled, able-bodied seamen who did the actual work of shiphandling—could make as much as £10 a month, depending on their rating, the men who did the back-breaking work of feeding the ships' coal-fired boilers typically made less than half that amount. The deck crew at least had some compensation in the knowledge of their hard-won skills in handling lines, taking soundings, hoisting and answering flag signals, reading Morse lamps, working the ship's machinery and mechanisms, or manning the helm if they were a qualified quartermaster. They were regarded with something approaching professional status by their working-class peers, if still disdained by the majority of their officers. But the men who literally brought power, heat, and electricity—in a word, life—to these ships were the poorest paid and least-regarded of any of the crew.

With the possible exception of the lot of a galley slave, it would be difficult to conceive of a task more demanding and demeaning, more backbreaking and more soul-breaking, than feeding the furnaces of a coal-fired boiler on a steamship. The confines of the hull meant that none of the bulky automated feeding mechanisms that fed boilers ashore could be installed in the ship. Instead the entire chore was accomplished through sheer human muscle power. The task began with the trimmers, who had to carry the coal from the bunkers to the foot of the firebox, using wheelbarrows to deliver great lumps of coal, measuring as much as twenty inches in length and eight inches thick. At the start of the voyage, with full bunkers, it was a relatively easy job, but toward the end of the crossing, as the bunkers began to empty, it was fiercesome work, for by then the coal might be 150 feet or more from the scuttle where it was loaded in the barrows. And for every trimmer carrying a load to the furnaces, there was one *inside* the bunker shifting coal. Despite the fact that the trimmers were at the very bottom of the hierarchy of the engineering department, there was a certain degree of skill required in their job as well. It was their responsibility to see that the coal was used in uniform amounts from each bunker, so that the weight of the remaining coal wouldn't unbalance the ship, upsetting her trim—hence the name "trimmers." Their world was an eerie one, even more poorly lit and poorly ventilated than their quarters, while temperatures ranged from the searing heat of the furnace door to the sea-chilled reaches of the farther bunkers. Once the coal was delivered to the firebox, the stokers took over.

Usually working stripped to the waist, like the trimmers their torsos and faces covered in coal dust, the stokers were eerily illuminated by the glow of the flames in the fireboxes and the flare of clinkers and slag as they went through an elaborate and exacting ballet of muscle and sweat. A stoker's first task was to break up the large lumps of coal brought by the trimmers into something more manageable. Using his shovel and slice bar, he would reduce the larger pieces into fragments roughly the size of a man's fist. Next, timing his movements to the roll and pitch of the ship, the stoker would swing open the door to a firebox and quickly thrust home his slice bar along the fire-grate, working it back and forth four times, once for each track of the grate, to improve the draft across the burning coals by breaking ashes and clinkers loose. These were quickly raked into a pit below the firebox and the fire-door swung closed again. On double-ended boilers the stokers worked in tandem so that doors at the opposite ends were never open at the same time, preventing back-drafts that could blow the fire out into the stokers' faces.

The fire-door would be opened again, and the stoker would shovel a layer of coal across the grate—a skilled stoker would usually feed in no more than four shovelfuls of coal, spreading them over the grate at a uniform depth of four inches. At the same time, other crewmen known as water tenders would keep a close eye on the water gauges, careful to keep a level of two inches in the boiler, a combination that maximized the amount of steam each fire-grate could produce.

The whole routine moved to the inexorable ringing of Kilroy's Patent Stoking Indicator, a mechanical timer that could be set for intervals between eight and thirty minutes. The higher the speed of the ship, the lower the interval between rings on the Indicator; the amount of time for which the Indicator was set was the total allotted to performing the entire cycle of breaking coal, slicing, clinkering, and stoking. The usual settings would be between eight and ten minutes for a complete cycle. At the end of each four-hour watch the stokers would finish by raking the ashes and clinkers out of the pits, hosing them down to cool them, then shoveling them into hoppers that mixed them with seawater and then ejected them out scuttles near the ship's waterline.

It's little wonder that, given the endless monotony and the sheer mindlessness of the work, along with the knowledge that they had little if any prospect of advancement from their station in society or aboard the ship, the "black gang" were often a surly, barely subordinate lot. More than one senior engineer had to be as adept at cracking heads as he was at repairing machinery. That such men rarely felt more than the most elementary loyalty to their officers and employers was inevitable. Over the years chilling tales, some of them confirmed to be true, would accumulate in waterfront bars of particularly despised officers who would be knocked senseless with the flat of a coal-shovel, then fed into the maw of a boiler, their ashes and bones emptied into the sea with the clinkers at the end of the watch.

Nor was it surprising that merchant marine officers usually held their crewmen in very low regard. A good captain, careful of how he exercised his authority, might dull the worst edges of the chasm between the wardroom and the fo'c's'le, but it could never be truly bridged. Even as generally decent a man as Arthur Rostron was not above the prejudice that the wardroom felt for the fo'c's'le. It was Rostron who said before a Board of Trade Inquiry that ". . . naturally an Officer is more on the *qui vive*; he is keener on his work than a man would be, and he knows what to look for. He is more intelligent than a sailor."

These, then, were the men who made up the crews of the British Merchant Marine. They were almost universally invisible men, for ashore they would congregate along the waterfronts, with their gambling dens, taverns, and brothels, while at sea they would rarely if ever be seen by the passengers of the transatlantic liners, their portions of the ship being carefully shut off from the accommodations of their "betters," the easier to make the liners appear to be showcases.

There was, of course, no need for the new Leyland ship to be a showpiece designed to attract passengers. As she was originally laid down, her owners had no intention that she should carry any passengers at all. It was only during the late stages of her construction that the upper bridge deck was lengthened, when nineteen staterooms were added by the line as an afterthought. These cabins were, of course, never intended to pay the ship's way like a true passenger liner's accommodations were designed to do; the additional money they brought to the Leyland Line would be regarded as a sort of corporate bonus.

And, curiously enough, the revenue created by these last-minute additions was not inconsiderable. While no glamour would ever accrue to Hull No. 159, there was a canny logic to the Leyland Line's decision to add the cabins. Then as now there was a segment of the traveling public which was singularly unimpressed by ornate and opulent public lounges, smoking rooms, dining saloons, and such. Grand staircases, Turkish baths, swimming baths, squash courts, and gymnasiums held little appeal to these folk; what they did enjoy was the experience of being at sea, in comfortable surroundings, traveling at a leisurely pace without any of the attendant fuss and complications which were inseparable from the social life aboard one of the crack transatlantic liners. They included small families, wealthy widows, retired businessmen, a surprising number of Midwestern socialites, young men, and occasionally chaperoned young ladies from middle-class families who were seeking adventure—in short, people who wanted to cross the Atlantic in comfort but were unwilling (or unable) to pay a premium price for passage on one of the big passenger liners.

This meant that the handful of passenger accommodations were devoted to quiet, low-key luxury: by the standards of the North Atlantic trade they were rated as Second Class—which by no means meant that they were second-rate. First, the whole ship was equipped with electric lighting, still something of a novelty on smaller ships on the North Atlantic. The smoking room had paneling in the finest English oak, the furniture was upholstered in embossed leather, and the floor tiling was made out of hard rubber, again something of an innovation in 1901. The dining room was done in Hungarian ash and satinwood, with teak frames about the windows, and the chairs and chaise lounges were upholstered in maquette. All in all, it was a quiet, comfortable way to travel—and surprisingly affordable: passage from London to Boston was £10, and from Boston to London, $50.

Certified to carry a maximum of forty-seven passengers, the nineteen staterooms were located on the port side of the bridge deck, at the top of the superstructure, while the dining saloon, smoking room, and galley, as well as the officers' and senior engineer's quarters, were situated on the starboard side. Apart from a small wireless office just below the bridge, quarters for the cooks, and lockers for the galley stowage, the rest of the ship was given over to cargo: the new vessel was destined for the American cotton trade. Her complement of fifty-five included a captain, four officers, one wireless operator, and forty-nine assorted crewmen. The new ship's name followed a Leyland Line tradition of naming their vessels as belonging to one of the forty-six United States. In this case, nine-inch-high brass letters under the ship's counter stern and on both sides of the forecastle proclaimed her to be the *Californian*.

The decision to add the passenger accommodations during her construction, made as it was almost at the last minute, was not made by the Leyland Line's board of directors. Instead it came from the line's new owner. While the *Californian* was still on the ways, the Leyland Line was bought outright by the American shipping combine known as IMM—International Mercantile Marine—under the leadership of Junius Pierpont Morgan, the American financier. Morgan, the greatest of a generation of trust builders, had conceived of a vast freighting monopoly that would control the shipping rates of goods and the fares of passengers being transported from Europe, from the moment they left the Old World until they arrived at their destination in the New. Since the American rail barons, especially Morgan, had already monopolized the U.S. railroads, all that remained for Morgan's dream to become reality was to gain control of the North Atlantic shipping lines.

Morgan's first move in that direction came in 1898, when he acquired the financially troubled Inman Line. Thomas Ismay, who had formed the White Star Line thirty years earlier and turned it into one of the powerhouses of the North Atlantic run, attempted to form a consortium of British shipowners that would keep Inman out of Morgan's hands, but the attempt fell apart because too few of Ismay's colleagues believed Morgan was serious. Dismayed at their lack of foresight, Ismay predicted that most of them would fall under

Morgan's sway after the American had crushed them in a fierce rate war.

He was right. In 1899, Morgan began acquiring stock in the two big German lines, Hamburg-Amerika and Norddeutscher-Lloyd, with an eye toward gaining a controlling interest in both. Within the next two years he also gained either ownership or control of the Leyland Line, the Dominion Line, and the Red Star Line, mainly by cutting fares until his lines were offering a Third Class passage to America for as little as £2. Morgan next set his sights on the two British shipping giants, the White Star Line and Cunard, the jewels in the crown of the transatlantic passenger trade.

When Morgan made his first advances to the White Star Line, Thomas Ismay's son and successor as owner and managing director, Bruce Ismay, was at first as determined as his father had been to resist the American. But Morgan received help from an unexpected ally: Lord Pirrie, the Chairman of the Board of Harland and Wolff, the huge Belfast shipyard that was the exclusive builder of White Star's ships. Pirrie was also, after Ismay himself, the single largest shareholder of White Star stock. Realizing that Morgan's rate war would leave White Star with little capital for building new ships, and having made Harland and Wolff heavily dependent on White Star for new construction, Pirrie began to pressure the younger Ismay to accept Morgan's offer to buy the line. Thomas Ismay would have told Lord Pirrie to be damned, and fought the "Yankee pirate" tooth and nail, but though Bruce Ismay was his father's son in many ways, he didn't possess the innate ruthlessness of his parent. Rather than stand up to Pirrie, the younger Ismay eventually caved in, and in late 1902 Morgan's shipping combine acquired ownership of the White Star Line.

All the while, IMM had continued its overtures to Norddeutscher-Lloyd and Hamburg-Amerika, seeking a controlling interest of each company's shares, while still allowing them to operate with a considerable degree of autonomy. The terms were carefully calculated to appeal to the German companies, which were heavily subsidized by the German government, and Morgan realized that these subsidies made them far less financially vulnerable than their British counterparts. Certainly he knew he wasn't dealing from the same position of strength as he had been with White Star, so no attempt was made to gain outright ownership of Hamburg-Amerika and Norddeutscher-Lloyd.

Cunard, meanwhile, under the canny leadership of its chairman, Lord Inverclyde, would soon skillfully exploit Morgan's purchase of White Star, and ultimately wring considerable concessions from the British government in order to keep the company in British hands. After almost eighteen months of intense negotiation, an agreement drawn up between the government and Cunard was signed in October 1902. His Majesty's Government agreed to finance the construction of two new ships—destined to become the *Mauretania* and *Lusitania*—at a cost of nearly £2,600,000, the sum to be repaid over a ten-year period at 2.75% interest, while an annual subsidy of £75,000 would help defray the operating expenses. In return Cunard guaranteed that control of the line would never pass from British hands—thus thwarting IMM in one deft stroke.

The *Californian*'s part in Morgan's grand scheme was, naturally, quite small. She was first and foremost a cargo carrier, destined for service between ports in England and the American Gulf Coast, as well as the Caribbean, with occasional crossings in the North Atlantic as well. The Leyland Line had acquired a well-earned reputation in the shipping world for being soundly managed and efficiently run, her ships earning the line handsome, if not extravagant, profits. Characteristically deep-laden, Leyland ships often sat so low in the water that it became something of a standing joke for other lines' vessels to report that they "Passed four masts and a funnel bound west, presumed Leyland's." All jests aside, Leyland ships were known to be reliable and sturdy money-makers.

The *Californian* went through her sea trials on January 23, 1902, and as soon as she was certified by the Board of Trade she was readied for her maiden voyage. On January 31, she left Dundee, Scotland, and arrived at New Orleans on March 3. Her return trip brought her to Liverpool, which was her company's home port, arriving on March 21. In April that same year, the Dominion Line—yet another acquisition of IMM—chartered the *Californian* for a series of five crossings between Liverpool and Portland, Maine. Once these were completed in December 1902, the *Californian* was returned to Leyland, which put her back on the southerly Atlantic crossings the following month.

For her first ten years in service, the *Californian* had four different captains. In 1911, she was given her fifth master, the man with whom her name would forever after be associated: Captain Stanley Lord.

Lord had been born on September 13, 1877, in Bolton, Lancashire, a British textile center (and near the birthplace of Arthur Rostron). He was the youngest of six surviving sons, a younger seventh brother having died at age seven; his family was middle-class, prosperous, and, according to Lord, his parents had plans for him to embark on a career as a businessman. But as so often happened in heyday of the British Empire, as a young boy Stanley Lord was captured by the romance of the sea, and he insisted that he was going to live the life of an officer in the British Merchant Marine. Even at a young age, Lord possessed a willful personality as well as considerable powers of persuasion, and he eventually won his parents' grudging approval to be apprenticed to a Liverpool shipping firm, the J.B. Walmsley Company. At the age of thirteen Stanley Lord put to sea aboard a barque, the *Naiad*, out of Liverpool, for the South American run.

Perhaps Lord sensed something in himself that his parents never recognized, for he took to the seafaring life as if he had been born with saltwater in his veins. Serious, studious, he quickly learned the ways of sail, as well as beginning his studies for his Mates certificates ("tickets"), the first stepping stone along the path leading to command. After seven years under canvas, he switched to steam, having already earned his Second and First Mate's tickets, signing on with the West India and Pacific Steam Navigation Company of Liverpool.

The degree of Lord's determination to succeed at his profession, as well as a measure of his skills, was demonstrated when, by the age of twenty-four, he earned both his Master's and Extra Master's ("any tonnage, any ocean") tickets, a feat many merchant officers five or even ten years his senior had yet to accomplish. The only blemish on Stanley Lord's otherwise spotless career was a notation in his Board of Trade file which read, "Mr. Stanley Lord is the holder of an OC [Officer Commanding] Certificate, No. 030740. He failed to join the *Barbadian* on 7 September 1899." It was far from the grievous offense it appears to be, and Lord had good reason not to join his ship: he had broken his leg and was physically unable to reach his ship before she sailed!

There was no doubt that Lord was a man who would go far in the shipping world, and would likely finish his career commanding one of the great passenger liners. Without exception Lord's employers had nothing but the highest praise for his professional abilities. There can be no doubt that Lord himself aspired to such heights; command of a large transatlantic liner was the goal of every rising officer in the British merchant marine. Command of one of these ships carried a special prestige, a cachet which was unmatched anywhere else in the civilian world. Only the peculiar "dash" that attached to officers of the more fashionable cavalry regiments in some of the European armies matched it. In a profession top-heavy with talent, to rise to command a passenger liner on the Liverpool- or Southampton-to-New York run was the pinnacle of professional achievement. It was everything Stanley Lord had gone to sea at the age of thirteen to achieve.

What is also beyond doubt is that Lord was clearly convinced of his own worth: when in 1901 he applied for a position with the White Star Line, he was told he would be taken on as either a Third or Fourth Officer and allowed to work his way up from there. Having already earned both his Master's and Extra Master's certificates, Lord felt, with some justification, that this was nothing short of an insult and chose to look elsewhere.

Eventually "elsewhere" became the Leyland Line, where in a little more than six years Lord worked his way up to a posting as Captain, earning £20 a month, with an annual bonus usually of £50. It was not a princely sum by any accounting. Captain Edward J. Smith of the White Star Line earned more than ten times that amount, but then Smith had gone to sea more than twelve years before Stanley Lord was born and was White Star's senior captain. But what mattered most about Lord's posting was that it gave him a command. Should he later choose to reapply with White Star, or possibly Cunard or the P. & O., he would be assured of rapid advancement, as they gave preferential treatment to officers who had previously held command with other lines. With a posting to one of them there was always the possibility of one day being given command of one of the crack transatlantic liners, the goal Stanley Lord had set out to attain when he went to sea as barely more than a boy.

Physically and temperamentally, Lord embodied the sharp social discrimination which separated merchant officers from merchant seamen. Nearly six feet in height—tall for those days—with a lean build and erect if somewhat rigid bearing, he was stern-looking, with deep creases at the corners of a thin-lipped, firmly set mouth. His nose was prominent, almost aquiline, while his eyes were narrowed from years of squinting into glaring sun and driving rain. All in all, he was an imposing figure, "a veritable Caesar in a sailor's suit," as one writer described him.

His character closely matched his appearance. Even given the social gulf which separated officers from the lower decks, Lord was noticeably aloof and autocratic, not only with his crewmen but with his officers as well. Though not overtly a bully, he was an intimidating presence, and not surprisingly, his crew generally feared him more than they respected him, in particular dreading his wrath should some job be performed to anything less than his exacting standards, for he had a particularly sharp tongue. Familiarity between Lord and his crewmen, of course, was quite simply impossible. In the British Merchant Marine the social gulf between the wardroom and the fo'c's'le was as great as that between the aristocracy and the working class ashore. All the same, Lord's austere, intimidating character made no allowance for the sort of avuncular command style which earned Edward Smith the respectfully familiar nickname "E.J." among his crewmen. Lord deliberately held himself as a distant figure of near-omnipotent authority.

This was not merely a pose: until the advent of wireless allowed some contact between ship and shore, the isolation which immediately enveloped a ship once it left sight of land endowed the ship's master with an awesome range of powers and an incredible weight of responsibility. The last true autocracy, the word of a ship's captain *was* the law at sea. He had the authority to conduct marriages (though with nowhere near the frequency that later romantics would suppose), to issue birth and death certificates, to place a crewman or passenger in irons for criminal infractions, and in extreme cases to administer capital punishment. The introduction of wireless created a notable abatement in a captain's authority, but tradition still imbued him with an aura of near-infallibility. Looking on his men as little more than a seagoing rabble, "underpaid, unwashed, indifferently fed, and overworked," a man like Stanley Lord felt no need to do anything to encourage personal loyalty among them. While some captains such as Cunard's Arthur Rostron or White Star's E.J. Smith felt inclined to treat their crews with something approaching a paternal, or at least benevolent, regard, such sentiments were not only beyond Stanley Lord's ability to inspire, they were beyond anything he desired.

Lord appears to have been well aware of the gulf between the bridge and the fo'c's'le, and to have almost reveled in it. One particularly telling—and ironic—incident early in his career throws a stark light on his personality. While serving as an apprentice officer aboard the barque *Iquique*, Lord attempted to give orders to a fellow crewman who, though he was some years older, he assumed to be another apprentice, or possibly even a deckhand. The other man turned out to be one of the ship's officers, and of course thoroughly outranked Lord; however, the officer was of a more collegial nature than Lord, and although he put the young apprentice properly in his place, nothing more was said about the incident. The officer's name was William Murdoch; neither man could have had any idea how Stanley Lord's life would become inextricably intertwined with William Murdoch's death.

In 1906 Stanley Lord was given his first command, the Leyland Line's *Antillian*. Having reached a point in his career where he could turn his thoughts to domestic life and a family, Lord married Miss Mabel Tutton on March 19, 1907; a son, Stanley Tutton Lord, was born on August 15, 1908. Meanwhile, over the next six years Captain Lord would be named the master of the *William Cliff* and the Leyland Line's *Louisianian*, before moving to the *Californian* in early 1912.

The *Californian*'s first crossing that year took her from her home port of Liverpool to New Orleans, where she loaded a cargo of cotton bales. Stopping in New York to take on additional cargo, she then made for Le Havre, France. It was not a good crossing. The weather was particularly rough, and some of the cargo suffered from the heavy seas—about six hundred bales of cotton were damaged to some degree. After calling at London on March 30 to unload more cargo, the *Californian* returned to Liverpool. From there she would be going back to Boston, her departure date set for April 5.

Preparations for the crossing were understandably hasty, although by no means incomplete, not with Stanley Lord on the bridge. There were some gaffes—Cyril Evans, the wireless operator, mistakenly obtained a map for the South Atlantic, rather than the North, for example—but for the most part they were readily corrected, and on April 5, the *Californian* left Liverpool bound for Boston as scheduled. Never a fast ship, she was given fourteen days to make the crossing.

Assisting Captain Lord with the watch-keeping duties on this crossing were three officers and one apprentice officer. The Chief Officer was George Frederick Stewart, who was 35 years old, the same as his captain. He held his Master's certificate but had yet to earn his Extra Master's ticket; until he did so he was unlikely to be given a command of his own. He was a competent, reliable seaman who had considerable experience on the North Atlantic run, something Captain Lord valued. The Second Officer (on a ship as small as the *Californian* there was no need for a First Officer) was Herbert Stone, a young man of 24, who was a newlywed. Stone was an intriguing individual, for while he gave the appearance of being a calm and competent officer, he was gravely insecure about himself, and worried constantly that he might lose his situation with the Leyland Line. His recent marriage caused him particular anxiety, for with a wife to support he could ill-afford, literally, to find himself "on the beach" without a posting. Not much is known about Stone's family, but something in his past caused him to look up to Captain Lord as a sort of father figure, for whom Stone would do almost anything in order to win approval.

Charles Victor Groves was the *Californian*'s Third Officer, and the most distinct and promising of the lot. Like Stone he was 24 years old, and although serving as Third Officer, he already had his Second Mate's ticket. Born in Cambridge, he had been educated in the Perse Grammar School, a British "public" school, or what would have been known as a private school in the United States. Not surprisingly, he possessed a better formal education than any other officer aboard the ship; indeed he was better educated than most officers in the British Merchant Marine. His apprenticeship was done with the steamship company of Runciman's, and he had already worked passages in the South Atlantic and the Mediterranean. Before joining the Leyland Line to gain experience in the North Atlantic he had spent some time with the P. & O. (Peninsular and Orient) Line. This meant that he alone of all of the *Californian*'s officers had any firsthand experience with large passenger liners. In many ways Groves was, with the exception of Captain Lord, the most experienced officer aboard. The Apprentice Officer was named James Gibson. Twenty years old, he had already spent over three years at sea, so that while he had not yet stood for any of his Mate's certificates, he was not entirely without experience.

Cyril Furnston Evans, to give him his full name, was typical of the wireless operators serving on the smaller ships who carried only a single Marconi man. His workday was usually sixteen hours long, beginning at 5:00 a.m. and lasting until 11:00 p.m., although he normally would not spend the entire time at his set. It was already well known among wireless operators and enthusiasts that their apparatus had much greater range at nighttime than during daylight hours, so Evans would work until lunch was served at mid-day, then take a nap until mid-afternoon, rising to go back to his set until 11:00 at night. By then almost all essential traffic would have been passed, and he would have some time for idle chatter with other operators, provided that he wasn't interfering with messages being transmitted or received.

The first eight days of the April 1912 passage proved to be uneventful, although the weather, while still mostly sunny and breezy, was growing steadily colder as the *Californian* progressed westward. On April 14, wireless activity seemed to increase, as more and more ships began reporting encounters with drift ice and icebergs. Due to the unusually warm winter in the Arctic, the amount of ice that broke off the Greenland glacier, as well as the pack ice which drifted down from the Arctic icecap on the Labrador current, was much greater than ususal. It also meant that because of the sheer volume of ice drifting down from the north, the resulting ice fields would stretch much farther south than usual.

It was 9:00 a.m. on the morning of April 14 when Evans took down a report from the Cunard liner *Caronia* that told of "bergs, growlers, and field ice at 42N, from 49 to 51W." It was a general report, not addressed to any specific ship, but Evans thought it important enough to take up to the bridge immediately. At twenty minutes before noon, the Dutch liner *Noordam* reported ice in much the same area, and at 1:42 p.m. a message from the *Baltic* was picked up which read: "Icebergs and large quantity of field ice in 41.51 N 49.9 W."

This one, too, went straight up to the bridge. A few minutes later the *Amerika*, a German ship, sent a warning about ice, mentioning that she had passed two large bergs at 41.27 N, 50.8 W.

The *Californian* made her own ice sighting later that afternoon. Just after 5:00 p.m., Third Officer Groves came up to the bridge to briefly relieve Chief Officer Stewart, who customarily took his dinner with Captain Lord. Groves found both Stewart and Lord on the bridge, scanning the horizon. About five miles to the south, three large bergs could be clearly seen, but no other ice was in sight. After a few moments, Lord and Stewart went below, the Chief Officer making a brief detour to the wireless office to instruct Evans to send out a message about the ice just spotted.

Evans tapped out the warning of his own at 6:30 p.m., when he signaled the *Antillian*, Captain Lord's old command, to tell her of the icebergs, giving the *Californian*'s position as 42.5 N, 49.9 W. An hour later he contacted the new White Star liner *Titanic* to inform her of "three large bergs five miles to southward of us," at 42.3 N, 49.9 W. Not long after that, yet another message arrived, this one from the Atlantic Transport liner *Mesaba*. She had sent out a detailed warning, reading, "Lat. 42 N to 41.25 N, Longitude 40 W to 50.30 W, saw much heavy pack ice and great number large icebergs, also field ice."

Evans' key went quiet again as he spent the next few hours listening to the traffic passing between other ships, as well as that being sent to and from Cape Race in Nova Scotia, which was just coming into range of the *Californian*. Quite a bit of it seemed to be coming from the *Titanic*, Evans noted, much of it paid, personal messages from passengers to friends and family ashore. Some of it seemed extraordinarily frivolous, one message reading, "NO SEASICKNESS. ALL WELL. NOTIFY ALL INTERESTED. POKER BUSINESS GOOD. AL." Evans could only marvel at the idea of having enough money to waste on sending such trivia.

At 8.00 p.m. Third Officer Groves returned to the bridge to take over the watch from the Chief Officer. Stewart relayed the gist of the wireless messages which had been received during the day, and then stood by for about a quarter-hour while Groves' eyes adjusted to the darkness before turning in. The Captain came to the bridge some time later, warning Groves "to keep a sharp lookout for this ice" and reminding him that extra lookouts had been posted far forward, at the extreme bow of the ship, a section known as the "eyes."

The night was extraordinarily clear, with the stars remarkably bright and distinct, and while there was no moon, visibility was excellent. The sea was unusually calm. And it was *cold*—by 10:00 p.m. the air temperature was down to 24 degrees Fahrenheit. The *Californian* continued steaming along at 11 knots on a course of S. 89 W. until a few minutes after 10:00 p.m., when Third Officer Groves spotted several small, white patches in the water dead ahead of the ship. Turning to Captain Lord, he remarked that it looked as if the *Californian* had encountered a group of porpoises.

Captain Lord knew better. One look was all he needed before he strode to the bridge telegraph and rang for FULL SPEED ASTERN on the engines. The white patches were ice—growlers and small bergs that were the fringe of a huge field ahead. Within minutes the *Californian*'s screw was biting hard into the water at it began churning in reverse, and the ship shuddered its entire length, pitching forward slightly, as she came to a stop. As always, prudence was Lord's watchword, and as the *Californian* came to a stop, he decided that he would rather deal with the problem of negotiating a passage through the ice in daylight. Another masthead light was illuminated, so that the *Californian* now showed two of them, the international visual warning of a ship "not underway."

At 11:00 p.m. Captain Lord went below to the chartroom, intending to pass the night stretched out on the settee there. He left specific instructions with Groves to be called if anything was sighted, although any disturbance seemed unlikely. "Absolute peace and quietness prevailed," Groves later recalled, "save for brief snatches of 'Annie Laurie' from an Irish voice which floated up from a stokehold ventilator." The ship drifted quietly on the current, her bows slowly swinging round until she was pointed almost due east. The sea was amazingly calm and the visibility was exceptional, the stars standing out in the night sky with diamond-like intensity.

At about a quarter past eleven, Groves noticed the glare of a ship steaming up over the horizon from the east. Ablaze with lights from bow to stern, the newcomer rapidly came abeam of the motionless *Californian*, passing along her starboard side some ten miles away.

Groves, who knew the look of a passenger ship well, could soon see that she was a large liner, with brightly lit decks piled one on top of the other. Around 11:30 he went down to the chartroom, knocked on the door, and told Captain Lord about the newcomer. Lord suggested that Groves try to contact her by Morse lamp, which he did, but gave up after a few moments when he received no reply.

About 11:40 Groves saw the big liner suddenly seem to stop and put out most of her lights. This didn't seem unusual to Groves; as an old hand of the Far East trade he was familiar with the P. & O. custom to dim their lights around midnight to encourage the passengers to take to their cabins and get to bed. It didn't occur to him that the stranger's lights might have disappeared because she had made a sudden, sharp turn, and was now sitting bow-on to the *Californian*.

Captain Lord too had been watching the new arrival from the port hole in the chartroom, but unlike Groves, who was standing one deck higher and had a much clearer view of the other vessel, Lord didn't believe the ship was much larger than his own *Californian*. He had stepped over to the wireless office at 11:15 and asked his operator, Cyril Evans, if he knew of any other ships nearby, but he made no specific mention of the ship to the south. When Evans replied, "Only the *Titanic*," Lord told him to warn her that the *Californian* had stopped and was surrounded by ice. Now, just a few minutes after the stranger had made that sharp turn, he was back on the bridge, peering intently at the distant ship through his glasses. When Groves informed him that the stranger was a large passenger liner, Lord remarked casually, "That doesn't look like a passenger steamer."

"It is, sir," Groves replied. "When she stopped she put most of her lights out—I suppose they have been put out for the night." Carefully Groves ventured his opinion that he thought her to be not more than ten miles off. Lord gave a noncommittal grunt, then announced he was returning to the chartroom, where he was to be informed if any other ships were spotted, the other ship changed bearing, or anything else unusual occurred.

Meanwhile, in the wireless office, as soon as the Captain had left, Evans slipped on his headphones, adjusted his set, and began tapping out to his friend Jack Phillips on the *Titanic*, "Say old man, we are surrounded by ice and stopped." Evans hadn't bothered to ask Phillips for permission to break into the *Titanic*'s traffic, give a position, or even properly identify himself, but just barged right in, so it was little wonder that Phillips tapped back furiously, "Shut up! Shut up! You are jamming me! I am working Cape Race!"

Despite the seeming harshness of Phillips' rebuke, Evans knew that it wasn't personal—he *had* interfered with the *Titanic*'s signals. Peeved at himself for making such an amateurish mistake, Evans pulled the headphones off and shut down his set. Captain Lord hadn't asked for an acknowledgment from the *Titanic*, and Evans wasn't about to face Phillips' ire a second time by asking for one, or—an even more frightening prospect—risking his captain's wrath by reporting the consequences of his mistake.

The *Titanic*, wherever she was, was so close that her powerful transmitter nearly blew his ears off when Phillips had responded. Evans had had enough; his day was done. So just a few minutes before 11:30, he pulled on his pajamas and settled into his bunk with a book. After perhaps a quarter-hour had passed, Evans put down the book, turned out his reading light, and drifted off to sleep. His workday was over. Certainly nothing was going to happen in the middle of the night that would require his services.

Chapter 4

S O S–*TITANIC*

It was half past eleven o'clock on the night of April 14, 1912, on the North Atlantic, about three hundred miles southeast of Halifax, Nova Scotia. The brand new White Star liner *Titanic*, the largest and most luxurious passenger vessel in the world, was gliding smoothly through the water on her maiden voyage, bound for New York. On the bridge, First Officer William Murdoch had the watch, and he was quietly confident that the remaining two-and-a-half hours before his relief would be quite uneventful.

Even should something unusual arise, Murdoch was a man well-equipped to handle the unexpected. A short, wiry man with a pleasantly plain face and a ready smile that heralded boundless good humor, Murdoch was a Scot from Dalbeattie in Galloway, raised in a seafaring family. Like the *Titanic*'s Second Officer, C.H. Lightoller, he had done his apprenticeship in sail, earned all his certificates, then joined the White Star Line, serving first in the Australian trade, then moving to the passenger liners of the North Atlantic. He had served on an impressive succession of distinguished ships: the *Arabic*, the *Adriatic* (under Captain Smith, now the captain of the *Titanic*), then the *Oceanic*. Most recently he had been Captain Smith's First Officer for two months on the *Titanic*'s sister ship, *Olympic*. Murdoch was a conscientious officer, and as he had amply demonstrated over the years, was an excellent seaman, with nearly faultless judgement and iron nerves. Captain Smith was certain to be glad Murdoch was on board.

Captain Smith, of course, was Captain Edward J. Smith, the commodore of the White Star Line. Solidly built, slightly above medium height, he was handsome in a patriarchal sort of way. His neatly trimmed white beard, coupled with his clear eyes, gave him a somewhat stern countenance, an impression that could be immediately dispelled by his gentle speaking voice and urbane manners. Respectfully and affectionately known as "E.J." by passengers and crew alike, he was a natural leader, radiating a reassuring combination of authority, confidence, and good humor.

Captain Smith had, like most of his officers and most skippers on the North Atlantic, gone to sea as an apprentice at the age of twelve, signing on as a cabin boy on a square-rigged ship. After getting his certificates he signed on with the White Star Line at the age of twenty-seven, and his career had been an uninterrupted series of successes ever since. The captain of a passenger vessel on the North Atlantic run was expected to mingle socially with the First Class passengers, and Smith's dignified manner and warm personality made him instantly popular on White Star ships. Some passengers thought so much of him that they booked crossings only on ships he commanded. White Star rewarded him for generating such a loyal following by giving him command of most of their new ships, so that a maiden voyage with Captain Smith in command became something of a tradition for the line.

He was also much admired among professional circles for his seamanship. "It was an education," Second Officer Herbert Lightoller would later recall, "to see him con his own ship up the intricate channels entering New York at full speed. One particularly bad corner, known as the Southwest Spit, used to make us fairly flush with pride as he swung her round, judging his distances to a nicety; she was heeling over to the helm with only a matter of feet to spare between each end of the ship and the banks." Despite such spectacular ship handling, Smith's career was remarkable for its near-total absence of any accidents or incidents—in contrast to, say, that of Second Officer Lightoller, who had already been shipwrecked twice. In 1907 after Smith brought the brand new *Adriatic* to New York on her maiden voyage, he granted a request by New York papers for an interview. When asked about his career at sea, he responded:

> When anyone asks me how I can best describe my experience of nearly forty years at sea, I merely say, uneventful. Of course there have been winter gales, and storms and fog and the like, but in all my experience, I have never been in any accident of any sort worth speaking about. . . . I never saw a wreck and never been wrecked, nor have I been in any predicament that threatened to end in disaster of any sort . . .

At the same time Smith was asked about the safety of the ships he commanded. He gave his answer with absolute assurance: "I cannot imagine any condition which would cause a ship to founder. I cannot conceive of any vital disaster happening to this vessel. Modern shipbuilding has gone beyond that."

It was just twenty minutes before midnight when Lookout Frederick Fleet, perched high in the crow's nest on the *Titanic*'s foremast with Frederick Lee, thought he saw something straight ahead. The object appeared quite small at first, but grew rapidly in size, and Fleet hesitated for only a few seconds to make sure of the object's identity before reaching up for the pull of the large bronze bell above his head. He gave three rings, the signal for "object ahead," then quickly grabbed the telephone in the box on the mast behind him. After a few anxious seconds, someone on the bridge answered. "What is it?" the voice in the earpiece asked.

"Iceberg right ahead!"

On the bridge, Sixth Officer Moody, who had taken Fleet's report, instantly relayed it to First Officer Murdoch, who reacted swiftly. "Hard a-starboard!" he snapped to the quartermaster who stood at the ship's wheel. Murdoch then rang for full speed astern on both engines. Up in the crow's nest it looked as if the ship would never turn in time, but at the last second the prow swung left, apparently missing the ice. Even so, it looked awfully close, and it seemed to Fleet that he could hear a distant, metallic ripping sound. On the bridge a faint trembling could be felt as the berg passed. Murdoch pulled the switch that closed the watertight doors to the boiler rooms and engine room, then stepped out onto the starboard bridge wing and watched the berg pass by the liner's hull. It was so close he felt he could almost reach out and touch it.

In his cabin, feeling that faint trembling, Captain Smith immediately knew that his ship had struck something, and was on the bridge just seconds after the impact. Imperturbable but with a serious air, he asked, "Mr. Murdoch, what was that?"

"An iceberg, Captain. I ordered hard-a-starboard and rang for full speed astern. I was going to hard-a-port around it, but it was just too close."

"Close the watertight doors."

"Already closed, Captain."

"All stop."

"Aye, Captain." Murdoch turned to the engine room telegraph and rang down for the engines to stop. Just then, Fourth Officer Joseph Boxhall came up to the bridge, and together with Smith and Murdoch, stepped out onto the starboard bridge wing, where for several seconds they peered vainly into the night trying to spot the iceberg. Stepping back inside, Smith sent Boxhall on a quick inspection of the ship. After just a few minutes Boxhall returned, saying he could find no damage below decks. His report didn't satisfy Captain Smith, who told Boxhall, "Go and find the carpenter and get him to sound the ship." As Boxhall ran down the bridge ladder, the carpenter, Jim Hutchinson, pushed past him on his way up to the bridge, blurting out, "She's making water fast!"

Right behind Hutchinson came one of the ship's postal clerks, Iago Smith, calling out, "The mail hold is filling rapidly!"

Boxhall worked his way down to the mail hold and for a minute or two watched the other four mail clerks, standing in water that was already almost knee deep, snatching letters from sorting racks and stuffing them into canvas bags, while around them floated other bags of mail, already full. Boxhall rushed back to the bridge to report what he had seen.

Chief Officer Wilde appeared and asked Captain Smith if it was serious. After hearing Boxhall's report, Smith turned to Wilde and said, "Certainly. It is more than serious." Smith asked for Thomas

Andrews, the *Titanic*'s builder who was making the ship's maiden voyage to help iron out any kinks in the new liner's operations, to be brought to the bridge. He then turned and checked the commutator, a device showing if a ship is listing to port or starboard, or down by the bow or stern. At that moment the commutator showed the *Titanic* listing five degrees to starboard and two degrees down by the head. Smith stared at it for some seconds, then softly muttered, "Oh, my God!"

Moments after Andrews arrived on the bridge, he and Captain Smith were making their own inspection of the damage. They found flooding in the forward cargo holds, the mail room awash, the squash court floor covered with water, and water flooding into boiler rooms 5 and 6. Once back on the bridge, Andrews explained the situation: the collision with the iceberg had left the first six of the *Titanic*'s sixteen watertight compartments opened to the sea. It was simply impossible for the ship to remain afloat with that many of her compartments flooded. Andrews gave the ship less than two hours to live.

But that was not the worst of it. That night the *Titanic* was carrying 2,207 passengers and crew, yet because of hopelessly outdated Board of Trade regulations, there were lifeboats for only 1,178 f them. If no other ship could reach her in time, Andrews' news was a death sentence for half the people on board the ship.

At 12:05 a.m., after issuing orders to uncover the boats and muster the passengers, Captain Smith left the bridge and walked back to the wireless shack. Inside, Senior Wireless Operator John Phillips and Junior Operator Harold Bride were completely unaware that anything had happened. Phillips was exhausted, having spent most of the day repairing a broken transmitter; once that job was done, he had been faced with a huge backlog of messages and was still desperately trying to get caught up. Mindful of Phillip's fatigue, even though he wasn't scheduled to come on duty until 2 a.m., Bride had offered to relieve Phillips at midnight to allow the senior operator to get some extra rest. Bride had just finished dressing when Captain Smith walked into the cabin.

"We've struck an iceberg," the captain announced without preamble. "You'd better get ready to send out a call for assistance, but don't send it until I tell you." By this time Bride had taken Phillips' place at the transmitter, and Phillips was behind the green curtain that separated their bunks from the wireless room itself. After hearing Captain Smith's announcement, Phillips began getting dressed again.

Smith then returned to the chartroom, and once again asked for Fourth Officer Boxhall. At age 30, Boxhall had been with the White Star Line for five years. He came from a seafaring family, and indeed there must have been something nautical in his genes, for he had already acquired a reputation as being an outstanding navigator. Captain Smith had so much confidence in his skill that he routinely assigned Boxhall the responsibility of keeping the ship's charts up-to-date, including any position, weather, or ice reports the *Titanic* might receive. Now he asked Boxhall to work out the *Titanic*'s current position.

There was no time for the complicated procedure of taking star sights, so Boxhall worked out the *Titanic*'s position through a process known as "dead reckoning." Actually the term is something of a misnomer, for the "dead" comes from a verbal shorthand for "deductive"—the ship's position would be "deduced" by starting with the last sun sighting taken that day (around 7:30 p.m.), then using the ship's speed to determine how far she had traveled along her given course since that time. Boxhall worked swiftly but competently; though his position would eventually be shown to be in error, that would be due to factors unknown to him at the time.

First, he based his speed calculations on the known performance of the *Titanic*'s sister ship, the *Olympic*. With her main engines making 72 turns per minute, as the *Titanic*'s had been at the moment of the collision, the *Olympic* made a speed of 22 knots. But the *Titanic*, with her propellors ("screws" the British called them) set to a different pitch than those of her sister, was slightly slower than the *Olympic*, and 72 r.p.m. on the main engines translated to a little over 21 knots. Boxhall also wasn't aware that the bridge clock hadn't been set back twenty minutes at the 10 o'clock change of watch, a customary adjustment done to compensate for the ship's westward travel. These factors, plus the presence of a northwest-to-southeast current of which Boxhall was unaware, meant that the *Titanic* had traveled about fourteen miles less than he estimated. When he finally handed his completed position to Captain Smith—41.46' N, 50.14' W—the latitude was essentially correct but the longitude actually placed the

Titanic to the west of where she actually was.

A few moments later Smith was back in the wireless office telling Phillips simply, "Send the call for assistance!" Phillips asked if he should send the regulation call, and Smith said, "Yes, at once!" Then he handed Phillips a slip of paper with the *Titanic's* position on it.

Phillips and Bride switched places again, and Phillips put the headphones over his ears. At 12:15 a.m. he began tapping out the letters "CQD"—the international signal for distress: "CQ—All Stations" "D—Distress"—followed by "MGY," the *Titanic's* call letters, and the position "41.46 N, 50.14 W."

"CQD...CQD...MGY...41.46 N, 50.14 W...CQD...MGY...."

It was a few minutes past midnight on the *Carpathia* when her wireless operator, Harold Cottam, left the bridge and returned to his wireless office, having just handed several routine wireless messages to First Officer Horace Dean. Once there he remembered some traffic he'd been listening to earlier that night, including a number of messages for the new White Star liner *Titanic*. He thought he would remind Jack Phillips, the new ship's senior operator whom he knew professionally, about those waiting messages. It took a few minutes for the set to warm up, then he politely tapped out a call to the *Titanic*, quickly receiving a curt "Go ahead."

"Good morning, old man [GM OM]. Do you know there are messages for you at Cape Race?"

What Cottam heard next made his blood run cold. Instead of the expected jaunty reply came the dreaded "CQD...CQD...SOS... SOS...CQD...MGY. Come at once. We have struck a berg. It's a CQD, old man [CQD OM]. Position 41.46 N, 50.14 W."

Stunned, Cottam did nothing for a moment, then asked Phillips if he should tell his captain. The reply was immediate: "Yes, quick." Cottam raced to the bridge and breathlessly told First Officer Dean. Dean didn't hesitate—he bolted down the ladder, through the chartroom and into the captain's cabin, Cottam hard on his heels.

For Captain Rostron, such indecorous behavior was a bit much. People were expected to at least knock before barging in on the captain, especially when he was asleep. But the reprimand died on his lips when a clearly anxious Dean told him about the *Titanic*. Rostron swung his legs out of bed and then seemed lost in thought for a few seconds as he digested the news.

"Mr. Dean, turn the ship around—steer northwest. I'll work out the course for you in a minute." As Dean sped back to the bridge, Rostron turned his attention to Cottam. "Are you sure it's the *Titanic* and she requires immediate assistance?" he asked.

"Yes, sir."

"You are absolutely certain?"

"Quite certain, sir."

"All right, tell him we are coming along as fast as we can." Cottam dashed back to his wireless set, and quickly began tapping out a message to the *Titanic*.

At 12:25 Phillips got his first piece of good news. While Cottam had missed the *Titanic*'s first CQD, he reacted quickly when Phillips brushed aside his question about the traffic waiting for the *Titanic* at Cape Race with a staccato "Come at once. We have struck a berg . . ." After a few moment's pause as the *Carpathia*'s operator rushed up to the bridge to inform his captain, he was back at his key with the welcome news that the *Carpathia* was only fifty-eight miles away and "coming hard." Phillips sent Bride to find Captain Smith and relay the news to him.

As soon as Cottam and Dean left his cabin, Arthur Rostron began donning his uniform, and as he dressed his mind was racing. This would be his first real test as a captain, as he had never faced this sort of emergency before. It isn't difficult to imagine his thoughts in those moments: exactly *how* should he prepare his ship for a rescue? And did the *Carpathia* even have room for as many as possibly three thousand extra people? The routine of putting on his uniform gave Rostron a valuable few minutes to organize his thoughts for the potentially daunting task ahead, and as he made his way to the *Carpathia*'s bridge, his mind was clear. There was no hesitation, no second guessing. Perhaps without even realizing it, he had gone into action the moment he heard the news from First Officer Dean. The first words out of his mouth had been the order to turn the ship around—*then* he had asked Cottam for confirmation. There had been no prevarication on Rostron's part, no instructions to Cottam to find out if there were any ships closer to the *Titanic* or better suited than the *Carpathia* to handle such an emergency. To Rostron, the *Titanic*'s CQD was a clear call to duty—he had no choice but to answer.

As he straightened his tie and set his cap square on his head, Rostron settled the last few details in his mind. Standing over the chart table before him, he began working out the *Carpathia*'s new course. Then he stepped out of the chartroom, climbed the ladder to the bridge, and strode over to the quartermaster. It seemed as though he gained confidence from each step he took, each act he performed. He gave the helmsman the new course—North 52 West—then called down to the engine room to order "Full Speed Ahead." At the *Carpathia*'s top speed of 14 knots she would cover the distance between herself and the *Titanic* in four hours, which was not good enough for Rostron. Now he really swung into action.

Returning to the chartroom he called for Chief Engineer Johnston, and explained the situation to the dour Scot. Speed, he told Johnston. He wanted more speed than the old *Carpathia* had ever mustered. Call out the off-duty watch to the engine room, he said, and get every available stoker roused to feed the furnaces. Cut off the heat and hot water to passenger and crew accommodations, and put every ounce of steam the boilers made into the engines.

Next he spoke to First Officer Dean and gave him a list of things to be done: all routine work was to cease as the ship prepared for a rescue operation, swing out the ship's lifeboats, to have them ready if needed; have clusters of electric lights rigged along the ship's sides; all gangway doors to be opened, with block and tackle slung at each gangway; slings ready for hoisting injured aboard, and canvas bags for lifting small children; ladders prepared for dropping at each gangway, along with cargo nets; forward derricks to be rigged and topped, with steam in the winches, for bringing luggage and cargo aboard; oil bags readied in the lavatories to pour on rough seas if needed.

Dean set to immediately and Rostron turned to the ship's surgeon, Dr. McGhee. The three surgeons aboard, McGhee, an Italian physician, and one who was Hungarian, were to be assigned to specific stations—McGhee himself in First Class, the Italian doctor in Second, and the Hungarian doctor in Third. All three were to be supplied with stimulants and restoratives, and first aid stations were to be set up in each dining saloon.

He said to Purser Brown: see that the Chief Steward, the Assistant Purser and the Purser himself each covered a different gangway to receive the *Titanic*'s passengers and crew; get their names and classes, and see to it that each one went to the correct dining saloon for a medical check.

Chief Steward Henry Hughes received an additional set of instructions: every crewman was to be called out; coffee was to be available for all hands. Also, soup, coffee, tea, brandy, and whiskey should be ready for those rescued; the smoking room, lounge, and library were to be converted into dormitories for survivors. All the *Carpathia*'s steerage passengers were to be grouped together; the extra space would be given over to the *Titanic*'s steerage passengers.

Finally, Rostron urged everyone to keep quiet. The last thing they needed was for the *Carpathia*'s passengers to be lurking about while there was work to be done. To help keep the passengers where they belonged, stewards were stationed along every corridor to shepherd the curious back into their cabins. An inspector, a master-at-arms, and several stewards were sent down to keep the steerage passengers in order—no one was sure if they would take too kindly to being herded about in the wee hours of the morning.

His instructions issued, Rostron quickly reviewed everything he had ordered, trying to think of what he had overlooked in his preparations. There didn't seem to be anything, so he quickly strode to the bridge and began posting extra lookouts. He was determined that the *Carpathia* would not meet the same fate as the ship she was rushing to aid. Rostron had an extra man posted in the crow's nest, two lookouts in the bow, extra hands posted on both bridge wings, and Second Officer James Bisset, who had especially keen eyesight, posted on the starboard bridge wing.

Now having done all he could do, Rostron faced the toughest task—waiting. But there was one last detail Rostron attended to. Second Officer Bisset noticed it first, then so did the others on the bridge—the Captain was standing toward the back of the bridge holding his cap an inch or two off his head, eyes closed, lips moving in silent prayer.

The order to uncover and swing out the *Titanic*'s lifeboats had been given by Captain Smith just after midnight. It was probably one of the most agonizing decisions of his career, for it brought him face-to-face with an awful truth only he and a handful of others aboard the sinking liner knew: the *Titanic* had lifeboats for barely half the people aboard her that night. The Board of Trade, which regulated such matters, had concocted a complicated formula for determining the lifeboat requirements of British-registered vessels. Specifically this stated that any ship over 10,000 tons must carry sixteen lifeboats with space for 550 people, plus enough rafts and floats to equal 75 percent of the capacity of the lifeboats. For the *Titanic* this worked out to a requirement for lifeboats for 962 persons.

Actually, her lifeboat capacity exceeded the Board of Trade requirements, since the White Star Line had added four Englehardt collapsibles, wooden keels with folding canvas sides, to the ship's complement of boats. Together with the required sixteen boats they gave the *Titanic* a capacity of 11,780 cubic feet, or room for 1,178 people. The nightmare that was about to confront Captain Smith was the fact that *Titanic* was carrying 2,207 passengers and crew. If help did not arrive in time, the collision with the iceberg was a death sentence for almost half the people aboard.

A sort of quiet, controlled frenzy swept over the *Carpathia* as her speed increased and her bow swung around to the northwest. Seaman Robert Vaughn was awakened by a sharp tug at the blanket he'd wrapped about himself when he'd settled into his bunk for the night, and an unseen voice told him to get up and get dressed. All about him his bunkmates were already pulling their clothes on—or so it seemed. The crew's quarters were pitch black, the lights either not working properly or else had gone missing, and Vaughn wondered aloud what was up. He was told the *Carpathia* had struck an iceberg.

It only took a quick glance out the porthole to put that rumor to rest—the ship was clearly driving hard through a slowly rising Atlantic swell. Once dressed, Vaughn and his shipmates quickly made their way to the upper deck, where First Officer Dean set them to work with a will. The first order of business was to swing out the lifeboats and have them readied for lowering. If the *Titanic*'s boats should

prove to be insufficient for the number of people aboard her, the
Carpathia's would have to ready to assist them. The time spent clear-
ing and swinging a boat out might be the difference between life and
death for some poor souls struggling in the freezing water. So the crew
swarmed across the *Carpathia*'s sixteen lifeboats, rolling up the canvas covers, undoing the lines lashing them to their deck cradles, check-
ing the oars and oarlocks, making certain the drainplugs were in place
and secure. With a series of creaks and groans from the block-and-
tackle sets suspending the boats from the davit arms, each lifeboat was
lifted free of its cradles, the blocks holding it in place knocked free,
and then in a carefully orchestrated series of movements, first the bow
then the stern of each boat was swung over the side, and snubbing
chains attached to keep them from swinging back and forth.

It was 12:34 by the clock in the *Titanic*'s wireless room when the
German liner *Frankfurt* responded, giving her position: 150 miles
away. Phillips asked, "Are you coming to our assistance?" The
German liner asked, "What is the matter with you?" Patiently, Phillips
tapped back: "Tell your captain to come to our help. We are on the
ice."

At this moment *Olympic* barged in. She was five hundred miles
away, but her powerful wireless easily put her in touch with her strick-
en sister. Phillips asked her to stand by. Captain Smith had just come
in the cabin to get a firsthand report of the situation. Phillips reminded him about the *Carpathia*.

"What call are you sending?" Smith asked.

"CQD," Phillips replied.

The exchange jogged Bride's memory. Recently an international
convention had introduced a new distress call to supersede the traditional CQD. It had chosen the letters SOS—not because they stood for
anything in particular, but because they were simple enough for even
amateurs to send and receive. Bride suggested to Phillips, "Send SOS;
it's the new call, and besides this may be your last chance to send it!"

Phillips, Smith, and Bride all laughed together, and at 12:45 a.m.
the *Titanic* sent out her first SOS. Phillips would continue to send the
new signal, interspersed with the traditional CQD call, as long as the
power lasted.

Down in the boiler room of the *Carpathia*, as word of the *Carpathia*'s mission spread, it soon seemed as if the entire "black gang" had been infused with Rostron's energy. The extra hands began shoveling coal into the furnaces of the boilers like they had never shoveled coal before. First the safety valves were closed off, then under Chief Engineer Johnston's careful guidance, the engineers began to systematically shut off steam to the rest of the ship, ducting it instead into the reciprocating engines. It was a scene straight out of Dante's Inferno, the sweating, grimy stokers, some wearing little more than their unionsuits and boots, shoveling coal into the glowing maws of the fireboxes, their faces and hands gleaming copper and bronze in the light of the fires. Wisps of smoke drifted through the gloom, while trimmers lugged their wheelbarrows back and forth between the bunkers and the fireboxes, determined that the stokers would never lack for coal.

Back in the engine room, the massive engines whirled, spun, and stroked as the *Carpathia* accelerated. The reciprocating steam engine at work was a spectacle of power the like of which has never been seen before or since, an intricate yet awesome ballet of power as the engines moved ever faster. It was Rudyard Kipling in his poem *McAndrews' Hymn* who most unforgettably captured the majesty of such engines:

> *To match wi Scotia's noblest speech yon orchestra sublime*
> *Whaurto—uplifted like the Just—the tail-rods mark the time.*
> *The crankshaft throws ghie the dimble bass, the feed pump sobs*
> *   an' heaves,*
> *An' now the main eccentrics start their quarrel in the sheaves:*
> *Her time, her own appointed time, the rocking link-head bides,*
> *Till—hear that note?—the rod's return whings glimmerin' through*
> *   the guides.*
> *They're all awa'! True beat, full power, the clangin' chorus goes*
> *Clear to the tunnel where they sit, my purrin' dynamos.*
> *Interdependence absolute, foreseen, ordained, decreed,*
> *To work, Ye'll note, at ony tilt an' every rate o' speed.*
> *Fra' skylight-lift to furnace bars, backed, bolted, braced an'*
> *   stayed,*
> *An' singin' like the Mornin' Stars for joy that they are made;*

While, out o' touch o' vanity, the sweatin' thrust-block says:
"Not unto us the praise, or man—not unto us the praise!"
Now, a' together, hear them lift their lesson—theirs an' mine:
"Law, Orrder, Duty an' Restraint, Obedience, Discipline!"
Mill, forge an' try-pit taught them that when roarin' they arose,
An' whiles I wonder if a soul was gied them wi' the blows.

And so the *Carpathia*'s engines pounded, pushing her, driving her forward with an urgency no steamship had ever known before, or would ever know again. Up, down, up, down, up, down, the pistons pounded, as Chief Engineer Johnston watched the revolutions steadily increasing. The gauges showed the ship going faster and faster as she drove ahead—14½ knots . . . 15½ . . . 16 . . . 16½ . . . 17 knots— the old *Carpathia* had never gone so fast.

(Decades later purists with a revisionist bent, citing a multitude of technical and technological details, among them the *Carpathia*'s size, hull form, engine design, and age, would claim––possibly correctly–– that the ship was never capable of a speed of 17 knots, and in all probability barely reached 16. It's a debating point certain to delight the most avid rivet-counter and technophile; but what remains unchallenged and unchallengeable is that in the early hours of April 15, 1912, the *Carpathia* was driven faster than her designers and builders would have ever believed possible.)

This was the sort of situation for which a man like Alexander Johnston was born. Fifty-nine years old, a burly man with a fine white moustache, he hailed from Scotland's western coast, a prototypical Scots "artifex"—engineer—reminiscent of "the auld chief engineer" who is the hero of "McAndrew's Hymn." He tended his boilers and engines with the same sort of devotion many men reserved for their children, knowing the strengths, weaknesses, quirks, and eccentricities of each piece of machinery in his charge. Yet it was his lavish care and attention to the details of their operations over the years that caused the *Carpathia*'s twelve-year-old boilers and engines to be equal to such an ordeal. Whatever claims might be made or denied about the speeds the *Carpathia* attained that night, what could never be denied was that her engines never missed a beat.

By 12:20, Captain Smith had given orders for the *Titanic*'s passengers to be put into the lifeboats—"Women and children first!"—and assigned the starboard side boats to First Officer Murdoch, giving the portside responsibilities to Second Officer Lightoller. Both men took their responsibilities very seriously, although their interpretation of their orders somewhat differed. Murdoch took "Women and children first!" to mean just that—they had first priority when a boat was being loaded. But when there were no women forthcoming, or those who were at hand refused to leave their husbands, he would relent and allow husbands and wives together into the boats. When there were no more married couples standing by, a handful of single men were given permission to climb into the lifeboats.

Lightoller, on the other hand, took "Women and children first!" a little further, interpreting it to mean women and children only. And sometimes he would be the one to decide where the line between child and adult was to be drawn. At one point, while putting passengers into Boat No. 4, he suddenly spotted a teenage boy, Jack Ryerson, climbing over the gunwale, and called out, "That boy can't go!" Jack's father, Arthur Ryerson bristled. Placing his arm around Jack's shoulders he said, "Of course the boy goes with his mother—he's only thirteen." Lightoller relented, but was heard to mutter, "No more boys."

The lifeboats were filled and launched haphazardly, as many women refused to leave their husbands, and passengers of both sexes questioned the wisdom of leaving the warm, brightly lit *Titanic* in order to splash about in mid-ocean in a open boat, especially when the air temperature was only about 25°, the water barely 28°. Eventually, at about 12:45, Boat No. 5, filled to about a third of its actual capacity, was lowered down to the water, the first lifeboat to get away from the sinking liner.

Once the *Carpathia*'s boats were readied, her officers divided the crew into work gangs, each assigned to a particular task. Seaman Vaughn found himself collecting unused blankets from throughout the ship and depositing them in the First Class Lounge, where he and several other crewmen began shifting tables, chairs, and sideboards; some of the men were busy transferring the contents of the liquor cabinet to the buffet. It was all so mysterious. Vaughn heard a rumor that Captain Rostron had given instructions that the ship be prepared to take on as many as 3,000 additional people, but where they were to come from, the crew had no idea—and they were too busy at the moment to try to figure it out.

Once the lounges were readied, the next job was preparing the gangways along the side of the ship. The first step in the task was to rig the electric lights. Rostron had calculated that the *Carpathia* would reach the *Titanic*'s position by 4:00 a.m., still complete darkness at those latitudes at that time of year. He was determined that there be no accidents due to passengers or crewmen from the *Titanic* trying to grope their way into the *Carpathia* in the darkness, so Dean's men hurriedly strung cables and affixed clusters of bright lamps to brackets on the liner's hull above each of the four gangways on each side of the ship. While this was being done, other seamen were busily rigging block-and-tackle at each of the gangways, with slings and heavy canvas bags at hand for use in lifting survivors aboard. Rostron was trying to cover every eventuality, and he realized that the people rescued from the *Titanic* might well be so physically and emotionally exhausted that they would be unable to climb any sort of ladder up the side of the ship from the bottom of a lifeboat. At the same time, he realized that some of them might be able to do just that, hence the presence of the rope ladders and cargo nets at the gangway doors.

The optimist and the pessimist existed side-by-side in the work the *Carpathia*'s crew was finishing. The ship's forward derricks were rigged and topped, with steam in the winches—the *only* steam generated by the ship's boilers that was *not* going to the engines, for in the event that the *Titanic* was still afloat when the *Carpathia* arrived, Rostron intended to do his best to bring as much of her luggage and cargo aboard as he could, particularly the Royal Mail. At the same time, gash-bags of oil were prepared, ready to be cut open and their contents pumped over the ship's side, in case the seas became rough. Rostron knew the North Atlantic well enough to know that it could be two entirely different oceans just sixty miles apart.

By 1:15 the *Titanic*'s wireless operator, Phillips, was beginning to worry. Where was everybody? It had been nearly an hour since the

Carpathia informed him that she was putting about and "coming hard," but that had been the only good news he'd had so far. And even that had come with a depressing qualification: the *Carpathia* was fifty-eight miles away and it would be nearly four hours before she arrived. Though Captain Smith hadn't said as much, in his heart Phillips probably knew that the *Titanic* didn't have four hours left to live. Anxiously he continued tapping away, hoping that some ship—any ship—would be closer and finally answer.

He was beginning to feel the strain. Perhaps it didn't seem possible to the other ships that the "unsinkable" *Titanic* could be in mortal danger, and in vain Phillips was trying to make them understand. When at 1:25 the *Olympic* asked, "Are you steering south to meet us?" Phillips tapped back in exasperation, "We are putting the women off in the boats," feeling that should make the situation clear enough to anyone. The *Frankfurt*'s operator, who appeared to ignore any communication not addressed directly to his ship, broke in with, "Are there any ships around you already?" Then, a few seconds later: "The *Frankfurt* wishes to know what is the matter? We are ten hours away."

This was too much for Phillips, who suddenly jumped up, tearing the headphones from his ears, and shouted, "The damn fool! He says, 'What's up, old man?'!" Furiously he tapped back, "You are jamming my equipment! Stand by and keep out!"

Every few minutes Captain Smith would drop by to see if Phillips was having any success raising a ship closer than the *Carpathia*, and to provide Phillips with further information. It was a quarter past one when Smith informed Phillips that the power was beginning to fade, maybe ten minutes later when he told him the water was reaching the engine rooms. At 1:45 a.m. Phillips again called the *Carpathia*, this time telling her, "Come as quickly as possible, old man; engine room filling up to the boilers."

On the *Carpathia*, now that the officers all had their assigned tasks and the crew was set to work, the navigation worked out, and perhaps most important of all for Rostron, prayers offered up to the Almighty, the most difficult part of this morning's sudden challenge began—the waiting. He was confident of his crew and ship, confident of the course he had laid out, confident of his skills as a navigator and ship handler. Yet there were still many things that could go wrong! Rostron was determined that no detail would go overlooked that might delay the *Carpathia,* or cost some poor victim their life once the ship reached the *Titanic*'s side; yet there was always the element of chance, the unknown, that could mean peril for the *Carpathia.*

For Rostron was under no illusion as to the fact that he *was* taking his ship, his crew, and his passengers into the unknown. The greatest threat was, of course, ice. Had the *Titanic,* by the most evil mischance, struck a solitary iceberg adrift in mid-ocean, or had she run deep into an icefield before coming to grief? When the *Carpathia* arrived at the *Titanic*'s position, would she be able to get close enough to help the sinking ship and her passengers and crew, or would the icefield intervene, forcing the *Carpathia* to stand off in the distance, impotent to do nothing more than watch the *Titanic*'s last moments?

On the *Titanic,* Phillips was still bent over the wireless key, mechanically tapping out his call, hoping that by some miracle a closer ship would suddenly respond. Even if the *Frankfurt,* the *Olympic,* or any of the other ships didn't realize it—though thankfully Cottam on the *Carpathia* had understood the seriousness of the situation—by now Phillips knew that the ship was doomed. Just a few moments earlier, he had been relieved by Bride while he took a turn around the Boat Deck. When he returned to the wireless shack a few minutes later, all he could do was shake his head as he took over from Bride again and mutter, "Things look very queer outside, very queer indeed." He had watched as the sea swept over the foredeck, washing past the foot of the foremast, swirling around the winches and cranes, flooding into the forward well deck. It was clear that the *Titanic*'s remaining time would be measured in minutes, not hours.

The news was spreading, however. Ships within range of the *Titanic* passed the word on to other ships that were not, and the Marconi station at Cape Race was able to pick up Phillips' signals directly. Soon the operator there began relaying the *Titanic*'s messages inland, where they were picked up by the wireless station atop the *New York Times* building in New York city. In Philadelphia, Wannamaker's department store had recently installed a wireless office, capitalizing on the public's interest in the new technology. The office had actually been set up in one of the store's front windows, and this was where a young wireless operator named David Sarnoff caught the signals from Cape Race. He in turn quickly passed the word on to other stations farther inland; slowly the New World was becoming aware of the unfolding tragedy in the North Atlantic.

By now there were precious few lifeboats left, and the situation began to get ugly. Earlier, a wave of male passengers had tried to force their way into Boat 14, and one of the *Titanic's* seamen used the boat's tiller bar like a club to drive them back. Furious, Fifth Officer Lowe drew his revolver and shouted at the malefactors, "If anyone else tries that this is what he'll get!" then fired three times along the side of the ship. Near the bridge a scuffle broke out around Collapsible C when a mob of stewards and Third Class passengers rushed the boat, trying to climb aboard. Purser McElroy drew his revolver and fired twice into the air to hold the rest of the crowd back, while First Officer Murdoch and two men from First Class began dragging the culprits out of the boat.

A few moments later, Second Officer Lightoller discovered a large group of men—passengers and crewmen—already huddled in Boat 2. Furious, Lightoller drew his revolver and leveled it at them, shouting, "Get out of there, you damned cowards! I'd like to see every one of you overboard!" There was a mad scramble as the men fled the lifeboat. They had no way of knowing that Lightoller's gun wasn't even loaded—and they had all heard shots fired further down the deck just a few minutes before. Not wanting to press his luck, Lightoller turned over Boat 2 to Fourth Officer Joseph Boxhall, who had been firing off distress rockets in the hope of attracting the attention of a ship sighted nearby not long after the collision. In short order Boxhall loaded the boat with twenty-five women, one male passenger from steerage, and three crewmen, and then had Boat 2 lowered to the sea below.

Aboard the *Carpathia*, Rostron's concern about the passengers getting underfoot during the crew's preparations for the rescue were well founded. Not that any of them would have deliberately gotten in the way or interfered with the crew's activities, but the *Carpathia*, for all of her lack of glamor, was a popular ship: many of her passengers had sailed on her many times, and had come to know the rhythms and routines of her Atlantic crossings. So when Mrs. Annie Crain awoke at 1:00 a.m. to the smell of fresh-brewed coffee wafting down the passageway outside her cabin, it aroused her curiosity, though not her apprehensions.

A few doors down from Mrs. Crain's cabin, it was different. There Mrs. Louis Ogden shook her husband awake, disturbed by the lack of heat in the cabin and the vibration that was shaking the entire ship. The Ogdens were experienced travelers, and Mrs. Ogden knew the *Carpathia* well enough to know that the liner was steaming as hard as she could, something which had rarely before happened. Once awake, Mr. Ogden agreed with his wife that it *was* an unusual situation—and the sounds from overhead didn't do much to reassure him. Various bumps, thumps, and creakings from machinery told him that the crew was doing *something* with the *Carpathia*'s lifeboats; Ogden didn't know just what, but when he opened his cabin door and peered down the corridor, the sight of stewards and stewardesses carrying blankets and mattresses didn't inspire much confidence.

On the other side of the ship, up on A-Deck, Howard M. Chapin had a similar experience. Awakened by a series of unfamiliar noises coming from the deck directly over his bunk, it took Chapin a few minutes to recall that a cleat used to tie off the falls of one of the *Carpathia*'s lifeboats was located in that exact spot: Chapin had idly made a mental note of it as he was walking the upper deck the day before. Now, he realized, someone was working the line tied off on that cleat. Looking about him, he noticed other details—the mattress of his bunk, which always seemed to vibrate gently in rhythm with the engines, was shaking harder than it ever had before, while the washstand basin and the glasses sitting beside it rattled in their brackets. All through the ship the plates creaked, the woodwork groaned, and the decks and bulkheads hummed as the *Carpathia* drove through the night.

All the lifeboats were gone by now and the *Titanic* was clearly only moments away from going under. There was one last, painful duty for Captain Smith to perform. Sometime around 2:10 a.m. he walked up the port side of the Boat Deck to the wireless shack, where he found Phillips still hunched over his key, tapping away. Quietly, Smith told Phillips and Bride, "Men, you have done your full duty. You can do no more. Abandon your cabin. Now it's every man for himself." Phillips glanced up at him, then went back to Morsing. The Captain continued: "You look out for yourselves; I release you. That's the way of it at this kind of time." Then he turned and left the wireless shack for the last time. Without a word, Phillips continued to tap out his distress call. The lights were starting to take on an orange glow as the power began slowly fading. Phillips was tinkering with the set, trying to adjust the spark to make it stronger. At 2:10 he tapped out two "V"s as a test; at 2:17, the *Virginian* heard a faint "CQD...CQ—" that ended abruptly. They were the last transmission anyone heard from the *Titanic*.

Aboard the *Carpathia*, little groups of passengers began huddling in obscure corners of the upper decks and superstructure. The crew had done their best to keep them in their cabins and out of the way, but the more resourceful among them managed to eventually elude the watchful eyes of their stewards and stewardesses and slipped out of their rooms. Some, like the Ogdens, had made fanciful leaps of logic about the ship's condition, which added to their desire to reach the open decks.

Ogden had seen some of the *Carpathia*'s stewards and stewardesses moving blankets and bedding down the corridors of the ship, but failed to receive an explanation for their unusual actions. In fairness to those crewmen, they didn't yet know why they were doing it either—Chief Steward Henry Hughes hadn't yet had time to explain to his staff why all of the bustle and urgency was necessary. It wasn't until almost an hour after Cottam had picked up the *Titanic*'s "CQD" that Hughes was able to call his people together and break the news to them. Hughes thought his people could do a better job if they had an idea of what was happening, so at 1:15 a.m. he gathered them in the main dining saloon, and quickly, quietly, told them about the *Titanic*. He explained how the rescue was up to the *Carpathia*, then paused dramatically, eyeing each man directly, and solemnly intoned: "Every man to his post and let him do his duty like a true Englishman.

If the situation calls for it, let us add another glorious page to British history." The stewards immediately set to work, determined that when they arrived at the *Titanic*'s side, they would be ready for anything.

But Louis Ogden knew nothing of this. When he tried to leave his cabin, he encountered the *Carpathia*'s surgeon, Dr. McGhee, who urged him to remain in his room. When Ogden pressed the doctor for details, the physician simply replied, "An accident, but not to our ship. Now, please go back to your room." A hasty conference between Mr. and Mrs. Ogden produced the slightly bizarre conclusion that the ship was on fire, and their only chance for safety lay in reaching the open decks. Quickly dressing, Ogden slipped into the corridor and out a side door onto the upper deck, where he encountered a quartermaster he knew from his frequent passages on the ship. Pressing the man for an answer, Ogden was finally told about the *Titanic*. He was frankly disbelieving, replying to the crewman, "You'll have to do better than that! We are on the southern route and the *Titanic* is on the northern!"

"We're going north like hell!" the quartermaster replied sharply. "Now, get back to your cabin!"

Subdued but undaunted, Odgen returned to once again confer with his wife, who, like her husband, refused to believe the quarter-master's story. Dressing as warmly as they could, they reached the upper deck and found a handful of other passengers gathered there in the shelter of the Promenade Deck. Huddling together, the little knot of passengers quickly pooled their meager amount of knowledge, and soon realized that they had all been told the same story—unbelievable as it may have seemed. The *Carpathia* was rushing to the aid of the stricken *Titanic*. Beyond that they knew nothing, but simply stood quietly, peering into the incredibly star-filled sky and the black water surrounding their ship.

The *Titanic* was gone now, slipping beneath the surface at 2:20 a.m. Now the stars that had watched her sink shone down on a scene of almost unbelievable horror. The sea around the spot where the *Titanic* had disappeared was covered with a mass of tangled wreckage, and struggling in the midst of it were hundreds of helpless passengers and crew, swept off the ship as she took her final plunge. Over everything hung a grey mist, just a few feet overhead. The water where the ship had gone under was still troubled, as every few seconds a bubble of air released from the wreck welled up from below, or more wreckage and debris popped to the surface.

The temperature of the water was only 28 degrees, cold enough to sap the life out of a human being in less than twenty minutes. Survivors would liken the sensation of being suddenly plunged into the water to that of "a thousand knives." One crewman was still shuddering and sucking in his breath years later when he described what he called the "stabbing cold." Hundreds of swimmers struggled in the water, clutching at the wreckage—and sometimes each other—desperately trying to stay afloat and fight off the insidious chill.

Twenty boats bobbed in the slowly rising swell, as across the water came the mingled cries of those struggling amid the wreckage. With the exceptions of Collapsible B, which had overturned as it was being launched, and where now more than fifty men were standing on its keel in a desperate gamble to survive, and Collapsible C, which was dangerously overloaded, there was room in the *Titanic*'s lifeboats for hundreds more people. Over and over again the cry "Save one life! Save one life!" was heard, rising above the nearly continuous pleadings of people in distress.

And yet, in what was probably the greatest tragedy of that terrible night, only one boat went back in an attempt to pluck swimmers from the freezing water. Fifth Officer Lowe ordered the boat under his command, No. 14, to return to the spot where the *Titanic* had gone under, but sadly accomplished little, pulling only three survivors from the water. The cold had taken the rest.

For them, death had come quickly. The cold swiftly numbed their hands, their feet, their heads, and within minutes they lost consciousness. The icy sea continued to sap the warmth from their bodies until after fifteen, perhaps twenty minutes at the most, their hearts could take no more, and, giving up the unequal struggle, finally stopped. Bodies floated motionless and silent, slowly being swept off by the current, away from the great ice floe, into the open waters of the North Atlantic.

Around 2:40, while talking to Dr. McGhee, the *Carpathia*'s Captain Rostron had caught a glimpse of green light—clearly a flare of some sort—on the horizon just off the port bow. "There's his light!" Rostron exclaimed. "He must still be afloat!" It would prove to be an optical illusion, however, as the light—actually a flare being set off in one of the *Titanic*'s lifeboats—was much farther away than Rostron surmised. The exceptional conditions of this night—the remarkable visibility coupled with near total darkness—had deceived him, as it caused any light to carry farther than it would have normally. On the other hand, the unusually good visibility was also now working to Rostron's advantage, as the *Carpathia* was now entering the edge of the icefield where the *Titanic* had come to grief.

A few minutes after Rostron saw the green flare, Second Officer Bisset spotted the first iceberg, dimly lit by the reflected light of a star. Moments later a second berg was sighted close by, then a third. The precaution Rostron had taken in posting extra lookouts was paying remarkable dividends, as the men in the bow and on the bridge were able to spot the bergs and growlers before the *Carpathia* approached dangerously near, allowing the ship to be maneuvered around them without any slackening of speed.

It was just one more irony on a night filled with them, because had Captain Smith posted extra lookouts in the same positions on the *Titanic* that Rostron placed his on the *Carpathia*, the little Cunarder's mission of mercy would have been unnecessary. Seamen had long known that at night, the closer a lookout was posted to the level of the sea, the better he could spot approaching objects—the occlusion of stars and sky by an object against the horizon was usually all that was needed to give away its position. Thus a man at deck level in the bow stood a much better chance of seeing danger ahead of the ship than lookouts posted high above the deck in the crows' nest. From that elevated position, a watcher would be looking down toward the sea as much as out toward the horizon, hoping to spot a black object against equally black water in time to warn the bridge of approaching danger. It had happened to the *Titanic*—Rostron, though he didn't know it yet, had taken precisely the precaution that would prevent such an accident from overtaking the *Carpathia*.

Carefully timing his helm orders, Rostron began working the *Carpathia* through the fringes of the ice field—but he never slowed down. Occasionally another flare would be seen, but no sign of the

Titanic herself. A little after 3:00, hoping to give some hope to those aboard the sinking ship, Rostron gave orders to begin firing colored rockets, interspersed with Cunard Roman candles, every fifteen minutes. Meanwhile, word that the sinking ship's lights had been seen quickly filtered through the crew. Down below in the boiler room, the stokers and firemen worked with renewed vigor; pressure gauges were pegged on every boiler. In the engine room, the big pistons of the *Carpathia*'s reciprocating engines still pounded up and down in a blur, crankshaft-throws spun in a flash of polished steel, linkheads rocked to and fro, and eccentric rods flicked back and forth, steam belching from the cylinder heads with every stroke of the pistons. Every plate, frame, and rivet in the ship shook with the exertion as the *Carpathia* thundered on. As one crewman later quipped, "The old boat was as excited as any of us."

According to the ship's clock on the *Carpathia*'s bridge, it was almost 3:30 and she was drawing close to the *Titanic*'s position. Captain Rostron was proud of his ship, and particularly proud of his officers and crew, his heart filled beyond words at their performance and dedication in bringing the *Carpathia* this far so quickly. Yet at the same moment his heart was sinking. Try as he might to keep his hopes up, he knew he was too late. Rostron was certain that the *Titanic* was gone. It had been nearly two hours since Cottam had last heard from her. The last message he received had been at 1:50 and had pleaded, "Come as quickly as possible, old man; the engine room is filling up to the boilers."

Cottam had told Rostron that the *Titanic*'s signals had been getting weaker; with that last message and the ominous silence afterward, Rostron feared the worst. Those flares, he decided, couldn't have come from the *Titanic* herself after all. At 3:50 he rang down to the engine room to "Stand By"; at 4:00 he rang for "All Stop." The *Carpathia* was at 41.46 N, 50.14 W. There was nothing to be seen but darkness. The *Titanic* was gone.

Chapter 5

BY THE ROCKETS' WHITE GLARE

Aboard the Leyland liner *Californian*, Second Officer Stone relieved Third Officer Groves at midnight. Passing through the wheelhouse, Stone encountered Captain Stanley Lord, and was given his orders for the middle watch. Lord, who hadn't returned to the bridge after his conversation with Groves about the unknown ship to the south, took time to draw Stone's particular attention to the steamer, which by now was almost abeam of the *Californian*, and also made a point of remarking about the loose field ice around their own ship, as well as the icefloes to the west and southwest.

When Lord pointed out the other ship to Stone, the Second Officer noticed that she was displaying her red (port) sidelight, along with a single masthead light and a few smaller lights; she also seemed to be showing a lot of deck lights. The glow from her lights seemed so bright that she appeared to be no more than five or six miles distant. Lord apparently didn't notice the change in the stranger's lights since he had first seen her—her green starboard sidelight was gone, her red port light showing, as if she had just made a sudden hard turn to the right. Lord then left Stone with specific instructions to notify him if the stranger changed her bearing or drew any closer to the *Californian*. Stone acknowledged his instructions and made his way up to the bridge. Lord headed for the chartroom settee.

Once on the bridge, Stone took Grove's report at the change of the watch, and was duly informed that the ship had stopped for the night and was drifting, but with steam up. Nothing particularly unusual had taken place during Grove's watch, and the only ship known to be nearby was the ship off the starboard, to the south, which Groves believed to be a big liner. He confirmed what Captain Lord had mentioned, that he, Groves, had tried unsuccessfully to contact the stranger by Morse lamp, but said that Stone was free to continue if he felt so inclined. As the two men talked, Stone was gradually getting his night-sight as his eyes grew accustomed to the darkness, and after a few more minutes of desultory conversation the watch-change was completed, and Groves went below.

While the two officers were conferring, they were joined by the apprentice officer, James Gibson, who brought with him welcome mugs of hot coffee. When he overheard Groves' remarks about the strange ship to the south of the *Californian*, Gibson trained his glasses on the stranger and could clearly make out her masthead light, her red sidelight, and the glare of white lights on her after decks, a detail that Groves had missed with the naked eye. Although he didn't know it at the time, the combination of visible lights Gibson was seeing confirmed that the stranger had made a sudden, sharp turn to starboard, toward the *Californian*. It would come to be an important point of detail in the days and weeks ahead. Gibson, picking up on the conversation between the Second and Third Officers, tried to raise the distant ship by Morse lamp, but was no more successful than Groves had been. A few moments later Groves left the bridge for the night, and Stone, as much to give the apprentice officer something to do as to actually get work done, told Gibson to fetch the gear needed to stream a new log line (a device which measured the ship's speed while she was underway), and then bring the ship's log up to date with the change of the watch.

While Gibson was gone, Stone paced back and forth across the bridge staring out into the night, frequently glancing over at the stranger to the south. At 12:40 Captain Lord called up the voice tube from the chartroom, asking if the other ship had come any closer. Stone replied no, that everything was the same as before. Lord informed him that he was going to lie down a bit on the chartroom settee. Stone resumed his pacing.

At 11:50 the lookout bell in the *Titanic*'s crow's nest had rung once, signaling that a ship was spotted nearby off to port. The stars had been so bright, even down close to the horizon, that the lights of this ship hadn't been clearly seen until the *Titanic* had turned around the iceberg and swung her bow around to the north. When the lookouts saw the other ship, they had immediately called the bridge, where Fourth Officer Joseph Boxhall ran out onto the port bridge wing and through his high-powered glasses saw a steamship that appeared to be about a third the *Titanic*'s size a half-point off the port bow, a position which would have made the *Titanic*'s red sidelight plainly visible to her. The stranger appeared to be motionless and not more than ten or twelve miles away, her port running light showing clearly.

Boxhall informed Captain Smith as soon as he had returned to the bridge from his inspection with the ship's designer, Thomas Andrews, a few minutes past midnight. Smith acknowledged Boxhall's report, then asked him to work out the *Titanic*'s position; once he was finished with that, Smith suggested, he might have a go at contacting the other ship by Morse lamp. Boxhall quickly complied, and moments later, at 12:15 a.m., Smith walked back to the wireless room, handing Jack Phillips the scrap of paper with the *Titanic*'s position and instructing him to send out the CQD.

After being relieved by Stone, Groves hadn't gone straight to his cabin, but instead made a short detour and stopped by the wireless office. Operator Evans lay back in his bunk, now glancing idly through a magazine, when Groves came in. Usually Evans welcomed visits from the Third Officer: young, keen Groves often stopped by to chat with Evans, picking up the latest news of the world or learning something more about wireless.

By this time, though, Evans' usual friendly demeanor was somewhat in abeyance. He'd had a long, hard day, and the brush-off from Phillips on the *Titanic* had been the last straw. When 11:30 came, the hour he usually shut down, Evans had wasted no time in getting off the air. Now he was ready to turn in and didn't much feel like being sociable. Groves tried anyhow: "What ships have you got, Sparks?"

"Only the *Titanic*," Evans replied, and Groves nodded, remembering the big passenger liner he had seen overtaking the *Californian* half an hour before. He picked up the headphones and put them on, hoping to catch some traffic. Groves' Morse was getting quite good— Evans was teaching him, and Groves joked that he could now catch one letter in three, though he was actually better than that—but he didn't know enough about the equipment to realize that the wireless set aboard the *Californian* was equipped with a clockwork-driven magnetic detector, and when he failed to wind it up, the detector picked up nothing, so he heard nothing. Disappointed, he put the headphones down on the desk and said good night to Evans, turning out the cabin light as he left. It was just after 12:15 a.m. and Jack Phillips had just sent out the *Titanic*'s first distress call.

Quartermaster George Rowe had been standing watch on the *Titanic*'s after, or auxiliary, bridge. This was often a hardship post, for the bridge was really just an open catwalk running across the poop deck at the stern, leaving Rowe completely exposed to the elements. Tonight, though, wasn't all that bad. The absence of any wind kept the cold from becoming unbearable, and Rowe was able to keep reasonably warm by pacing to and fro across the bridge. As he paced he noticed a curious sight: thousands of tiny ice splinters that gave off bright colors as they caught and refracted the glow of the deck lights, a phenomenon that sailors call "Whiskers 'round the Light." It stuck in Rowe's mind because it usually occurred only near ice fields.

His reverie was suddenly broken by an interruption in the motion of the ship, as the steady beat of the engines changed. Stepping to the starboard side of the auxiliary bridge, he peered forward, startled to see what appeared to be a full-rigged ship, with sails set, passing perilously close by the *Titanic*'s starboard side. After a second or two, Rowe realized that he was actually looking at an iceberg, one that towered over the auxiliary bridge, itself nearly sixty feet above the water. As Rowe watched, the berg passed by swiftly and vanished. Within moments after the berg glided by, he felt the ship stop, and shortly after that the funnels began venting steam. But the activity on the Boat Deck hadn't yet attracted his attention, and so he was quite startled when about fifteen minutes before 1:00 a.m. he saw a lifeboat, only about a third filled, float by on the starboard side.

He telephoned the bridge and asked if they knew there was a lifeboat adrift. The voice at the other end, Fourth Officer Boxhall, with a distinctly disbelieving tone, asked who he was. Rowe explained and Boxhall realized that in the excitement Rowe had been forgotten. Boxhall told him to come to the bridge immediately and bring some distress rockets. Rowe pulled a box containing twelve white rockets from a locker on the poop deck, then began making his way forward.

When he arrived at the bridge a few minutes later, he found Boxhall, who had had no success in raising the stranger to the north by Morse lamp, talking with Captain Smith, who turned and instructed Rowe to begin firing his rockets, and continue to fire them off, one every few minutes. The rockets Rowe carried were manufactured by the Cotton Powder Co. Ltd., of a type known as "socket distress signals"; that is, they were constructed to be fitted into a specially-made socket attached to a bulkhead or railing, and launched from there. Designed to fly as high as eight hundred feet, the rockets would then burst in a shower of white stars perhaps two hundred feet across. Rowe quickly fitted one of them into the launching socket on the port bridge wing, and struck a match. With a bright yellow flash and a loud "whoosh" the rocket sped up into the sky, where it burst with a near-deafening "BANG" and a brilliant flash of fiery white light.

Around 1:00 a.m. on the bridge of the *Californian*, Stone was startled by a flash of white light above the other ship. Taken by surprise and unsure of exactly what he had seen, he watched the stranger closely, and after a few minutes, was rewarded with another white flash—and this time he was able to identify what he was seeing: a white rocket bursting high above the unknown vessel, sending out a shower of white stars. Several minutes later he saw another—then later still another—and still another. Five white rockets . . .

There had been little urgency on the *Titanic*'s Boat Deck, with passengers climbing into the lifeboats in the most leisurely manner, most people believing that the fuss was just precautionary. Very few knew the extent of the damage done by the iceberg; even fewer knew that there were boats for only half as many people as were on board. Only Phillips, Bride, and the *Titanic*'s officers knew that the ship was sending out the international distress call. From bow to stern the *Titanic*, sitting motionless in the water, was ablaze with bright lights, their glow lighting the ocean for hundreds of yards in every direction. The ship's orchestra had come up on deck and begun playing bouncy, up-tempo ragtime, while passengers and crew milled about in a calm, unhurried fashion. The ship was beginning to list noticeably down by the head, but even that didn't seem to cause much concern. Certainly few people aboard considered the situation dangerous.

All that changed in an instant a few minutes before 1:00 a.m., just as Boat 5 was being lowered. Without warning a bright flash and a loud hiss came from the starboard bridge wing, and a few seconds later an explosion of brilliant white stars burst high over the Titanic with a tremendous bang. Moments later a second rocket went soaring into the sky, another one a short time after that. In the words of Lawrence Beesley, a passenger aboard the *Titanic*, the flash of the exploding rockets "split the night"—in every respect a textbook example of a visual signal of distress. Now everyone knew that the *Titanic* needed the help of any ship close enough to see her. She was in mortal danger.

At around 1:30 Stone decided that it was time he informed Captain Lord. Calling down the voice tube that connected the bridge to the chartroom, where Lord was napping on the settee, Stone quickly told Lord that he had watched the stranger to the south fire rockets.

"Are they company signals?" Lord asked.

"I don't know, sir, but they appear to me to be all white."

"Well, go on Morsing."

"Yes, sir."

"And when you get an answer, let me know by Gibson."

"Yes, sir."

So began a series of exchanges, actions, and inactions that have no parallel in maritime history. From this moment on, the words and actions of Captain Stanley Lord have baffled maritime authorities for nearly a hundred years. The language and terminology that Second Officer Stone used in his report to Lord were very precise and very clear: the ship to the south was firing "white rockets"—Stone repeat-ed this fact twice. It was a significant detail, for in 1912, the governing convention for the use of signals at sea was Article 31 from the International Rules of the Road, which was accepted in total by the British Board of Trade. The Article stated, among other provisions, that *"Rockets or shells, throwing stars of any color or description, fired one at a time at short intervals"* were to be regarded as a signal of distress. "Distress" at sea has one meaning, and one meaning only—somebody, somewhere, is about to die.

Yet somehow, despite Stone's report, from this moment onward, Lord never appeared to consider the idea that the rockets seen by Stone and Gibson were actually a distress signal—in fact, his actions (or more correctly, his inactions) appear as if Lord deliberately refused to entertain the idea. How or why he refused to do so would never be adequately explained, by himself or anyone else, for nearly a century.

That it did not immediately occur to him that the rockets might indeed be a distress signal was nothing inexcusable; sometimes the most obvious answers to a mystery are the most readily overlooked for just that reason. But the answer to Lord's next question—"Are they company signals?"—should have made clear to him that what Stone and Gibson were seeing was not simply an attempt by the stranger to the south at identifying herself. The regulations of the British Board of Trade issued to the masters of all ships calling at British ports listed registered company signals. These were pyrotechnics that ships sometimes used to identify themselves to other vessels they encountered—and made it clear that the complicated arrangements of lights and shapes and colors of those signals were nothing like "rockets throwing stars of any color or description."

To further remove any possible misunderstanding, the preface to the Board of Trade regulations publication was clear: "Note—if these signals are used in any other place, for any other purpose than stated, they may be signals of distress, and should be answered accordingly by passing ships, and claims sent in for payment of salvage." In other words, when in doubt, take no chances—investigate.

Yet when Stone answered, "I don't know, sir, but they appear to me to be all white," Lord's response—"Well, go on Morsing"—would damn him for all time. Later he would maintain that he barely recalled this exchange with Stone, claiming that he had been half-asleep throughout and responded to his Second Officer in monosyllables, yet the recollections under oath of both Stone and, later, Gibson, was that their captain was alert and lucid each time they spoke with him.

For the next hour, until the strange ship to the south had disappeared, Stanley Lord, who as a certified Master Mariner was fully cognizant of the Board of Trade regulations, would studiously avoid any use of the word "distress" in his exchanges with Stone and Gibson—not a minor point, for even mentioning the word would acknowledge that possibility, compelling Lord to take action. Likewise he would avoid any suggestion that Cyril Evans, the wireless operator, be awakened to see what he might learn, lest Evans receive a message of such an unambiguous nature that it laid a moral and legal obligation on Lord to respond. It was as if by a careful evasion of even the idea that the distant ship might be in distress, he would never have to confront the responsibility that went with it, or the potential dangers it might entail to him personally. Whatever his specific motives, a dark side of Stanley Lord's character, one that he may have never realized existed, was being awakened in those early morning hours. By the time it reached its full dimensions, it would become a frightening persona indeed.

Lord returned to his nap on the chartroom settee and Stone returned to studying the distant ship. The *Californian* continued to drift, slowly turning to starboard, her bows gradually coming around until they were bearing directly on the other ship, both her red and green running lights now visible to the stranger. About this time Gibson returned to the bridge, and Stone told him about the strange ship firing rockets. Gibson raised his glasses to his eyes and as he focused on the unknown vessel he was rewarded with the sight of another rocket being fired off. Gibson's glasses, which were more powerful than Stone's, allowed him to see detail Stone couldn't pick up: the white detonating flash . . . the fiery trail of the rocket streaking up into the sky . . . the near blinding white flash as the rocket burst . . . the spray of slowly falling white stars . . .

On the *Titanic*'s Boat Deck, the mood had shifted dramatically once the rockets started going up. The lights were still bright, the music was still cheerful, but Lightoller and Murdoch found that they no longer had to coax people into the lifeboats. Captain Smith went out to the starboard bridge wing were Fourth Officer Boxhall and Quartermaster Rowe were firing off the rockets. The young officer still hadn't accepted the fact that the *Titanic* was sinking. "Captain, is it really serious?" he asked.

"Mr. Andrews tells me that he gives her an hour to an hour and a half."

Back in the wireless room, Phillips was all too painfully aware of how little time the *Titanic* had left to live. Anxiously he continued tapping away, hoping that some ship—any ship—closer than the *Carpathia* would finally answer. It is easy to imagine Phillips wondering just where was that damned fool who had nearly blown his ears off just a couple of hours ago.

Up on the bridge Captain Smith seethed with a frustration similar to Phillips' as he continued to stare at the lights of the ship on the horizon, so tantalizingly close. Smith, Fourth Officer Boxhall, and Quartermaster Rowe all agreed that it was a ship. While all three men watched as the rockets were being fired, she had slowly swung around, as if drifting on the current, so that by the time Rowe had fired the sixth rocket both her starboard and port sidelights showed, indicating that she was bows on to the *Titanic*. For a moment Boxhall thought this meant she was steaming toward the stricken liner, but it soon became disappointingly clear that this wasn't the case. Yet even if that ship couldn't hear the tremendous bangs of the *Titanic*'s rockets bursting, surely she must be able to see the rockets themselves. Why didn't she respond? Boxhall finally gave up on trying to reach her by Morse lamp, but Rowe was eager to try, so Captain Smith gave him permission. Once he thought he saw a reply, but after studying the stranger through the captain's glasses he decided it was only her masthead light flickering. Discouraged, Rowe went back to firing off the rest of his rockets.

It seemed strange, Stone thought, that a ship would fire rockets at night. As the two officers on the *Californian* watched, a seventh rocket climbed into the sky and burst above the stranger. Stone borrowed Gibson's glasses and studied her for some minutes, then handed them back to the apprentice officer, remarking, "Have a look at her now. She looks very queer out of the water—her lights look queer."

Gibson peered at the stranger carefully. She seemed to be listing, and had, as he later described it "a big side out of the water." Stone noticed her red sidelight had disappeared: did that mean her bearing had changed and the light was obscured, or had the light simply vanished—submerged in the Atlantic? The *Californian* continued her slow, drifting turn to starboard until the stranger was now off her port bow. Gibson suddenly realized that the *Californian* was continuing to swing with the current, and her bow was now pointing to the east, as if she has turned completely around, 180 degrees. The other ship would now only be able to see her green sidelight. About 1:40 a.m. they saw an eighth rocket burst over the ship.

"A ship is not going to fire rockets at sea for nothing," Stone remarked, and Gibson agreed. "There must be something wrong with her." Gibson said he thought she might be in some sort of distress. It was a pivotal moment, in hindsight throwing into stark relief the characters of the three men around whom so much attention would focus in the weeks and years to come: Gibson, a mere apprentice officer, lacking the authority to take any action; Stone, possessing such authority, but personally insecure, hesitant, and vacillating despite his experience as a watch-keeping officer; and Lord, autocratic, overbearing, passionately concerned with his own self-protection, his oppressive personality a brooding presence on the bridge that effectively crushed any initiative the two junior officers might have shown.

Another rocket shot up into the sky from the *Titanic*'s bridge. Quartermaster Rowe had fired off a half-dozen already, going to the Morse lamp occasionally, still vainly trying to get the attention of that ship on the horizon. Like Rowe, Captain Smith, was convinced that she couldn't be more than ten or twelve miles away, and had come by and muttered something to Rowe about wanting a six-inch naval gun to "wake that fellow up." Rowe didn't catch all of the captain's remark, but he silently agreed with the gist of it. Rowe's frustration, like Phillips' in the wireless room, was beginning to build, but like the wireless operator, he kept at his work, hoping for a miracle.

As the men on the *Californian* continued to watch, the stranger slowly began to disappear. Stone would later suggest that she had seemed to be steaming away from the time she began firing the rockets, and now she seemed to be changing her bearing. He couldn't see her red sidelight anymore—Gibson hadn't noticed any bearing change, though he too decided that she was gradually disappearing. He didn't think she was steaming away. He had no idea what exactly the stranger was doing, but he remarked that it was curious how the stranger had always shown her red sidelight but never her green, as would have been the case with a ship steaming away to the southwest.

At 2:00 a.m. Stone sent Gibson down to wake up Captain Lord. "Tell him that the ship is disappearing in the southwest and that she had fired altogether eight rockets." Gibson knocked on the chartroom door, opened it, and relayed Stone's message. Sleepily, Lord asked, "Were they all white rockets?"

"Yes, sir."

"What time is it?"

"2:05 by the wheelhouse clock, sir."

Lord nodded, turned out the light, and went back to sleep, and Gibson went back to the bridge. At 2:20 Stone thought he could still faintly make out the strange ship, then her lights seemed to fade away completely.

The *Titanic*'s lights were glowing a dull red now, and it was difficult for those in the lifeboats to see what was happening aboard the ship. The stern began swinging up into the sky, the ship's hull shrieked with agony, subjected to stresses it was never designed to withstand, as bulkheads, frames and hull plates began to sheer and break under the strain.

With a long moan of tortured metal, the *Titanic* stopped moving. The lights, which had been glowing a dark red, suddenly went out completely, snapped on again with a searing flash, then went out again forever. From the fourth funnel aft, the *Titanic* stood almost perpendicular, a huge black shape silhouetted against the impossibly bright stars, suspended as it were between the sea and the sky.

The noise died away and a pall settled over the scene. Then the weight of the water-filled forward half of the ship began to drag the liner down. She seemed to sag for a moment, as the stern settled back somewhat toward the sea. The over-strained hull finally gave way and began to break apart, causing some of those watching in the boats to imagine that somehow she would miraculously right herself, leading others to believe that she had broken completely in two. The *Titanic* began to slip under, gathering speed as she went, as if to hurry and bring an end to this final indignity. Standing on an overturned lifeboat, less than fifty yards from the *Titanic*, Second Officer Lightoller heard a sound that would haunt him for the rest of his life: as the ship began her final plunge, he could hear people—husbands and wives, brothers and sisters, parents and children—crying out to one another, "I love you."

Little more than twenty seconds after the liner began its plunge, the waters of the North Atlantic closed over the Blue Ensign at the Titanic's stern. An eerie silence settled over the sea for some seconds, as if everyone, passengers and crew, those in the boats and those in the water, were momentarily unable to accept that the ship had vanished. Finally, in Boat 5, Third Officer Pitman glanced at his watch and quietly announced, "It is 2:20 a.m."

By 2:40 Stone was certain that the stranger was gone, and whistled down the speaking tube to the chartroom. When Lord answered, Stone told him that the other ship had disappeared to the southwest and was completely out of sight. One last time Lord asked about the rockets, and Stone assured him that there were no colors, "just white rockets." Lord told Stone to record it in the log, then went back to sleep.

With the stranger, for whatever cause or reason, having stopped firing her rockets and apparently vanishing, Stone and Gibson resumed their watch. For the next hour nothing happened. Then at 3:30 a.m., Gibson suddenly saw another rocket, this one off to the south-southeast and farther away than the other rockets had been. Drawing Stone's attention to it, Gibson watched as a second, then a third rocket was launched. The ship firing these rockets was still below the horizon, so the two officers hadn't yet actually seen her, but both men immediately noted that these rockets were company signals, not the white rockets the other ship had fired earlier. Oddly, Stone did not report these new rockets to the captain.

At 4:00 a.m., Chief Officer George F. Stewart appeared on the bridge, relieving Stone. Stone described the night's events—the strange ship to the southwest, the eight white rockets she fired, the ship slowly disappearing, and his informing Captain Lord of these events three different times.

As Stone was talking, Stewart raised his glasses and, peering southward, spotted a four-masted steamer with one funnel and "a lot of light amidships" as she hove into view. He asked Stone if this was the ship that had fired the rockets, and Stone replied that he had not seen this ship before, and that he was sure it was not the same one that had fired the first eight rockets. With that, Stone went below, leaving a somewhat bemused Chief Officer Stewart alone on the bridge.

Stewart had an uneasy feeling, a vague sense that "something had happened." Knowing that rockets at sea sometimes meant distress, Stewart couldn't help but think that may have been the case here. Even so it was not until 4:30 that he did anything, and that was to awaken Captain Lord at his accustomed hour. Knocking politely on the chartroom door, Stewart began recounting the night's events as told to him by Stone. About halfway through this recitation Lord stopped him, saying, "Yes, I know. Stone's been telling me."

Once he had donned his greatcoat, scarf, and hat, Captain Lord went up to the bridge and began to describe to Stewart how he intended to work his way through the icefield that lay ahead of the *Californian*, Stewart asked him if he was going to first try to learn something about the ship that had been firing rockets off to the southwest. Lord raised his glasses and studied the four masted steamer off to the southeast and said, "No, she looks all right. She's not making any signals now." Inexplicably Stewart did not mention to his captain that the ship he was looking at was not the one Stewart was referring to and was not at all the ship that had fired the eight white rockets.

Over the course of the next hour, conversation on the bridge was desultory as the two men waited for the dawn. Finally the feeling that had been nagging at Stewart caused him to run down to the *Californian*'s wireless room and wake up Cyril Evans with the words "Sparks, there's a ship been firing rockets in the night. Will you see if you can find out what is wrong—what is the matter?"

Evans jumped from his bunk, pulled on his trousers and a pair of slippers, and quickly settled in at his apparatus. Winding up the magnetic detector, starting the brush motor, he slipped on the headphones and tapped out a quick "CQ": "Any station—come back." Within seconds, the *Frankfurt* answered, stunning Evans: "Do you know the *Titanic* has sunk during the night, collided with an iceberg?"

Evans immediately asked for the *Titanic*'s position, which the *Frankfurt* readily provided—41 46' N, 50 14' W. No sooner had Evans thanked the German operator than the *Virginian* called, asking, "Do you know the *Titanic* had sunk?" Evans replied, "Yes, the *Frankfurt* has just told me." A quick exchange of signals then followed, and Evans asked, "Please send me official message regarding *Titanic*, giving position." Here Evans was being justifiably careful: asking that the communication take the form of an official message transformed its contents from simple idle exchange between operators into hard fact on which the captain of the *Californian* could act.

The position for the *Titanic* given by the *Frankfurt* and the *Virginian* were identical, and no sooner had Evans transcribed the *Virginian*'s signal than Chief Officer Stewart had it in his hand, and he and Evans were racing up the stairs to the bridge, shouting to Captain Lord that a ship had gone down.

Thrusting the message at Lord, Stewart stood by, anticipating that the captain would order the ship to get under way immediately. Instead, Lord took one look at the position, then shook his head in disbelief. "No, no, this can't be right," he said, handing the message slip back to Evans. "You must get me a better position than this."

It was a cryptic remark, and one of frightening significance, for as soon as he uttered it, Stanley Lord began a journey down a dark and lonely road, which would only end fifty years later with his death as a disappointed, bitter man. For better or worse, Lord himself was never called upon to explain it, perhaps fortunately for himself, for there can only be one reason for his sudden exclamation, "You must get me a better position than this." It had already been confirmed by two ships, the *Frankfurt* and the *Virginian*, and it would be absurd to suggest that Lord meant one was more precise. Boxhall's position of 41 46' N, 50 14' W. had proven to be more than adequate for the *Carpathia*, as well as the *Mount Temple,* another ship that had come racing from nearly a hundred miles to the southwest, in the hope of reaching the *Titanic*.

The *Carpathia*'s Captain Rostron had even taken a moment to congratulate Boxhall on what he called "a splendid position." Captain James Moore of the *Mount Temple* had no trouble reaching the scene where the *Titanic*'s lifeboats were being recovered by the *Carpathia* based on that same position. Though later discoveries would find the error Boxhall had made in his calculations which put the *Titanic*'s estimated position roughly twelve miles west of where she actually was, for all practical purposes it was a small enough error to be inconsequential.

So was there a significance to Boxhall's position that Lord immediately recognized, of which Evans, who knew nothing of navigation, would not have suspected? It's a disturbing possibility, and given Lord's subsequent actions, quite likely. Given that Lord was a skilled, if occasionally sloppy, navigator, and already knew the *Californian*'s actual position during the night, one glance at the figures given by Boxhall would have made it clear that the *Californian* was uncomfortably close to the spot where the *Titanic* sank—uncomfortable, that is, for the captain of a vessel whose officers had seen white rockets fired from a nearby ship during the night and done nothing to investigate them. The implication of the remark "You must get me a better position," then, is chilling, for it demonstrates that at this precise moment Lord suddenly became aware of the colossal, tragic blunder he had made during the night by not responding to the nearby ship as her rockets went off. He was suddenly hoping that the "better position" for which he was asking would put the *Titanic* farther from the *Californian*—far enough to excuse Lord's inactivity.

All of Lord's subsequent actions and statements for the next half-century are explicable, if not forgivable, only if he understood the significance of Boxhall's position—its proximity to his own ship during those crucial hours when the *Titanic* was sinking. Indeed, almost every action Lord took that morning seemed to indicate exactly that: Stanley Lord knew the moment he read the position that the *Californian* was already so near it as to be within sight of the spot—*and that the ship his officers had watched fire off the white rockets during the night had been the doomed* Titanic.

Chagrined, Evans returned to the wireless office, only to return to the bridge minutes later with a second slip of paper, this one confirming the accuracy of the first position he had given Lord: 41   46' N, 50   14' W was the only position anyone had for the *Titanic*. This time Lord accepted it without comment, and proceeded to work out a course to bring the *Californian* to that spot. The steamer to the south-southeast was, apparently, forgotten, and Lord never bothered to ask Evans if he had any information about any other ships in the vicinity. Again, in retrospect, it was a significant lapse, for had he done so, Lord would have soon learned that the ship to the south-southeast was the *Carpathia*, and that she was picking up the lifeboats holding the *Titanic*'s survivors.

Saying nothing further to Evans, Lord immediately rang down to the engine room for "Slow Ahead" and began steaming toward the *Titanic*'s last reported position. For some inexplicable reason—about which he was never subsequently questioned and so never was compelled to make clear—Lord chose to steam *west*, taking the *Californian* into and through the icefield and out into the clear water beyond. In light of later developments it was a curious decision, to say the least, for the overnight position recorded in the log of the *Californian* placed her well to the north-northwest of the *Titanic*'s wireless position, and northwest of where the lost liner's lifeboats were waiting. Steaming *into* the icefield then actually took the *Californian* farther away from the scene of the *Titanic*'s disaster, rather than bringing her closer. Even had the position in the *Californian*'s log been correct—and it would be subsequently shown to be patently false—there was nothing but open water to the south and southeast, where both the real and estimated positions for the *Titanic* lay.

It was slow going for the first four or five miles as Lord picked his way through the heavy field-ice that had drifted in during the night and which was frequently studded with bergs. He moved at what he deemed a maximum safe speed—four knots. The *Mount Temple,* a ship which had come racing up from the southwest, almost a hundred miles distant, in a valiant but vain effort to reach the *Titanic* before she went down, was still on the west side of the icefield when, at around 6:00 a.m., her captain saw the *Californian* moving through the icefield some six miles north of his ship. Sometime between 6:30 and

7:00 a.m., the *Californian* reached clear water and carefully worked her way up to her top speed of fourteen knots, heading due south.

Intriguingly, it was Evans who would provide the first proof of just how close the *Californian* had been to the sinking *Titanic* during the night. At 6:10 a.m. the *Virginian*'s wireless operator contacted Evans at the request of her master, Captain G.J. Gambell, asking for details about conditions at the wreck site. According to Gambell, Evans "immediately" advised him that the *Carpathia* was in sight and could be seen picking up survivors from boats. This meant that even before 6:30 a.m. the *Californian* was already within seven miles—visual distance—of the wreck site, though she was by this time on the other side of the icefield because of Captain Lord's inexplicable maneuvering. The irrefutable proof comes from Evans' identification of the *Carpathia*, information which could have only come from the bridge, meaning Captain Lord himself.

What Evans didn't say was that they were looking *across* the icefield to the *east*. This was a strange signal, to say the least, for it shows that Captain Lord and the *Californian*'s officers were already aware of the *Carpathia*'s identity and position, as well as what she was doing. Complying with Lord's instruction to keep him informed, Evans had relayed to the bridge exchanges between the *Carpathia* and other ships, allowing Lord to identify the ship he had originally seen to the southeast as the *Carpathia*. This makes the *Californian*'s traverse of the icefield even more inexplicable if Lord's real intention was to render whatever aid he could.

The whole crew of the *Californian* was roused by now. Additional lookouts were posted, and lifeboats were swung out. Lord would at one point claim that he went so far as to put a stoker in a coal basket, which was then hoisted up the foremast, where, at a height above the crows' nest, he could act as an extra lookout, although later no one would remember this actually being done, and none of the *Californian*'s company ever came forward as that crewman. Third Officer Groves, remembering the big steamer he had seen stopped to the south of the *Californian* before midnight, went by Second Officer Stone's cabin to ask if it were true about the *Titanic*. "Yes, old chap," Stone assured him, "I saw rockets on my watch."

Groves then returned to the bridge, and at 6:50 a.m. he noted that the *Carpathia* was directly east of the *Californian,* yet the Leyland liner was still steaming southward. Around half past seven, after having crossed at most some eight miles of open water, Captain Lord decided that he had arrived at the *Titanic's* wireless position, but the ship was nowhere to be seen, nor were any lifeboats. There wasn't even any wreckage. Only the *Mount Temple* was nearby; some six miles to the east of these two ships sat the Cunard liner *Carpathia,* clearly visible across the icefloe. Lord now decided to make for the rescue ship to see if he could be of any assistance.

Captain Lord would later maintain that intervening ice again made a direct course toward the Cunard ship impossible, so the *Californian* had to take yet another roundabout route, coming up on the *Carpathia* from the southwest. As his ship approached the *Carpathia,* Lord noted that the Cunard vessel had four masts and a single funnel, but gave no indication that he recognized her as the same ship he had earlier misidentified as the mysterious rocket-firing ship of the early morning hours. Instead, Lord seemed most intent on establishing beyond any doubt that reaching the *Titanic's* position was an arduous, difficult, and time-consuming undertaking for his ship.

In the meantime, Evans began making up for lost airtime. He began cluttering up the already overladen ether with an endless series of questions and comments about the *Titanic*; only the Telefunken operator aboard the *Frankfurt,* near-hysterical and endlessly transmitting in a garbled combination of German and English, was more annoying. What Evans did not know was that a Marconi Inspector, Gilbert Balfour, was aboard the *Baltic,* and overheard every word. Soon Balfour had enough of Evans chatter and tapped out an angry reprimand to the *Californian's* operator for misuse of his wireless, effectively silencing Evans for most of the remainder of the day.

At 8:30 the *Californian* hove to a few hundred yards away from the *Carpathia,* and soon an exchange of flag signals began between the two ships—it was obvious to the skippers of both that there was simply too much wireless traffic at the moment for them to talk intelligently to each other through that medium. Eventually it was decided that while the *Carpathia* would immediately head for New York, the *Californian* would continue to search for survivors. The Cunard liner had just picked up what Second Officer Lightoller assured Captain

Rostron was the last of the *Titanic*'s lifeboats, but the methodical Rostron, though he knew how unlikely the possibility, was taking no chances: if there were any boats unaccounted for or anyone clinging to a bit of wreckage, the *Californian* would be able to pick them up. As the *Carpathia* steered southwest and began to make her way out of the fringes of the icefield, the *Californian* began a slow traverse of the area.

There was little enough to see; unlike disasters on land, catastrophe at sea leaves little to mark its passage, and none of it is permanent. There were large pieces of reddish cork from the *Titanic*'s ruptured bulkheads, steamer chairs, cushions, lifebelts, rugs, sections of wood panels from the ship's public rooms, bits of clothing, the odd life ring or two, the abandoned lifeboats, the red and white striped barber pole; an amazing array of debris and yet surprisingly little left to mark the passage of the largest ship in the world. Within hours it would begin to disperse and within days most of it would be lost to wind and waves. Captain Lord would later claim that he didn't find any bodies at all. It is doubtful that he looked very hard, for the sea was littered with them, and for the next several days liners would report sighting bodies, some singly, others in groups, in an ever-widening circle around the spot where the *Titanic* went down.

The superficial nature of the *Californian*'s search should have come as no surprise to anyone, though. Third Officer Groves later maintained that the search was broken off by 10:30 a.m., though Captain Lord would maintain that it was continued until 11:40. Lord's version was the one that went down in the *Californian*'s log, of course, but then Captain Lord's version of many things would find their way into the *Californian*'s log. Nowhere, for example, did the ship's log mention anything about her officers sighting white rockets in the early hours of the morning of April 15, 1912. If the *Californian* departed the area earlier than her captain maintained, it was understandable: few men would ever have as much reason as Stanley Lord to put as much distance as possible between himself and the place where the *Titanic* sank.

Chapter 6

RESCUE AT DAWN

Standing on the keel of Collapsible B, Second Officer Lightoller struggled to keep the two dozen or so survivors still perched atop the upturned boat alive. Within minutes after the *Titanic*'s stern had disappeared, as many as sixty men, possibly more, had been desperately trying to stand upright on the wallowing keel, but their numbers steadily dwindled as cold and fatigue took their toll. Lightoller wasn't a ruthless man, or hard-hearted, but a lifetime of adventures had put more steel into his soul than most, which often allowed him to view even the most difficult circumstances with an unemotional detachment. Yet even the strong-willed sailor had to brace himself each time he heard the soft thud of knees hitting the keel, followed seconds later by a sibilant splash as yet another man collapsed and fell into the water. Unlike so many who had remained aboard the doomed liner to the end, these weren't men who had given up, or resigned themselves to their fate, but who instead had fought for their survival, only to have their bodies give out before their spirits faltered.

One of these victims proved to be Phillips. Intelligent, intense, and high-strung, the young wireless operator's reserves of strength were exhausted by the combination of a near-eighteen hour workday and the stress of the two hours spent at the wireless key while the *Titanic* was slowly sinking. With almost his last breath Phillips had told Lightoller the *Carpathia* was steaming hard from the south. Moments later he collapsed and slid off Collapsible B's keel, his body vanishing in the darkness.

It was sometime around 3:30 when the Second Officer saw a flash of light to the southeast, followed some seconds later by a faint "boom." Lightoller hoped it was a signal from an approaching ship. That flash had been seen in the other lifeboats as well. In Number 13, Fred Barrett, a stoker, who was nearly unconscious from the cold, suddenly sat bolt upright and shouted, "That was a cannon!" In Boat 6, where the passengers had been bickering with the eternally morose and uncooperative Quartermaster Hitchens all night, Margaret Martin saw a brief glimmer of light on the horizon and cried out, "There's a flash of lightning!" Hitchens only muttered pessimistically, "It's a falling star." But a few minutes later another flash was seen, and shortly after that, the masthead light of an oncoming steamer.

Soon the ship's green and red sidelights could be seen as the vessel loomed over the horizon, still firing rockets, still coming hard. In Boat 9, Paddy McGough, a big, strapping deck hand, called out, "Let us all pray to God, for there is a ship on the horizon and it's making for us!" and nobody dared disagree with the suggestion. In Boat 3, someone lit a rolled up newspaper and waved it wildly as a signal, followed a few minutes later by a passenger's straw hat. In Number 8, Mrs. J. Stuart White swung her cane with its battery-powered light in the tip over her head for all she was worth. In Boat 2, Fourth Officer Boxhall lit a green flare.

Captain Rostron's heart leaped when he saw the flare light up directly ahead of the *Carpathia*. If he was too late to reach the *Titanic* before she went down, he wasn't too late to save those souls who were bobbing about on the open sea in the lifeboats. In the flare's pale wash of light he could make out a boat less than a quarter mile away. He immediately rang down "Slow Ahead" on his engines and began to swing the ship to starboard, so he could pick up the boat in the shelter of his portside, which was to leeward. No sooner had the *Carpathia*'s bow begun to swing to the right then Bisset spotted a huge dark iceberg to starboard, and Rostron had to put his helm over to avoid it. The boat was now on his windward side, and as the morning breeze picked up, the swell had become choppy, causing the boat to bob up and down like a cork. As Rostron moved out onto the starboard bridge wing, megaphone in hand, a voice called up to the *Carpathia*, "We have only one seaman in the boat, and can't work it very well!"

"All right!" Rostron shouted back, and began edging the liner closer to the boat. Turning to Bisset, he told him to go down to the starboard gangway with two quartermasters and guide the lifeboat as it came alongside. "Fend her off so that she doesn't bump, and be careful that she doesn't capsize."

"Stop your engines!" A new voice floated up from the boat below, that of Fourth Officer Boxhall, and Boat 2 was now gently drifting toward the *Carpathia*'s starboard gangway. Suddenly yet another voice, a woman's, cried out, "The *Titanic* has gone down with everyone on board!"

Boxhall turned to the woman, Mrs. Walter Douglas, and told her to shut up. She lapsed into silence, but apparently no one aboard the *Carpathia* heard her anyhow. (Boxhall later apologized; Mrs. Douglas graciously refused to take offense. Both understood that they were desperately overwrought by what they had just endured.) Lines were dropped and the boat was made fast. A rope ladder was let down from the gangway, along with a lifeline that Boxhall would secure under the arms of each passenger before they began climbing up.

The first to be brought aboard was Elizabeth Allen who, as she neared the gangway, was lifted onto the *Carpathia* by Purser Brown. She stepped aboard at 4:10 a.m. Brown asked her what had happened to the *Titanic*, and she told him it had sunk. More survivors followed her up the ladder, the last being Boxhall. Rostron sent word that he needed to see Boxhall on the bridge immediately.

When the *Titanic*'s Fourth Officer appeared, Rostron, hoping to get this painful duty over with as quickly as possible, asked him directly, "The *Titanic* has gone down?"

"Yes"—here Boxhall's voice broke with emotion—"she went down about 2:30."

"Were many people left on board when she sank?"

"Hundreds and hundreds! Perhaps a thousand! Perhaps more!" Boxhall went on, his voice breaking as grief began to get the better of him. "My God, sir, they've gone down with her. They couldn't live in this cold water. We had room for a dozen more people in my boat, but it was dark after the ship took the plunge. We didn't pick up any swimmers. I fired flares . . . I think that the people were drawn down deep by the suction. The other boats are somewhere near."

Rostron nodded, the formalities taken care of, and sent Boxhall down to the First Class Dining Saloon. The emotional exchange with the *Titanic*'s Fourth Officer had left Rostron deeply moved, and now a profound sadness swept over him, strangely coupled with relief and satisfaction. It was a sadness brought on by the knowledge that for all he had done, he had arrived too late to save the hundreds of lives that were lost when the *Titanic* went down. The relief came from the realization that he had been able to rescue the more than seven hundred survivors, so his efforts were hardly in vain. Finally, satisfaction at knowing that he, his crew, and his ship had done a superlative job in carrying out the rescue.

The *Carpathia* had performed flawlessly despite being driven harder than she had ever been—or ever would be again—a tribute to the meticulous shipwrights at Swan-Hunter who had built her a decade earlier. The crew had risen above themselves, impelled by the knowledge that an untold number of lives were depending on their every action—and they had done everything right. It would be fair to say that no skipper on the North Atlantic had ever been more proud of his crew, or ever had more reason for his pride, than Arthur Rostron in those moments before sunrise on April 15, 1912.

Dawn was breaking and now the *Carpathia*'s captain could begin to see the rest of the *Titanic*'s boats, spread out across four or five miles of sea. The *Carpathia*'s passengers were beginning to stir now, and those who were already up were lining the rails, looking down at the pitiful handful of survivors in Boat 2, or gazing out across the water at the other boats. Mrs. Louis Ogden, a First Class passenger on board the *Carpathia*, would later recall that the lifebelts most of the survivors wore made everyone look as if they were dressed in white. She remembered what her husband had told her about the *Titanic*— he had heard the news from a quartermaster in the early hours of the morning, but both he and his wife had been skeptical—seeing the White Star emblem on the side of Boat 2 now made the awful truth clear. She felt heartsick.

In the growing light, maybe five miles off to the west, stretching from the northern horizon to the western, was a vast, unbroken sheet of ice, studded here and there with towering bergs, some as much as two hundred feet high. Smaller bergs and growlers dotted the open water between the ice floe and the ship, presenting the passengers of the *Carpathia* with a spectacle they would never forget. The sun edged over the eastern horizon, its morning rays playing across the ice, turning it shades of pink, blue, grey-green and lavender, lending a perverse beauty to its menace.

For some it was a disconcerting sight. One of the *Carpathia*'s passengers, Charles Hurd, an extraordinarily heavy sleeper who hadn't been aroused by the ship's thundering dash north, awoke to find her inexplicably stopped in the middle of the ocean with those whacking great chunks of ice floating nearby. He hunted up his stewardess to demand an explanation. The woman was weeping, and before Hurd could say anything, she pointed to a cluster of haphazardly-dressed women making their way into the Dining Saloon, and through her tears said, "They are from the *Titanic*. She's at the bottom of the ocean."

The sky was brilliantly clear, with the sun's first golden rays now reaching above the horizon and fanning out across the blue; the pale sliver of a new moon appeared. As the growing dawn made it clear to those in the lifeboats that the *Carpathia* had indeed stopped to rescue the *Titanic*'s survivors, shouts of relief rose up from some of the boats. Others gave organized cheers as they began pulling for the liner. In Boat 13 they sang "Pull for the Shore, Sailor" as they rowed toward the *Carpathia*. But some boats were very, very quiet. In Boat 7, Lookout Hogg told his charges, "It's all right, ladies, do not grieve. We are picked up." The women, though, just sat there, speechless with relief.

There were no cheers from the freezing men on Collapsible B either—it took too much effort just to stay afloat. As dawn broke, Lightoller spotted Boats 4, 10, and 12, along with Collapsible D, tied together just as Fourth Officer Lowe had left them, about a third of a mile away. Concerted shouts of "Ship ahoy!" produced no results, but when Lightoller found an officer's whistle in his pocket and gave it three sharp blasts, that got the attention of everyone.

Seaman Clinch in Boat 12 and Quartermaster Perkis in Boat 4

quickly cast off from the other two boats and pulled alongside Collapsible B. The overturned boat was wallowing badly now, the men almost knee deep in water, and when Boat 4 came alongside, it nearly washed everyone off. (One of them, Harold Bride, the *Titanic*'s junior wireless operator, would suffer for weeks from severe frostbite in both feet, caused by standing for hours in the icy water atop Collapsible B.) Lightoller, taking no chances, especially now that rescue was so close at hand, warned the men not to jump all at once. One by one, they scrambled into two waiting lifeboats, some afraid of losing their footing and being pitched into the water, others so cold that they were oblivious to everything and everyone around them. Lightoller was the last man off Collapsible B, carefully climbing into Boat 12, taking charge of the now dangerously overloaded boat, and guiding her toward the *Carpathia*.

Fifth Officer Lowe was busy as well. He had hoisted the sail aboard Boat 14 as soon as the *Carpathia* hove into view, taking advantage of the early morning breeze. Not every sailor could do that, for as he later explained at the Senate Inquiry, "Not all sailors are boatmen, and not all boatmen are sailors." Lowe was both, and taking advantage of the skills he had learned sailing up and down the Gold Coast, he soon had Boat 14 cutting along at close to four knots. He noticed that Collapsible D was particularly low in the water, and swung his boat over toward her.

Thinking that the Fifth Officer was going to transfer more passengers to the already wallowing collapsible, one of those aboard called out to Lowe, "We have about all we want!" To the relief of everyone else in the collapsible, Lowe quickly told them to tie Boat 14's painter to Collapsible D's bow, and he would tow her to the *Carpathia*. They gratefully complied.

Lowe then spotted Collapsible A, almost a mile and a half off, looking like it could sink any minute. More than half the thirty people who had taken refuge in Collapsible A during the night had frozen to death and fallen overboard. Now only thirteen were left. Lowe wasted no time trying to take the boat in tow, instead getting its occupants into Boat 14 as quickly as possible, then putting about for the *Carpathia*.

The whole straggling flotilla of lifeboats was now converging on the Cunard ship. It was 4:45 when Boat 13 tied up at the portside gangway, a half hour after that when Boat 7 pulled alongside. At 6:00 survivors from Boat 3 began to climb aboard the *Carpathia*. Some used the rope ladders, children were hoisted up in mail sacks, and some of the women, not strong enough to negotiate the rope ladders, were lifted aboard in slings. As Elizabeth Shutes found herself swung up into the air, she heard a voice from somewhere on deck call out, "Careful fellows, she's a lightweight!"

Henry Sleeper Harper stepped into the gangway, accompanied by his wife, his dragoman Hassan Hassah, and his prize Pekinese, only to be met by an old acquaintance, Louis Ogden. What occurred next was so surreal that it might have been lifted from a scene in a Durrenmat play. As if it were the most natural thing in the world to meet under such circumstances, Harper walked over to the astonished Ogden and said, "Louis, how do you keep yourself looking so young?" Ogden, stunned by the morning's events and Harper's sudden appearance, was speechless.

It was about this same time that Second Officer Bisset, still keeping a wary eye on the ice, caught sight of a four-masted ship with a single pale-red funnel some seven or eight miles to the north-northwest of the *Carpathia*. At almost the same moment, First Officer Dean, to whom Rostron had given the duty to scan the water for the rest of the *Titanic*'s lifeboats, spotted the same vessel. The *Carpathia*'s Third Officer, Eric Rees, and Fourth Officer, John Geoffrey Barnish, both saw her as well. She was just getting under way and heading west, into the icefield, and she was briefly brought to Captain Rostron's attention. But there were more urgent matters immediately to hand, and Rostron, Bissett, Dean, and the other officers gave the ship little notice, apart from making note of her appearance and bearing.

Collapsible C tied up below the *Carpathia*'s gangway at 6:30, and Fifth Officer Lowe carefully brought Boat 14 alongside ship just before 7:00, with Collapsible D still in tow. By now the crew of the *Carpathia* had fallen into a routine while bringing the passengers and crewmen aboard, and the two lifeboats were quickly unloaded.

There was by now a lot of frantic activity on the small liner's deck (although many of the *Carpathia*'s passengers and crew were later to remark how quiet the *Titanic*'s survivors seemed) as family members sought one another out, or peered anxiously over the railing as each boat came alongside, looking for familiar faces. Usually the outcome was predictable: the sought-after loved one wouldn't be in any of the boats and the agonizing reality would set in. But sometimes there would be a happy reunion. Dr. Washington Dodge was reunited with his wife and son. They had been separated on the *Titanic*'s Boat Deck when Dr. Dodge insisted they get into a boat, but he remained on board himself; later, an officer ordered him into another boat to man an oar. Billy Carter, who had been in Collapsible C, stood staring down at Boat 4 as it came alongside, spotting his wife and daughter, but was still searching frantically for his son. Finally he called out, "Where's my boy?"

Recognizing his father's voice, ten-year-old William, Jr. lifted the brim of a girl's hat he was wearing and looked up, saying, "Here I am, Father."

Not all the reunions were as happy. When Mrs. John B. Thayer and her son, Jack, saw one another, they rushed into each other's arms. After a minute though, Mrs. Thayer asked Jack, "Where's Daddy?" All the young Thayer could say was, "I don't know." The elder Thayer had died on the *Titanic*'s Boat Deck.

Sadder still was the plight of an Italian woman, a steerage passenger, who broke down completely in the Third Class dining room, weeping hysterically, shouting out, "*Bambino!*" over and over again. Gradually it was realized that she was pleading for her baby, from whom she had been separated somehow in the lifeboat. The child was soon found and brought to her, but if anything the woman became more agitated as she held up two fingers to show that a second child was missing. This one was found, too—in the pantry, on the hot press. Someone had put it there so its little body would thaw out.

By 8:15 all the boats were alongside, except for Boat 12, which was still a quarter mile away and moving slowly. The breeze was freshening, and with the boat as overloaded as it was—seventy-four people in a boat designed to hold sixty-five—Lightoller wasn't about to take any chances. Rostron nudged his engines to life and brought the *Carpathia* forward slowly, swinging his bows to starboard a bit to bring the boat into the ship's lee. As he turned the wind kicked up a squall and a couple of waves crashed over the boat, covering everyone with spray. Gingerly, Lightoller put his tiller over, and Boat 12 slipped into the sheltered waters by the *Carpathia*'s side. At 8:30 she made fast to the ship and Lightoller began unloading his passengers. As he did so, he was startled to hear a voice above him sing out, "Hullo, Lights! What are you doing down there?" Looking up, Lightoller saw the smiling face of the *Carpathia*'s First Officer, Horace Dean, peering over the side of the ship. The two men were old friends—Dean had been the best man at the Second Officer's wedding. No one could have anticipated that they would ever meet again under such circumstances.

By 9:00 a.m. all of the *Titanic*'s survivors were aboard the *Carpathia*. Now Captain Rostron had to figure out what to do with them. Though collecting and confirming the names of all the survivors would take most of the rest of the day, by 9:30 a.m. the Purser and his assistants were able to give Rostron a fairly accurate tally: 705 survivors had been brought aboard—meaning that more than fifteen hundred people had died with the *Titanic*. Heartsick, the deeply religious Rostron decided that while nothing could be done for those lost, a brief religious service—a combined memorial and thanksgiving— might go a long way toward helping the survivors begin to sort out their grief. Approaching the Reverend Father Roger Anderson, an Episcopalian minister who was one of the *Carpathia*'s passengers, Rostron broached the subject. Reverend Anderson thought it a noble idea and agreed to preside. The service would be held that afternoon in the First Class lounge.

While there is no way of knowing exactly what thoughts were in Rostron's mind at those moments, it isn't difficult to surmise what they might have been. While like most skippers on the North Atlantic run Rostron wasn't much given over to being deeply introspective, he was quite capable of profound reflection. The remark he would make in the days ahead that "There was another Hand than mine on the helm" certainly showed that he was aware of how he, his crew, and his ship had become an integral part of what was far more than just a great ocean-going drama, but that instead was one of the great tragedies of the sea. He had no way of knowing exactly how many passengers and crewmen had been aboard the *Titanic*, but it would not have been difficult to calculate that the *Carpathia* had saved not even a third of the White Star liner's capacity. Moreover, the number of boats his ship had recovered would have told him that there was little if any hope that there were still survivors unaccounted for.

Still, there would have been no self-recrimination, no dwelling on "what-ifs" and "might-have-beens." Rostron would have wasted no time wondering what might have happened had the *Carpathia* heard the *Titanic*'s distress call sooner. He knew that he had acted with remarkable alacrity; he also knew the distance between the two ships. Even given the *Carpathia*'s heroic burst of speed, she would have never been able to arrive in time to save everyone. And even as he watched the rescue unfolding that morning, he would have understood that for the living, everything which could have been done had been done: not a single survivor was lost or injured being brought aboard the *Carpathia*. For those who had gone down with the *Titanic*, save for reverencing their memory at the memorial service later that day, there was nothing more that he or anyone else could do. Rostron's duty now was as he always saw it: to the living.

A quick conference with the Purser and an inventory of the *Carpathia*'s supplies of food and linen told him that there was no way the ship could continue her voyage eastward across the Atlantic; Italy would have to wait. His only choice was to turn around and go back to New York. Reminding the Purser to do all he could to make the *Titanic*'s survivors as comfortable as possible, Rostron returned to the chartroom to work out his new course.

As the *Carpathia*'s crew set to work, her passengers did all they could, too: helping the crew wherever and however they could, finding extra clothes for the survivors, giving up their spare toiletries and toothbrushes. Some made room in their cabins for survivors, others doubled up with other passengers so that those families and fragments of families which survived could be together in some semblance of privacy. But there were some burdens that the *Carpathia*'s passengers, no matter how good their intentions, could never ease, never share. As Mrs. Ogden was taking a tray of coffee cups over to two women sitting by themselves in a corner of the *Carpathia*'s upper deck, they shook their heads and gently waved her off, never taking their eyes from the ice-littered sea. "Go away," they murmured listlessly. "We've just seen our husbands drown."

Meanwhile Rostron returned to the bridge, and ordered as many of the *Titanic*'s boats brought aboard as possible. Six were slung in the *Carpathia*'s davits, seven more were stowed on the foredeck; there was no room for more. These boats would be returned to the White Star Line when the ship reached New York; the other seven, including all four collapsibles, were set adrift. While the boats were being hoisted aboard, the *Mount Temple*, another vessel that had come rushing to the *Titanic*'s assistance, hove to about six miles to the east, having passed through the southern end of the icefield from the west. Rostron, who was expecting her arrival, quickly appraised Captain Moore of the *Mount Temple* of the situation, and asked her to continue the search for survivors. Then he returned to the chartroom to work out a course for New York.

It was about 9:15, as he was down in the charthouse laying out his new course, that Rostron was called back to the bridge. A second ship—a four-masted freighter with a single pale-red funnel—had appeared, steaming up from the southwest. First Officer Dean and Second Officer Bissett both recognized her as the ship they had earlier seen off to the north-northwest; Rees and Barish also recognized her. Rostron didn't, not immediately, and he wondered where she had come from, since Cottam had assured him that, apart from the *Mount Temple*, there wouldn't be any other ships arriving for some time. A brief exchange of flag signals followed, and the stranger identified herself as the *Californian*.

Rostron was too busy to give any further thought to whence she had come, or how she had appeared on the scene unannounced—it would only be later that afternoon that he remembered seeing her earlier that morning, some eight or so miles off to the north-northwest. Quickly determining that the newcomer had no survivors aboard, Rostron then informed the master of the *Californian* that since the *Carpathia* had picked up all the survivors there were, his ship was immediately headed for New York. As a precaution he asked that the *Californian* take one last look around, so that it would be absolutely certain no one was being left behind. With that the Cunard liner put about, and slowly steamed away.

As the *Carpathia* began making her way toward New York, Rostron began dealing with the thousand and one unexpected details suddenly arising from bringing aboard over seven hundred survivors.

It was sometime on April 19, the day after the *Carpathia* docked in New York, that Rostron sat down and wrote a report to the Cunard home office of the actions he took to rescue the Titanic's survivors, as well as what transpired on the return to New York. The document paints a vivid picture of those four remarkable days.

R.M.S. *Carpathia*,
April 19, 1912.
General Manager Cunard Steamship Company, Ltd., Liverpool.

Sir: I beg to report that at 12.34 A.M. on the 15th inst. I was informed of urgent distress message from *Titanic*, with her position. I immediately ordered ship turned around and put in course for that position; we being then fifty-eight miles S. 42 E. (T) from her. Had heads of all departments called and issued what I considered the necessary orders to be in preparation for any emergency.

At 2.40 A.M., saw flare half a point on port bow, taking this for granted to be ship. Shortly after we sighted our first iceberg (I had previously had lookouts doubled, knowing that *Titanic* had struck ice, and so took every care and precaution).

We soon found ourselves in a field of bergs, large and small, and had to alter course several times to clear bergs; weather fine and clear, light airs, calm sea, beautifully clear night, though dark.

We stopped at 4 A.M., thus doing distance in three hours and a half, picking up the first boat at 4.10 A.M.; boat in charge of an officer and he reported to me that *Titanic* had foundered. At 8.30 A.M. last boat picked up. All survivors aboard and all boats accounted for, viz fifteen lifeboats alongside, one lifeboat abandoned, two Berthon [collapsible] boats alongside (saw one bottom upward among wreckage) and according to second officer not been launched, it having got jammed, making sixteen lifeboats and four Berthon boats accounted for.

By the time we had cleared first boat it was breaking day, and we could distinguish the other boats all within an area of four miles. We also saw that we were surrounded by icebergs, large and small, and three miles to the N.W. of us a huge field of drift ice with large and small bergs in it, the ice field trending from N.W. round by W. and S. to S.E., as far as we could see either way.

At 8 A.M. the Leyland S.S. *California* [sic] came up. I gave him the principal news and asked him to search and I would proceed to New York; at 8.50 proceeded full speed. While searching over vicinity of disaster and while we were getting people aboard I gave orders to get spare hands along and swing in all our boats, disconnect the falls and hoist us as many *Titanic* boats as possible, in our davits; also, get some on fo'castle deck by derricks. We got thirteen lifeboats, six on forward deck and seven in davits.

After getting all survivors aboard and while searching I got a clergyman to offer a short prayer of thankfulness for those saved and also a short burial service for those lost.

Before deciding definitely where to make for I conferred with Mr. Ismay, and though he told me to do what I thought best I informed him, taking everything into consideration. I considered New York best.

I knew we should require more provisions, clean linen, blankets and so forth, even if we went to the Azores.

As most of the passengers saved were women and children, and they were very hysterical, and not knowing what medical attention they might require, thought it best to go to New York; also thought it would be better for Mr. Ismay to get to New York or England as soon as possible and knowing that I should be out of wireless communication with anything very soon if I proceeded to the Azores.

Again, passengers were all hysterical about ice, and pointed out to Mr. Ismay the possibility of seeing ice if we went to Halifax. Then I knew from the gravity of the disaster that it would be desirable to keep in touch with land stations all we could.

I am pleased to say that all survivors have been very plucky. The majority of the women, first, second and third

classes lost their husbands, and considering all have been won-
derfully well. Tuesday our doctor reported all survivors physically well.

Our first class passengers have behaved splendidly, giving
up the cabins quite voluntarily and supplying the ladies with
clothes and so forth. We all turned out of our cabins to give
them up to survivors, saloons, smokerooms, library and so
forth also being used for sleeping accommodations. Our crew
also turned out to let the crew of the *Titanic* take their quarters.

I am pleased to state that owing to preparations made for
the comfort of the survivors none are the worse for exposure
and so forth.

I beg to specially mention how willingly and cheerfully the
whole of the ship's company have behaved throughout, receiving the highest praise from everybody, and I can assure you,
that I am very proud to have such a ship's company under my
command.

We have experienced very great difficulty in transmitting
news, also names of survivors. Our wireless is very poor, and
again, we have had so many interruptions from other ships,
and also messages from shore (principally press, which we
ignored). I gave instructions to send first all official messages,
then names of passengers, then survivors' private messages,
and the last press messages, as I considered the three first items
most important and necessary.

The consultation with Bruce Ismay had been a particular chore: no
sooner had the Chairman of the White Star Line been brought aboard
than he was taken to Dr. McGhee's cabin, where he remained until the
Carpathia docked in New York. His meals were brought to him, and
aside from brief visits from two fellow survivors and Rostron, when
the captain felt it necessary to seek his advice on some point, Ismay
refused to see anyone. Possessed of a more fragile nature than anyone
really suspected, Ismay had undergone a terrible shock when the
Titanic went down. Certainly he was aware that his own survival
would become an ugly issue, when so many other men in all three

classes aboard the *Titanic* had died—the mortality rate among the men in Second Class alone had exceeded 90%. That he was also the chairman of the White Star Line would only make a bad situation appear worse; Ismay knew he would be pilloried in the American press, and there was no reason to believe that the British press would be any kinder. Then there was the sheer horror of what he had just witnessed: no one could have watched more than fifteen hundred people die without recoiling from the experience.

When Rostron first approached Ismay, it was to seek his approval for a return to New York, the captain's thought being to do whatever was best for the survivors. Ismay immediately agreed; in fact whatever Rostron proposed was fine, Ismay said. No sooner had Rostron begun making his plans for the return to New York than Cottam reappeared on the bridge, bearing a message from the *Olympic*: her captain, H.J. Haddock, was suggesting that the Titanic's passengers be transferred to his ship. Rostron thought this an appalling idea: just the sight of the *Olympic*, virtually a twin of the vanished *Titanic*, might well be enough to send some of the survivors into hysterics. Going back down to Dr. McGhee's cabin, he broached the idea to Ismay, who simply shuddered at the suggestion. Rostron returned to the bridge and sent a signal to Captain Haddock, politely declining his offer.

As Rostron said in his report, the *Carpathia*'s passengers and crew were exemplary in their conduct toward the *Titanic*'s survivors. Despite being unexpectedly rousted out of their staterooms and shifted to other, smaller, less comfortable cabins, the Cunard passengers were nothing but helpful to their White Star counterparts. Likewise the crew, doubling up in already confined quarters, were never heard to begrudge the spaces given over to the *Titanic*'s crewmen. All of them, passengers and crew alike, understood that they were suddenly part of an extraordinary event, which required extraordinary conduct.

Not unexpectedly, most of the survivors held themselves somewhat aloof from the passengers aboard the *Carpathia*, not from any sense of snobbery, but rather because most of them were in varying degrees of shock, some physical, some emotional. The enormity of what they had experienced was such that no one aboard the Cunard ship, no matter how sympathetic, could ever understand it. And so the *Titanic*'s survivors were polite, and accepted the *Carpathia*'s passengers' assistance with genuine gratitude, but the gulf was always there.

The worst moment of the trip to New York came through the actions of one of the surviving couples, Lady and Sir Cosmo Duff Gordon. They had been part of a group of twelve—five passengers and seven crewmen—who had gotten away from the *Titanic* in Lifeboat No. 1; they would soon become nortorious for having refused to return to the sinking ship, despite the fact that there was room for an additional thirty people in the boat. Apparently, once safely aboard the *Carpathia*, Lady Duff Gordon had what to her seemed to be a smashing idea: why not have a group picture taken of herself, her husband, her secretary, the other two passengers, and the seven crewmen who had manned Boat Number 1 for them? So, the day after they were rescued, all twelve gathered on the *Carpathia*'s foredeck, the crewmen conspicuous in their lifebelts. Other survivors stared in disbelief as Dr. McGhee, the *Carpathia*'s surgeon, prepared to take the picture with the words, "Now, smile everyone!"

Predictably perhaps, wireless messages presented a problem. The world was desperate for news of the disaster, families anxious for word of the fates of their loved ones, survivors intent on letting them know they were alive. The result was what appeared to be a hopeless muddle. Precisely what happened is still open to debate, but what is clear is that some of the troubles were technical in nature, and some were manmade. Captain Rostron, who had a keener appreciation of wireless than many of his colleagues, was determined to keep the idle chatter to a minimum; only the most essential messages were to be sent. He instructed Cottam to give first priority to communicating news to the Cunard and White Star offices, in particular in sending the names of the survivors, then passing along any brief personal messages they might have. Messages sent by the *Carpathia*'s own passengers would have to wait; there would be no time to answer incoming inquiries from the press.

In the wireless shack Cottam set to work. Once Harold Bride had gotten medical attention for his badly frostbitten feet, and a few hours rest, he began to periodically relieve Cottam at the key, but it was a long process. After sending the *Olympic* a brief synopsis of what had happened, along with an estimate of the numbers of passengers and crew lost as well as rescued, Cottam and Bride essentially ignored any incoming requests for news for the next three days.

One of the first messages Cottam sent was to Philip A. S. Franklin, Vice President of the White Star Line in New York:

> "Most desirable *Titanic* crew should be returned home earliest moment possible. Suggest you hold *Cedric*, sailing her daylight Friday. . . . Propose returning in her myself. YAMSI."

"YAMSI" was of course a transposition of Ismay, though why the Chairman of the Line chose to employ such a transparent subterfuge is anyone's guess: he always signed his cables that way. No matter what the signature read, the contents of the message quickly became an object of suspicion in some circles, for there seemed to be something irregular about the haste with which Ismay wanted to get the *Titanic*'s crewmen—and himself—away from the United States. Ismay always maintained that his sole motive in sending the cable was to get the crewmen back to England as quickly as possible so that they could go back to work if they wished, because their pay stopped the moment the *Titanic* sank. Critics of Ismay then and since would be quick to point out that White Star could have kept their pay going, but such benevolence was of course alien to the nature of British shipowners. Given his colleagues' overall level of avarice, Ismay's gesture of repatriation was surprisingly considerate.

It has also been suggested that he was trying to evade American jurisdiction by spiriting the surviving *Titanic* crew out of the country, before any formal inquiry could be launched. Unfortunately for those who sought to pillory Ismay at any turn, this theory doesn't hold up. Not only would Ismay, isolated on the *Carpathia*, have lacked knowledge that any such inquiry was pending in America (one was), but he certainly knew that a formal Board of Trade inquest would be called in Great Britain. It makes little sense to suggest that Ismay was trying to flee from the possible reach of one investigation only to fly into the certain arms of another. Nevertheless, the contrived signature coupled with the contents of the message would create a flurry of suspicion among the American press, eager as always to name a scapegoat regardless of the facts, and lead to Ismay facing a grueling three-hour cross-examination before a sub-committee of the United States Senate.

The Ismay tempest-in-a-teapot aside, there was very little real information available to an American press suddenly desperately hungry for any news regarding the *Titanic*'s fate. A series of garbled wireless transmissions from ships in the vicinity of the *Titanic* had left the newspapers thoroughly confused. With the *Carpathia* refusing to answer any queries, there was little hard information to go on, and the headlines the morning of April 15 were filled with varying degrees of speculation.

Only one New York paper seemed to grasp the enormity of the events unfolding in the North Atlantic. Sometime around 1:20 in the morning of April 15, the wireless station on the roof of the editorial offices of the *New York Times* received a bulletin from Cape Race in Newfoundland, which read:

> Sunday night, April 14 (AP). At 10:25 o'clock [New York time] tonight the White Star Line steamship *Titanic* called "CQD" to the Marconi station here, and reported having struck an iceberg. The steamer said that immediate assistance was required.

The *Times'* managing editor, Carr Van Anda, immediately called the New York office of the White Star Line, then contacted the *Times'* correspondents in Montreal and Halifax in an effort to learn more. At the moment the facts were sparse, the situation unclear. About a half-hour before midnight (New York time), the Allen Line had received a transmission from their steamer, the *Virginian*, which had picked up one of the *Titanic*'s early distress calls and had altered course to rush to the stricken liner's aid. The White Star ships *Olympic* and *Baltic* were also putting about, as were the *Birma*, the *Mount Temple*, and the *Carpathia*. Cape Race was monitoring the wireless transmissions between these ships as well as keeping a close watch on the messages coming from the *Titanic*. Cape Race had heard nothing from the sinking liner since 12:27 a.m., when a blurred CQD was heard, and abruptly cut off.

Van Anda had a good head for news, and quickly began reshaping the morning mail edition of the *Times*. The political feud between

President Taft and Theodore Roosevelt which had dominated the news for the past three months and had originally been given preeminence on the front page was instantly relegated to the inside pages, and taking its place would be the accident to the *Titanic*. Van Anda sensed that a tremendous story was breaking, though at the same time a terrible dread began looming in his mind. At that point, the *Titanic* hadn't been heard from in nearly an hour—as more reports came in, it was learned that the women and children were being put into the lifeboats and that the ship's engine room was flooding. What Van Anda began to suspect was the worst—the "unsinkable ship" had sunk.

There was no confirmation yet, so the story Van Anda prepared for the early edition was cautious. He simply presented the bare facts as they were known at that early hour, as well as whatever information was available about the ship and her passengers. But the four-line headline itself shouted:

NEW LINER *TITANIC* HITS AN ICEBERG;
SINKING BY THE BOW AT MIDNIGHT;
WOMEN PUT OFF IN LIFEBOATS;
LAST WIRELESS AT 12:27 A.M. BLURRED

That would do for the morning editions, but now Van Anda decided to play his hunch: when the city edition went to press, it announced that the *Titanic* had sunk. It would be several hours before he would know for sure, but if he was right, then the *New York Times* would have "scooped" every other paper in the country—quite an accomplishment for a newspaper that in 1912 was just another New York daily. Although he had no way of knowing it, Van Anda had just claimed a position of preeminence for the *New York Times* among American newspapers which it would not relinquish for the rest of the century.

But while the *New York Times* was prepared to announce in its latest edition that the *Titanic* had sunk, based on the prolonged silence of her wireless, no other editor was willing to follow Carr Van Anda's lead. Consequently the White Star offices were besieged by reporters seeking additional information.

At first, Phillip Franklin was confident, telling his questioners, "We place absolute confidence in the *Titanic*. We believe that the boat is unsinkable." At the same time though, as rumors were gaining strength and doubts began to grow, he was having messages sent addressed to Captain Smith, asking for information about the ship and its passengers.

Yet the story being told to the public sounded so convincing. The myth that the *Titanic* was unsinkable had been repeated so many times by so many different sources that it had become accepted as a truth. It was impossible to imagine that any serious accident had happened to her. When the *Evening Sun* ran a banner-sized headline that declared "ALL SAVED FROM *TITANIC* AFTER COLLISION," the paper was merely giving voice to what the public—and White Star officials—believed to be true. The latest story had it that the *Titanic*'s passengers were being transferred to the *Parisian* and the *Carpathia*, while the *Virginian* took the wounded liner in tow, bound for Halifax.

The White Star Line's positive posture was maintained all through the day of April 15. True, Franklin admitted to reporters, there were rumors that the *Titanic* had sunk and that the loss of life was heavy, but these were rumors, not reliable news. Wireless operators—in some cases amateurs—were catching snippets of transmissions and relaying them on. The news they were hearing wasn't good. But the ships actually involved, actually *there*, the *Carpathia*, the *Virginian*, the *Parisian* and others, weren't within wireless range yet, so for news as important as this, Franklin understandably wasn't willing to settle for second- or third-hand information.

When the official word came at 6:15 p.m., it was like a body blow to Franklin: the *Olympic*, her transmission delayed for some hours by technical problems, reported that the *Titanic* had sunk at 2:20 a.m., with more than 1,000 passengers still aboard; the survivors had been rescued by the *Carpathia* and were being brought to New York. It took nearly three-quarters of an hour before Franklin could muster the self-control he needed to face reporters. With his anguish visibly playing across his face, he told them, "Gentlemen, I regret to say that the *Titanic* sank at 2:20 this morning."

That was all he would—or could—say at the moment. It is remarkable that he was able to hold onto his composure for so long, but gradually he admitted that the report "neglected to say that all the crew had been saved," then later that "probably a number of lives had been lost," which eventually became "we very much fear there has been a great loss of life." At 9:00 p.m. Franklin broke down completely. Sobbing, he told the stunned reporters that there had been a "horrible loss of life"—it would be possible, he said, to replace the ship, but "never the human lives."

In the years to come critics would have harsh words to say about Franklin's apparent lack of candor with the press. Some would hint, for instance, that he had withheld confirmation of the *Titanic*'s loss until after trading had ceased on Wall Street for the day, allowing IMM shareholders with inside knowledge to sell off stock which was sure to plunge in value the next day. Yet it's difficult to give too much credence to the idea. So many rumors, half-truths, and theories were flying about on April 15 that Franklin's restraint in making any announcement until the truth was confirmed appears more admirable than sinister. Garbled, incomplete, and sometimes irrelevant messages were being picked up by wireless operators up and down the Eastern Seaboard, each one being given varying degrees of credence by the Eastern press, and adding to the confusion. The best example of this was how the story that the *Titanic* was being towed to Halifax after her passengers had been safely transferred to other ships got its start: two garbled messages about incidents involving other ships, which had nothing to do at all with the *Titanic*, were somehow thrown together and reported as the latest news about the stricken White Star liner.

And at the same time it's difficult not to feel a certain sympathy for Franklin once the truth was known: here was disaster on an unprecedented scale, an event so huge that it was difficult to assimilate. Close to a century later, after two world wars, numerous smaller wars, police actions, and global terrorism, humanity has become, if not desensitized, then at least resigned to death on a massive scale. In 1912, all the horrors of the 20th century were still to come, and the Edwardian world was still in so many ways naive and innocent. That so many people—and soon word on the street was that the death toll had reached 1,200 (no one yet suspected that it would climb still higher)—could lose their lives in a single stroke of fate was nearly unimaginable. It was, in Walter Lord's memorable phrase, "as if an entire small town had been wiped off the map." It should come as no surprise, then, that Franklin struggled to communicate the truth to the press. It was so devastating that he could barely manage to comprehend it himself.

Nonetheless, news began to trickle in, especially when Cottam and Bride aboard the *Carpathia* began transmitting lists of survivors along with their personal messages. As their messages arrived at the White Star offices in New York, messengers quickly brought it to men who were standing by outside, chalk in hand, ready to post the latest news on hastily erected chalkboards set up ten or more feet above the street, so that the growing crowds could read it for themselves. Similar chalkboards appeared above the offices of most of New York's newspapers.

People had begun gathering in front of the White Star offices around 10:00 a.m. on April 15, just a few hours after the morning papers broke the news of the *Titanic*'s accident. Some of those gathered were relatives of passengers on board the ship, others were friends, some were mere curiosity seekers. A few family members were admitted into the building—Ben Guggenheim's wife; John Jacob Astor's son, Vincent; Astor's father-in-law, W.H. Force—along with a handful of influential people who had a particular interest in the fate of the ship, among them J.P. Morgan. When they emerged from Franklin's office, their faces would be grim; Vincent Astor left in tears. The crowd outside the White Star building began to fear the worst, and the word soon spread across the city, then into the rest of the country.

A few more days would pass before it became clear how bad the loss really was—and it was very bad. Captain Rostron's muster had shown that he had 705 survivors aboard the *Carpathia*—but there had been 2,207 passengers and crew aboard the *Titanic* when she struck the iceberg. When the numbers were written down, the sums added up, the "t's" crossed and the "i's" dotted, 1,502 people had lost their lives. In First Class, 123 passengers out of 325 died; in Second Class the figure was 167 out of 285; in Third Class, there had been 706 aboard and 528 were lost. That so many more Third Class passengers had been lost in proportion to their First or Second Class counterparts would soon lead social critics to lay charges of discrimination against the White Star Line, echoes of which, however strained or unfounded, can still be heard today.

Critics would be quick to point out that a greater percentage of First Class men were saved than Third Class women, raising a great cry of indignation that a third of the men in First Class survived the disaster. But statistics can be misleading and manipulative: if one-third of the First Class men lived, that can only mean that two-thirds of them died with the ship. Nearly all of the First Class men who got away left the ship in the first four or five boats, when there was little sense of urgency or danger and only a handful of officers knew that there weren't enough lifeboats for everyone on board. Even as the awful truth slowly became apparent, most of them stayed on board the *Titanic* voluntarily. And though it is true that none of the First Class men who made it into a lifeboat would later relinquish his place to another passenger, it is significant, perhaps, that not one of the First Class men would demand that someone else give up a seat in deference to him.

These are the facts, and for the truly detached observer there is no need to attempt to burnish the image of the First Class men. They left their own unique memorial, in a handful of unforgettable vignettes. There was Daniel Marvin, reassuring his eighteen-year-old bride of two weeks, "It's all right, little girl," as he helped her into the lifeboat; or Colonel Archibald Gracie, working as hard as any crewman to help launch the last two lifeboats. There were Bjorn Steffanson and Hugh Woolner helping Purser McElroy stop a rush of passengers on Collapsible C. There was John Jacob Astor, meekly standing aside from Lifeboat No. 4 when Second Officer Lightoller refused to make an exception to "Women and children only" for him. Astor's final words to his wife, who was three months pregnant, were, "To please me, get in the boat. The ship is fully equipped and everyone will be saved. I'll see you in the morning." He then turned away, knowing he would never see his unborn child.

There was Isidor Strauss, refusing to get into a boat before any other man; and Benjamin Guggenheim, who after standing for some moments on the Boat Deck, returned to his cabin and doffed the heavy sweater, winter coat, and homburg hat his steward had insisted on his wearing. Reappearing on the Boat Deck dressed in evening clothes, complete to white tie, tails, and silk hat, his secretary at his side simi-larly attired, he stopped a passing steward and gave the man a farewell message to pass on to his wife: "I am willing to remain and play the man's game if there are not enough boats for more than the women and children. . . . No woman shall be left aboard this ship because Ben Guggenheim was a coward. We've dressed in our best and are pre-pared to go down like gentlemen."

The last anyone saw of John B. Thayer, Arthur Ryerson, Clarence Moore, Charles Hayes, George Widener, or Walter Douglas—six of the wealthiest and most influential men in North America—was of them standing in a small group near the portside railing on the for-ward Boat Deck, none of them going anywhere near a lifeboat. It was almost as if they had come to some collective conclusion that part of the price for living well was an obligation to die well. It might be too much to call their action heroism, but it would be cruel and wrong to pretend that their *sang froid* was not admirable.

And yet, the discrepancy between the percentage of First Class men and Third Class women who were saved existed. Though it would become the recurring theme of egalitarian social critics and lev-elers for more than nine decades, simple class discrimination was not responsible—far more subtle and insidious influences were at work. Wynn Craig Wade, a clinical psychologist from Michigan State University, wrote of the fate of Third Class with rare insight in *Titanic: The End of a Dream*: "Undoubtedly, the worst barriers were the ones within the steerage passengers themselves. Years of conditioning as third-class citizens led a great many of them to give up hope as soon as the crisis became evident."

It was this apparent helplessness that August Wennerstrom, a Third Class passenger himself, had observed and about which he later made the bitter observation: "Hundreds were in a circle with a preach-er in the middle, praying, crying, asking God and Mary to help them. They lay there, still crying, till the water was over their heads. They just prayed and yelled, never lifting a hand to help themselves. They had lost their own willpower and expected God to do all their work for them."

Generations of being at the bottom of the social strata, being told where to go, what to do, and when to do it, had produced a mentality almost bereft of initiative among many of the people who comprised Third Class.

This doesn't mean that the steerage passengers simply stood by and let themselves be drowned because they couldn't think of anything better to do. Third Class never got the chance to show their own peculiar brand of courage and self-sacrifice. Unlike the crew, they lacked leadership and an example to action, because no one inside or outside Third Class provided it for them. A handful of men and women in Third Class did succeed in reaching the Boat Deck on their own, but they were lucky—when they left Third Class they had no clear idea where they were going or how they would get there. No one will ever know how many others who tried to do the same got lost inside the ship or were trapped in dead ends and taken down with the *Titanic* when she sank. As for the rest, they fell back on old habits, and simply waited in vain for someone "in charge" to come along and lead them to safety.

Their sacrifice, then, would be measured in different coin from those of the officers and crew or the men in First Class who stayed behind, terms far less glamorous, far more harsh. They had put their trust, however misplaced, in the belief that their "betters"—the people in charge, whoever they might be—knew what they were doing. It had always been thus, and they had been raised to believe it would always be so. The steerage passengers didn't know, couldn't know until it was too late, that the circumstances had overwhelmed the very people they were relying on to protect them.

And somehow, amidst all the hue and cry over the respective plights of the First and Third Class passengers, the men and women in Second Class are all to often overlooked or, worse, ignored. Of the 285 Second Class passengers aboard the Titanic, only 118 survived. Among them were only 14 men—154 men from Second Class had down with the ship. There had never been a more dramatic expression of "Women and children first!" since the troopship *Birkenhead* ran on the rocks off the South African coast in 1852. As that ship foundered, the soldiers' commanding officer, Colonel Seton, ordered his men to "Stand fast!" in close-formed ranks and allow the women and children aboard to take to what few lifeboats there were. The troops' ranks held steady even as the ship went under. Nine officers, three hundred forty-nine other ranks, and eighty-seven of *Birkenhead*'s crewmen were lost: all the women and children survived. Aboard the *Titanic*, nine of every ten men in Second Class died with the ship, a fact which would all too often be overlooked by social critics in the years to follow.

Yet what was perhaps the greatest tragedy of the *Titanic* disaster was one of which most Americans were unaware, and would remain so. What is so often overlooked in the telling of tales of the *Titanic* is the loss of so many of the crew, and the price paid by their families. Out of 891 crewmen aboard the ship, only 207 survived—684 were lost with the ship. More than three quarters of the *Titanic*'s crew died when the ship went down, a greater loss, proportionately, than suffered by any of the passenger classes. But what that number doesn't tell—cannot tell—is the overwhelming burden of grief it brought to a single city in England. It is here that the genuine tragedy of the *Titanic* disaster is seen in full measure, and the guilt of those who ignored the sinking liner's calls for help is shown in all its clarity.

Four out of every five crewmen aboard the *Titanic* came from the city of Southampton, a proud old seafaring town whose ties to ships and the sea date back to Roman times. Entire streets were hung with black crepe in the weeks following April 15, whole rows of houses bereaved. That afternoon a crowd began to gather outside Ocean House, the White Star Line's offices in Southampton, just a few score yards from the Ocean Dock, from which the liner had departed only a few days before. It consisted almost entirely of women: young women with bright-eyed babies in their arms; middle-aged women with hands red and worn from work; old women, wrinkled and gray; all of them waiting for news of their menfolk, husbands, fathers, sons. Names were posted as quickly as they came in, but all too often, when one of the women would leave to go home, she would be sobbing, leaning on the arm of a friend, a daughter, a mother-in-law. Sometimes, saddest of all, she left alone. In the April 23 issue of the London *Daily Mail* an unsigned article described how those anxious days closed:

> . . . in the afternoon hope died out. The waiting crowds thinned, and silent men and women sought their homes. In the

humbler homes of Southampton there is scarcely a family who has not lost a relative or friend. Children returning from school appreciated something of tragedy, and woeful little faces were turned to the darkened, fatherless homes.

The story went on to tell of the working class streets in Southampton and the loss they had suffered. It told of Mrs. Allen, whose husband George was a trimmer on the *Titanic*; of a woman on Union Street with three small children; of Mrs. Barnes, who lost a brother; of Mr. Saunders, whose two boys were firemen; of an old man on Cable Street who had four sons aboard the ship; of a young girl, half-mad with grief, whose husband had been a steward—they had been married only a month; of Mrs. Gosling, who lost a son; of Mrs. Preston, a widow, who lost her son as well. But the most heartbreaking may have been Mrs. May, whose husband Arthur and eldest son, Arthur, Jr., had both gone down with the *Titanic*. There were ten children left behind to care for, as well as young Arthur's wife and six-week-old baby. The oldest of her children was nineteen, the youngest was six months old.

> Many women who wait for hour after hour outside the White Star offices pathetically cling to hope that their men . . . have escaped in one of the boats. . . . One drooping woman was leaning on a bassinet containing two chubby babies, while a tiny mite held her hand. "What are we waiting for, Mummy? Why are we waiting such a long time?" asked the tired child. "We are waiting for news of your father, dear," came the choked answer, as the mother turned away her head to hide her tears.

Not a hint of this despair would have reached the *Carpathia*, of course. There, a grimly determined Cottam and Bride continued to send out lists of survivors' names, along with any personal messages they might have. The two wireless operators steadfastly refused to answer any requests for information, no matter what the source, not even those from the cruiser USS *Chester*, dispatched by a worried President Taft. Taft had sent out the *Chester* expressly to contact the

Carpathia, whose wireless didn't have the range to reach New York directly. But despite her repeated attempts, all in the name of the President, the *Chester*'s queries went unanswered, as did those of the various newspapers and wire services hungrily waiting for news.

Both wireless operators aboard the *Carpathia* would later claim that the wireless man aboard the *Chester* was so ham-handed that his signaling was almost unintelligible—he also used American Morse, which neither of the British operators said they knew. Before long, though, it would be revealed that there were other reasons for their reluctance to respond to the *Chester* or any of the New York press' inquires.

Deprived of information, the New York papers quickly turned their ire on the *Carpathia*. The *World*, for example, proclaimed with calculated petulance, "CARPATHIA LETS NO SECRETS OF THE TITANIC'S LOSS ESCAPE BY WIRELESS." The *Evening Mail*'s frustration was even more obvious: "WATCHERS ANGERED BY CARPATHIA'S SILENCE." The tone of the other New York papers were similar.

In reality, both Cottam and Bride had been advised by the Marconi office in New York that Guglielmo Marconi himself had concluded a deal with the *New York Times* on behalf of the two young operators that would reward them handsomely for providing an exclusive for the *Times*. For a couple of young men earning the equivalent of $40 a month or less, the promise of several thousand dollars in exchange for a few hours spent talking to a reporter was irresistible, so sending only survivors' names and messages provided a convenient excuse for turning aside any other inquiries.

Neither Bride nor Cottam, nor Marconi himself for that matter, were aware that Marconi's apparently benevolent action could appear to be a deliberate attempt to withhold information from an anxious public solely for the *Times*' benefit. It would take some weeks before the whole story would be sorted out, though in the end it was shown that Marconi himself received nothing from the *Times* and had indeed been looking out for the best interests of his two young operators. Still, it was an awkward situation that resulted in some embarrassing moments for Marconi, including an appearance before a Senate Subcommittee. He would be chastised for exercising poor judgment, but cleared of any wrongdoing. In any case, it soon became quite clear that in the meantime nothing more would be learned from the little Cunarder until her arrival in New York, which was scheduled for Thursday night, April 18.

Chapter 7

NEW YORK AND BOSTON

In New York, Thursday night, April 18, 1912, was cold and drenched with rain, the whole of New York Harbor shrouded in a thunderstorm. A crowd began gathering, mindless of the weather, on the Cunard pier around 6:00 p.m., small at first, only a few hundred, but slowly growing until by 9:00, more than 30,000 were standing along the east bank of the Hudson River. At the tip of Manhattan, huddled in the cold April downpour, another 10,000 were lining the Battery. Peering through the gloom and mist, at a few minutes past 9:00 they spotted a ship in the Ambrose Channel. It was the *Carpathia*. She was first greeted by a small fleet of steam launches, tugboats, ferry boats, and yachts, led by a large tug containing an official party of the mayor and several city commissioners.

As the *Carpathia* hove into sight the mayor's tug let loose a shrill blast from its steam whistle, followed by the bells, whistles, and sirens of every other boat in the harbor, all in salute of the gallant Cunard ship. Captain Rostron stood on the bridge, staring out at the flotilla of boats surrounding his ship and dimly making out the throng gathered at the Cunard pier awaiting his arrival. Until this moment he had no idea, as he put it later, of "the suspense and excitement in the world:

"As we were going up Ambrose Channel, the weather changed completely, and a more dramatic ending to tragic occurrence it would be hard to conceive. It began to blow hard, rain came down in torrents, and, to complete the finale, we had continuous vivid lightning and heavy rolling thunder. . . . What with the wind and rain, a pitch-dark night, lightning and thunder, and the photographers taking flashlight pictures of the ship, and the explosion of the lights, it was a scene never to be effaced from one's memory."

At pierside, people began weeping quietly, but there was little hysteria. The most frenzied behavior was exhibited—surprise!—by the huge numbers of reporters who had gathered along with the crowd on the pier, or had gotten aboard one of the boats that had sailed into the channel to meet the *Carpathia*. When the liner stopped to pick up the pilot, five reporters were able to clamber from their boat over the railing onto the pilot boat, then attempted to force their way up the boarding ladder and onto the *Carpathia*.

Captain Rostron, once he saw the reception awaiting his ship, anticipated such an eventuality, and had stationed Third Officer Rees at the foot of the boarding ladder. Rees watched in bemused fascination as the small craft gathered around the pilot boat, the reporters shouting questions up to the decks of the *Carpathia* through megaphones, the photographers setting off their magnesium flashes as they took picture after picture. But when one of the newsmen tried to shove the pilot aside and rush up the boarding ladder himself, Rees sprang into action. Grabbing the pilot by the arm, Rees hauled him onto the boarding ladder, then turned and punched the reporter in the mouth, sending him sprawling.

"Pilot only!" he said, in case the other newsmen hadn't got the message. Apparently one missed it, for he immediately started raving about his sister, crying about how he had to see her; when Rees didn't believe his story, he tried to bribe the Third Officer, offering him $200 to be allowed on board. Rees refused, the boarding ladder was raised, the pilot was taken up to the bridge, and the journey up the channel resumed.

Somehow one reporter did slip aboard, but he was quickly cornered and brought to the bridge. Rostron, who had no time for such nonsense, informed the man that under no circumstances could he speak with any survivors before the *Carpathia* docked. The man was left on the bridge, after giving his word he would abide by the captain's instructions. "I must say," Rostron later admitted, somewhat astonished, "he was a gentleman."

The crowd gasped with surprise when the *Carpathia* steamed past the Cunard pier toward the White Star dock and stopped there. Amidst the nearly continuous lightning and photographers' flashes, the crew of the *Carpathia* could be seen manning several lifeboats and putting them into the water. After a moment the suddenly apprehensive crowd realized what was happening: they were the *Titanic's* lifeboats, being duly returned to their rightful owners. It was a heartbreaking sight.

After a painfully slow turn, the *Carpathia* made her way back to the Cunard pier, and was carefully warped alongside and made fast. The canopied gangways were hauled into place, and a procession of passengers began to make their way down from the ship to the dock. After a few seconds, the stunned crowd realized that these neatly dressed people weren't from the *Titanic*. Captain Rostron had decided that it would be unfair to his passengers to make them wait and wade through the tumult that would inevitably greet the survivors, so the *Carpathia's* passengers disembarked first.

Then there appeared a young woman, hatless, eyes wide as she stared at the waiting crowd, the first of the *Titanic's* survivors. At the foot of the gangway stood a solid phalanx of reporters, each one hungry for a story. Standing unrecognized among them was one man who was after the biggest story of them all: a diminutive figure flanked by two U.S. Marshals, he was Senator William Alden Smith. The appearance of the Senator and the marshals marked the beginning of a turning point in the lives of Captains Rostron and Lord. The Senator was the Chairman of the Senate subcommittee formed to investigate the loss of the *Titanic*; the lawmen were there to serve Federal subpoenas to Bruce Ismay as well as several surviving members of the *Titanic's* crew.

A similar scene would be enacted in Boston aboard the *Californian* a few days later. It was the beginning of a process which, by the time it had run its course, would put Arthur Rostron firmly on the path that would lead him to become the Commodore of the

Cunard Line; and at the same time it would slowly destroy Stanley Lord's professional standing and career.

The *Californian* docked in Boston Harbor on April 19 virtually unnoticed and with no fanfare whatsoever. By coincidence it was the same day that the first hearings of the Senate Investigation into the *Titanic* disaster began in New York. The only incident which marked the ship's arrival as unusual was the appearance of a corporate representative from the Leyland Line at dockside. As soon as a gangway was lowered into position he came aboard and immediately closeted himself with Lord in the captain's cabin. No one would ever know the reason for the company representative's visit, but it was an event that had never taken place before during Lord's tenure as captain of the *Californian*.

That does not mean that the ship's completion of its passage to Boston was without incident. On April 18, the day before the *Californian* was to arrive, two extraordinary incidents took place. At separate times during the day, Captain Lord called Second Officer Stone and Apprentice Officer Gibson into his quarters, and there demanded that each record a sworn, written statement describing the events of the morning of April 15. Both men complied, and when they had finished handed their statements to Lord, who promptly locked them in *Californian*'s safe. No word of explanation for his demand was offered by Lord, nor, apparently, sought by Stone or Gibson, who by now were resigned to their captain's sometimes overbearing ways.

No sooner had the Leyland Line ship tied up at the dock and the crew allowed to go ashore than rumors began flying about the waterfront that the *Californian* had been near enough to the *Titanic* on the night of April 14–15 to watch the doomed White Star liner go down. It didn't take long for the tale came to the ears of Boston reporters, hungry, like newsmen all across the country, for more stories about the *Titanic*. Before the day was out, the *Boston Traveler, Boston Evening Transcript,* and *Boston Globe* had sent representatives to talk to Captain Lord, who met them in the *Californian*'s chartroom.

Appearing confident and authoritative, Lord began spinning out details and snippets of information which cast him in the best possible

The Royal Mail Steamer (RMS) *Titanic*, the largest and most luxurious passenger liner of her day, and one of the most beautiful ships ever built.

Captain Edward J. Smith. After 47 years at sea, the *Titanic*'s maiden voyage was to be his last Atlantic crossing before retirement.

John ("Jack") Phillips (left), the senior wireless operator aboard the *Titanic*; Harold Bride (right) was the junior operator.

Captain Smith in the starboard bridge-wing cab of the RMS *Olympic*, the *Titanic*'s sister ship. Note the Morse lamp on top of the cab. A similar light was mounted on the port wing. The *Titanic*'s installation was identical to the *Olympic*'s.

The RMS *Carpathia*, a modest Cunard passenger liner that was on her way to Trieste, Italy, when the *Titanic* sent out her wireless distress call.

Captain Arthur Rostron (seated, center) and the officers of the *Carpathia*. First Officer Dean is sitting to Rostron's left, Chief Engineer Johnston stands behind Rostron's right shoulder, Second Officer Bisset is standing second from the left, in profile.

Harold Cottam, wireless operator aboard the *Carpathia*. He was technically off-duty when the *Titanic*'s distress signals went out, and caught the "CQD" by chance.

The SS *Californian*, seen from the *Carpathia* about 9:15 a.m. on the morning of April 15, 1912, as the *Carpathia* was collecting the last of the *Titanic*'s survivors.

Captain Stanley Lord, captain of the *Californian*. At the age of 35 he had already spent 22 years at sea.

"Women and Children First"—a contemporary illustration of the *Titanic*'s Boat Deck as she was sinking. Despite some romanticized elements, it is a surprisingly accurate representation of the atmosphere that filled those desperate two hours and forty minutes as the *Titanic* sank.

Lifeboat No. 14 towing Collapsible D (the last boat to be lowered from the *Titanic*) as it approaches the *Carpathia* on the morning of April 15, 1912.

Collapsible C pulling alongside the *Carpathia*. The dark-clad figure immediately below the man at the tiller is believed to be Bruce Ismay.

Lifeboat No. 6 struggling to reach the *Carpathia*. There were only two men in the boat; the women spent much of the night rowing in an effort to keep warm.

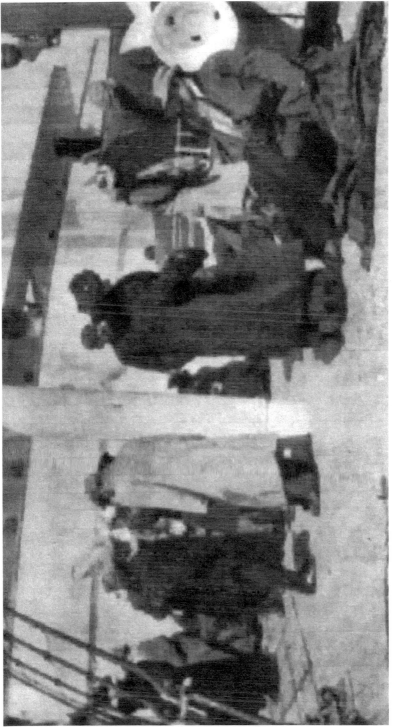

Some of the *Titanic's* survivors huddled in the *Carpathia's* forward well deck. Stunned by their experience, they kept to themselves during much of the voyage to New York.

Above: The offices of the New York American; like most of the New York papers, a huge chalkboard was erected above the sidewalk, where hourly updates of the latest news about the *Titanic* were posted.

April 16, 1912. Newsboy Ted Parfett hawking editions of the London Evening News outside the White Star Offices on Trafalgar Square.

Part of the crowd lining the approaches to Cunard's Pier 54 in New York, awaiting the arrival of the *Carpathia*.

The *Titanic*'s lifeboats, returned to the White Star Line in New York by the *Carpathia*. Within days of their arrival, the name *Titanic* was removed from each, and they were pressed into service on other White Star ships.

William Alden Smith, the junior United States Senator from Michigan, who chaired the Senate investigation into the *Titanic* disaster.

The Senate hearings in session in New York. Compared to the British Inquiry, the American investigation was a very informal affair.

Lord Mersey (right) on his way to one of the sessions of the British
Inquiry, accompanied by his son.

The British Board of Trade Inquiry into the loss of the *Titanic*, held in the
London Scottish Drill Hall.

Second Officer C.H. Lightoller and his wife Sylvia. Lightoller was the
senior surviving officer from the *Titanic*'s crew.

light, and which cast carefully structured aspersions on the characters of anyone who dared suggest that the captain's conduct in the wee hours of April 15, 1912 were anything less than exemplary. Perhaps the most revealing of these comments was Lord's derisive observation, when asked if the *Californian* had actually been close enough to the sinking *Titanic* to see her lights, that "Seamen will say almost anything when they're ashore."

Lord's assumed air of calm authority for the most part seemed to give the lie to the rumors, although one comment he made seemed so unusual to the reporters of the *Boston Traveler* and the *Boston Evening Transcript* that both newspapers printed it. When pressed about the *Californian*'s position during the night of April 14–15, Lord refused, claiming such information was "state secrets." He declined to show his log entries for that night, and informed the reporters that "the information would have to come from the company's office." Lord's use of the term "state secrets" struck a jarring note at the time—it still does—for its hyperbole. The Leyland Line was a business, not a sovereign nation, and ships' logs had always been, as a matter of common practice, if not actual law, available for public inspection at any time. The conclusion that there were entries made— or missing—of which Lord did not want the public to know was then, and remains, inescapable.

Nevertheless, the reporters took Lord at his word, and the story was buried on the inside pages of the handful of papers that carried it. The Boston press immediately turned its attention to the U.S. Senate investigation into the loss of the *Titanic*, which was just getting underway in New York. And so the strange mix of falsehood, deception, and fabrication about the events of April 15, 1912, which would come to surround Stanley Lord for the rest of his life, had begun.

The world might have never been the wiser had it not been for an obscure New England newspaper which featured an astonishing lead story in its April 23, 1912 edition. The Clinton, Massachusetts, *Daily Item* ran a banner headline which read:

CALIFORNIA [sic] REFUSED AID
Foreman Carpenter on Board this Boat Says Hundreds
Might Have Been Saved FROM THE TITANIC

Two men in Lord's crew weren't so easily dispatched by his casual dismissal of their veracity as he might have hoped. The first was the ship's carpenter, James McGregor, who confided in his cousin, who lived in Clinton, that the *Californian* was close enough to the sinking *Titanic* to have actually seen the doomed liner's lights and distress rockets. The account McGregor gave was so detailed, and tallied so closely with what had actually transpired on the *Californian*'s bridge and in her chartroom that there was no chance of his account being a fabrication.

According to McGregor, the officers on watch had seen an unknown ship to the south firing white rockets for the better part of an hour very early in the morning of April 15, and had duly reported their sightings to Captain Lord, who refused to take any action. It was shameful to McGregor to be associated, however indirectly, with such conduct, and his bitterness was palpable when he said, "The captain [Lord] will never be in command of the *California* [sic] again," and that he would "positively refuse to sail under him again and that all of the officers had the same feeling."

Not having any idea that Carpenter McGregor had already been talking to a reporter, but after reading his captain's disparaging remarks in the Boston papers, Ernest Gill, one of the *Californian*'s assistant engineers, took a reporter and four fellow engineers to a notary public and swore out a lengthy affidavit, in which he maintained that he personally had seen a ship firing rockets just after midnight on April 15. Moreover, he claimed that the ship firing the rockets was no more than ten miles away, and that he had heard the *Californian*'s second officer saying that he too had seen the rockets, and that the ship's captain had been told about them.

The affidavit was printed in its entirety on the morning of April 23 by the *Boston American*, which also wired a complete copy to Senator Smith in New York. Carpenter McGregor's story appeared in the *Clinton Daily Item* the same day. For Smith, it was a remarkable turn of events, for he had, quite by accident, only the day before discovered that there had been an unknown ship within sight of the sinking *Titanic* which failed to respond to her distress signals. Smith was determined to find that ship.

William Alden Smith, the junior Senator from the state of Michigan, suddenly took center stage amid the public's fascination with the *Titanic*. A classic Horatio Alger "rags to riches" success story, Smith had been born in 1859 in tiny Dowagiac, a run-down logging town in the southwest corner of Michigan's lower peninsula. In early adolescence, after his family had moved to the city of Grand Rapids, he developed what would be a lifelong fascination with railroads. He also developed an acute business sense while earning his living at a variety of jobs, including work as a newspaper correspondent and as a page in the Michigan legislature. That position unlocked a passion for politics in Smith; he had studied law and been admitted to the Kent County, Michigan bar, and began a lucrative practice in railroad law. The next step came in 1892 when he was elected to Congress, where he would represent the state of Michigan in either the House of Representatives or the Senate for the next thirty-five years.

William Alden Smith was short, about five feet six, and had a curiously expressive face, capable of changing from fierce rage to warm affection in seconds. He possessed a great deal of personal charm, a remarkable memory from which he could pluck information almost effortlessly, and an oratorical style that was half persuasive, half coercive. Though he was nominally a Republican, within a short time everyone in Congress knew that William Alden was his own man, bound by no party dogma. He was the quintessential political maverick, and Smith gloried in the role. He was an American Midwesterner, writ large, with all the altruism, naivete, dreams, hopes, fears, and prejudices of the American heartland. He was not a dupe, for before he became a politician he had been a successful lawyer and businessman; nor was he a rube, for though largely self-educated, he was a more learned man than many of his colleagues.

Although Smith's political enemies would attempt to portray his investigation into the *Titanic* disaster as sheer opportunism and self-promotion, the accusation rings false. Then as much as now, Congress was a haven for ambitious mediocrities, leaders prepared to follow where the people led, and first-class intellects and talents were always objects of suspicion and hence ridicule. Many times before and after the *Titanic* Inquiry, Smith was to fight lonely battles for causes—

including racial equality and women's rights—that many considered
lost or hopeless. The *Titanic* inquiry would be Smith's one moment to
stand on the world's stage, and he would make the most of it, not for
his sake, but for the ideals and people he represented.

When the news of the *Titanic*'s fate reached Washington, Smith,
like everyone else, was aghast at the enormity of the tragedy. It was
almost impossible to grasp the concept, let alone the reality, that more
than 1,500 lives had been lost in less than three hours. In those innocent days such carnage was unknown, barely imaginable. It was, as
historian Walter Lord once observed, as if a violent battle had been
fought and lost. Newspaper editors, using charts, photographs, and
any other visual aid they could find, tried to give some meaning to the
number and to make the enormity of the casualty list comprehensible
to the man on the street; but it was no easy task, for there had never
been a maritime disaster anything like the loss of the *Titanic*.
Compounding this sense of incredulity was the fact that ocean travel
had seemed to be so safe: in forty years only a handful of passengers
had lost their lives crossing North Atlantic. Within days of the news
breaking about the sinking, government officials, newspaper editors,
and the public were all demanding explanations as to how such a
tragedy could happen.

This was a challenge tailor-made for an analytical mind like
Smith's, and he would not rest until he knew how 1,500 people could
be left behind on the decks of the sinking liner. In the years before he
was first elected to Congress in 1892, Smith had served as general
counsel to two midwestern railroads, and learned firsthand how utterly dependent were the passengers on a railroad's owners for their safety. He discovered that most railroad owners were inclined toward
excessive penny-pinching to maximize profits, with many railroads
operating worn-out equipment on poorly maintained rail networks.
The results were frequent accidents which left passengers and railroad
workers alike dead or maimed, with little if any recourse for their loss
and suffering. Aside from a standard track gauge, there was little in
the way of industry-wide standards for engines, rolling stock, equipment, or signals; regulation of working hours and conditions for engineers, firemen, and brakemen; or uniform operating procedures.
There were no standard tariffs for passenger fares or freightage. The

railroads of the 1880s were, by any measure, very much *laissez-faire* operations.

In Congress, William Alden Smith worked non-stop to bring an end to this haphazard state of affairs. To Smith's mind, because it was the railroads which were the sinews that bound the United States together, and on which the nation's economy depended, they were as much a public trust as private property. The railroad barons had an obligation to serve the people as much as they had an opportunity to fill their coffers. The first ten years of Smith's Washington career were spent successfully imposing a body of Federal regulation on the nation's railways. In the process he made fearful political enemies among men like J.P. Morgan, E.H. Harriman, and Jay Gould, men who felt that not just their profits but their authority should be privately held, and who fought all of Smith's proposed legislation hammer and tongs. But popular sentiment was on Smith's side, not to mention other American business interests, large and small, which stood to benefit from a rationalization of the American railroad industry, and his legislative efforts ultimately succeeded.

Yet Smith was no populist, as some biographers have tried to paint him; nor did he have socialist leanings, although he wasn't particularly hostile to some of their ideas. Smith was the genuine article, a self-proclaimed "maverick" who would just as readily buck his party's line as toe it, but one who chose his battles carefully, not for the sake of making a name for himself but rather because of the inherent rightness of the cause.

It was his experience with the railroads that prompted Smith to take a close look at the transatlantic passenger trade in the days following the *Titanic* disaster. A review of the existing legislation showed that the steamship lines on the North Atlantic were run in much the same *laissez-faire* manner which had characterized American railways two decades earlier. When Smith discovered, in particular, the relationship between J.P. Morgan's railroad interests and Morgan's holdings in International Mercantile Marine, he became determined to launch a full-scale inquiry. Morgan was still a bitter political foe, and Smith found himself wondering if the same casual, offhand manner in which Morgan had once run his railroads was how he now ran his steamship lines.

In Smith's view, there was little if any difference between the public trust held by the American railroads and the steamship lines which crisscrossed the North Atlantic. If anything, the steamship lines bore an even greater responsibility, for they served the nations of Europe as well as the United States. He was determined to bring the steamship companies into line much the same way he had done with American railroads, with a healthy dose of practical, commonsense legislation. But Smith's practical turn of mind would not allow him to take action without first learning the facts, hence his determination for a full-scale Senate investigation to be empanelled. He wasn't sure if there was any evidence of negligence in the *Titanic*'s navigation, or in her safety equipment, or in how the ship's officers and crew handled the evacuation of the ship; but if there was, he would find it. Quickly he pushed a resolution through the Senate that authorized the formation of a subcommittee from the Committee on Commerce, of which Smith was a member, naming him as chairman. Smith carefully composed the subcommittee with members chosen to make it a politically balanced body, and he was careful to ensure that it possessed the power to issue subpoenas, including those for foreign nationals.

At 3:30 p.m. on April 18, Smith, the other six members of the subcommittee, and two U.S. Marshals boarded the *Congressional Limited* at Union Station in Washington, D.C. and arrived in New York just in time to be rushed across the city to Cunard's Pier 54 to meet the *Carpathia* as she tied up. Subpoenas were served to Bruce Ismay, Chairman of the White Star Line, as well as all of the *Titanic*'s surviving officers. Her surviving passengers as well as the *Carpathia*'s officers were invited to make themselves available for testimony. The hearings would begin the following morning, at 10:00 a.m. in the East Room of the Waldorf-Astoria Hotel.

Senator Smith's inquiry lasted nearly six weeks, during which time eighty-two witnesses were called, including all of the *Titanic*'s surviving officers, as well Captains Rostron and Lord and the wireless operators of both the *Titanic* and the *Carpathia*. Significantly, of the eighty-two witnesses called, twenty one of them were passengers. Smith was determined from the start to find out what really happened on the night of April 14–15, and he knew that the passengers, who owed no loyalty to the White Star Line and so would have no reason to hide, alter, or shade facts, would go far in helping his committee form a complete and balanced picture of the *Titanic*'s sinking. Moreover, and in this he was probably acting on the advice of his colleague Senator Burton, who had considerable experience with maritime matters, Smith was determined that the investigation would not degenerate into an endless round of technical discussions, which would only leave matters more confused, and by introducing the passengers' testimony he was able to avoid that pitfall.

There were admittedly times when Senator Smith's ignorance of nautical matters seemed to lead to him to ask remarkably odd questions, since the answers appeared to be perfectly obvious. At one point in the course of Lightoller's testimony, when the Second Officer was describing how the *Titanic*'s forward funnel had collapsed, falling on a knot of swimmers, Smith asked anxiously, "Did it kill anyone?" Later, when he was pursuing the subject of watertight compartments, he asked Lightoller if he were able to say "whether any of the crew or passengers took to these upper watertight compartments as a final, last resort?" Lightoller, not believing that Smith had actually asked such a question, replied that he wasn't sure. Still later, he asked one witness if the ship sank by the bow or by the head, and when the feisty Fifth Officer Lowe was testifying, Smith asked him if he knew what an iceberg was made of. "Ice, I suppose," was Lowe's flippant reply.

It was apparent gaffes like these that at first made the Senator look rather foolish, although as the hearings progressed the logic behind his methods gradually became apparent. Far from being the bumbling incompetent or the complete rube that critics of the investigation depicted Smith to be, the Senator was being crafty. When he asked, "Did the ship go down by the bow or the head?" he was effectively depriving the *Titanic*'s officers and owners of one of their more useful defensive ploys, that of falling back on technical jargon and nautical terminology in their answers while hoping to confuse the hapless landlubber.

When asking Lightoller if any of the passengers and crew might have sought refuge in one of the ship's watertight compartments, Smith was not asking for his own enlightenment. In 1911, he had been given a tour of the *Olympic*, conducted by Captain Smith himself, and the Senator had seen firsthand what watertight compartments were on a ship. But there were many thousands of Americans who had never seen an ocean liner and had no idea what a watertight compartment was, who had horrible visions of some huddled knot of survivors trapped at the bottom of the ocean, slowly suffocating in the darkness. Smith had asked a question that he knew to be slightly ridiculous simply to allay those fears.

Nor was Smith above taking steps to educate himself on subjects of which he knew little. On May 25 the Senator, along with Rear Admiral Richard Watt, Chief Constructor of the U.S. Navy, and a navy stenographer boarded the *Olympic* in New York harbor. There, escorted by the *Olympic*'s skipper, Captain H.J. Haddock, they witnessed crewmen demonstrate the method for loading and lowering one of the lifeboats. Smith and his party then made a trek down to Boiler Room 6, where they examined the watertight doors and surveyed the sections of the ship that had been fatally damaged in the *Olympic*'s sister.

Similarly, when the Senator asked Fifth Officer Lowe what an iceberg was made of, it was to seek an explanation for those who wondered how an object that was merely frozen water could inflict a mortal wound on a ship with steel sides nearly an inch thick. Fourth Officer Boxhall, when asked the same question, saw what Smith was getting at and replied that he believed that some icebergs did contain rock and such debris, but nothing large enough to matter.

At 10:30 a.m. on April 21, Smith opened the proceedings. Bruce Ismay was the first witness called, and in his cross examination, which ran to fifty-eight pages in the official transcript, Smith served notice to everyone that he was determined to find the truth of what had happened aboard the *Titanic*. The next witness called was the *Carpathia*'s Captain Arthur Rostron. He instantly impressed everyone with his courage, clear-headedness, thoroughness, and his compassion. Rostron's dignified and disciplined bearing impressed everyone on the committee, and when he described the memorial service held aboard the *Carpathia*, as well as the funeral for four victims who had perished in the lifeboats before the *Carpathia* arrived, there were tears in his eyes. At the obvious sorrow of this sunburnt seaman, many in the hearing room openly wept.

Senator Smith then asked Rostron to recount in detail the events of the night of April 14–15, and how the *Carpathia* responded to the *Titanic*'s distress call. During the course of describing the *Carpathia*'s frantic dash north to the aid of the *Titanic*, Rostron was asked what preparation he had made to handle the survivors. Almost as if he had anticipated the question, Rostron drew a typewritten list from his coat pocket, on which he had recorded all the orders he had given to ready the *Carpathia* for a rescue operation.

Smith then had Rostron describe the task of recovering the *Titanic*'s survivors, and the trip back to New York. The alacrity with which Rostron had responded to the *Titanic*, the comprehensive preparations he made, and the courage he had shown by steaming full speed into the ice field to pick up the survivors left an indelible impression on Smith and the other committee members, making Rostron the yardstick by which other ship's captains would be measured.

The *Titanic*'s Fourth Officer, Boxhall, was called before the committee on the third day of the hearings, April 23, the same day that the story of the *Californian* broke in the two New England newspapers. Boxhall's testimony would prove to be some of the most lucid and informative of the entire investigation. Questioned primarily by Senator Smith, but also at times by Senators Burton and Bourne, Boxhall carefully described the *Titanic*'s lifeboats, the watch-keeping routine of her officers, the conditions on the night of the collision, the collision itself, and the process of loading and lowering the *Titanic*'s lifeboats. It was during this part of his testimony that the Fourth Officer first mentioned that another ship had been close by the *Titanic* as she was sinking.

"You remained on the upper deck?" Smith asked.

"On the upper deck."

"Where these lifeboats were?"

"Where these lifeboats were. . . . Generally assisting.

"Assisting in lowering these lifeboats?

"Not in lowering them, sir."

"In manning them?"

"Yes, sir, in manning them; but my attention until the time I left the ship was mostly taken up with firing off distress rockets and trying to signal a steamer that was almost ahead of us."

So startling was Boxhall's revelation that he had to mention it twice before Smith realized the significance of what he was saying—that there was another ship which was close enough to see and be seen by the *Titanic* as the White Star liner was sinking. There is no record of Smith's reaction, if any, to Boxhall's words, although surprise, followed by disbelief and then consternation would have been understandable. In any case, Smith wasted no time in following this new thread of information.

Boxhall quickly described the unknown ship's lights, saying that he could see her masthead light and her red sidelight, that she seemed to be bows-on to the *Titanic*, and appeared to be only about five miles distant. He then went on to describe how Captain Smith told him to try to contact the stranger by Morse lamp, which Boxhall did, but, "I can not say I saw any reply. Some people say she replied to our rockets and our signals, but I did not see them."

When other witnesses confirmed Boxhall's testimony, Smith became determined to find that ship and find out why. What Smith would discover would create a sensation and a controversy which would still remain unsettled and unresolved nearly a century later.

Chapter 8

THE AMERICAN INVESTIGATION

When Senator William Alden Smith read the articles in the *Boston American* and the *Clinton Daily Item* alleging that the *Californian* had been close enough to the *Titanic* to have seen her distress rockets, he immediately realized that she could have been the "mystery ship" of Boxhall's dramatic revelation. He promptly sent his marshals up to Boston, to serve Engineer Gill, Captain Lord, and the *Californian*'s officers with subpoenas to appear before his committee on Friday, April 25, in Washington DC, where the hearings were being moved. The press, which by now was following the committee members and their assistants everywhere they went, quickly picked up the scent of a good story in the making, and that Friday morning the hearing room was packed.

The Inquiry had shifted to Washington for the simple reason that the facilities at the Waldorf-Astoria were inadequate to the committee's needs; also, the public's interest was threatening to turn the hearings into a circus. At one point, on the third day of the Inquiry, a group of women collectively marched into the hearing room, and not finding enough room for them to be seated together as a body, immediately began rearranging the furniture to suit their convenience. Smith, tight-lipped and furious, promptly ordered the ladies to cease their disruptive behavior, on pain of being forcibly removed from the hearings. Returning to Washington would allow the committee to sit in a more controlled, subdued, and ultimately productive environment.

So it was that Thursday, April 25, was the last day of the New York hearings. When they reopened in Washington the next day, all of the subpoenaed *Californian* officers and crew were present. Without a doubt the story that would be related by Ernest Gill would create a sensation, and Smith, who had some doubts about Gill's credibility, suddenly found himself hesitant to bring the engineer to the witness stand, lest his testimony ultimately prove to be an embarrassment to the committee. Smith decided to have a brief private interview with the engineer before he appeared before the committee. At one point in their conversation the Senator asked Gill outright how much he had been paid for the story. Gill, with perfect candor, replied $500, but then explained that he would most likely lose his job after his testimony was made public (within days he did), and he had to do something to secure an income as he had a family to support. But when pressed by Smith about the veracity of his affidavit, Gill budged not an inch—it was all true, he said, and he just wanted to set the record straight about what went on aboard the *Californian* that night.

Grateful for the man's forthrightness, Smith had Gill testify to the whole committee. He was taken step by step through his entire affidavit, clarifying some points and expanding on others, with an emphasis placed on the ship firing the rockets. "I am of the general opinion that the crew is," Gill concluded in his testimony, " confident that she was the *Titanic*."

Captain Lord was the next to testify. Before leaving Boston he had arrogantly told the *Boston Journal*, "*If* I go to Washington, it will not be because of this story in the paper, but to tell the Committee why my ship was drifting without power, while the *Titanic* was rushing under full speed. It will take about ten minutes to do so." To his chagrin, it took a good deal longer than ten minutes. The gist of Lord's testimony was that he personally never saw the other ship, yet he was absolutely certain that the ship his officers saw, which didn't appear to be in any danger, was too small to have been the *Titanic*. Instead, that unknown ship stopped some ten to twelve miles from the *Californian* about twenty minutes before midnight, then had steamed off around half past two. That was also the ship the *Titanic* saw, and not the

Californian, which was too far away to be seen. Lord also told the Senators that his officers had reported to him only once that the other ship was firing rockets. Why that ship should be sending up rockets Lord had no idea, but he maintained that he was quite convinced that they weren't distress signals, and that the vessel was in no danger.

Smith then began a careful cross-examination, quietly and methodically, which would ultimately shred Captain Lord's story. Throughout the first part of his testimony, the same arrogance Lord had displayed in Boston began to assert itself, and believing that in Smith he was dealing with a fool—or at least a credulous rube—he assumed that he could play on the Senator's relative ignorance of maritime matters to his own advantage. Having no idea of Smith's skills in cross-examination, which were terrific, Lord rattled on with his answers, while Smith carefully drew a noose around him. At one point, Smith asked Lord about the icefield the *Californian* encountered: "When you notified the *Titanic* that you were in the ice, how much ice were you in?" Lord replied, "Well, we were surrounded by a lot of loose ice, and we were about a quarter of a mile off the edge of the field." A few minutes later, Smith asked, "How badly were you interfered with by the ice on Sunday evening?"

"How were we interfered with?"

"Yes."

"We stopped altogether."

"What did you stop for?"

"So we would not run over the top of it."

"You stopped your ship so that you might avoid the ice?"

"To avoid the ice."

"And did you avoid it?"

"I did."

A few moments later, after probing about the *Californian*'s movements through the icefield once she had received news that the *Titanic* had sunk, in the middle of a series of questions about lookouts, Smith suddenly asked, "If you had received the C.Q.D. call of distress from the *Titanic* Sunday evening after your communication with the *Titanic*, how long, under the conditions which surrounded you, would it have taken you to have reached the scene of the catastrophe?" Lord's reply was quite firm: "At the very least, two hours."

"Two hours?"

"At the very least, the way the ice was packed around us, and it being nighttime."

Unexpectedly Smith changed tack, and began questioning Lord about the *Carpathia*, and drawing conscious and deliberate, if rather subtle, comparisons between her actions and performance in the early morning of April 15 and those of the *Californian*. Often overlooked in assessments of the US Senate Investigation is the fact that Smith was a gifted cross-examiner, with a phenomenal memory. He was particularly adept at using the tried-and-true tactic of returning to a subject previously covered in questioning, to see if the witness's story changed. As would soon become evident, Stanley Lord's story of the morning of April 15, 1912, changed with every retelling.

Lord did not realize it, but Smith suddenly begun to have suspicions about the captain's veracity. Already he had contradicted himself by telling the Senator that his Second Officer had indeed seen at least one white rocket fired by a ship to the south of the *Californian*, when he had denied this (as Smith well knew) to the Boston newspapers. Now Lord was giving three different descriptions of the ice conditions his ship had encountered—that the *Californian* was variously "surrounded by loose ice," or had "avoided the ice," or that the ice "was packed around" the ship. In doing so, Lord had aroused a suspicion in Smith that he wasn't being told the whole truth. Next he asked Lord if the captain had ever seen the *Titanic*; Lord replied that he had never seen her, only her sister, the *Olympic*, in daylight from a distance of about five miles. After asking about the *Californian*'s wireless procedures, Smith then turned to the issue which everyone in the hearing room had been anticipating.

"Captain, did you see any signals of distress on Sunday night, either rockets or the Morse signals?"

"No, sir, I did not. The officer on watch saw some signals, but he said they were not distress signals."

"They were not distress signals?"

"Not distress signals."

"But he reported them?"

"To me. I think you had better let me tell you that story."

"I wish you would." And with that, Smith handed Lord enough

rope for the captain of the *Californian* to figuratively hang himself. Lord's account was so filled with deliberate falsehoods that it deserves to be presented in its entirety.

"When I came off the bridge," he began, "at half past 10, I pointed out to the officer that I thought I saw a light coming along, and it was a most peculiar night, and we had been making mistakes all along with the stars, thinking they were signals. We could not distinguish where the sky ended and where the water commenced. You understand, it was a flat calm. He said he thought it was a star, and I did not say anything more. I went down below. I was talking with the engineer about keeping the steam ready, and we saw these signals coming along, and I said, 'There is a steamer coming. Let's see what the news is.' But on our way down I met the operator coming and I said, 'Do you know anything?' and he said 'The *Titanic*.' So, then, I gave him instructions to let the *Titanic* know. I said, 'This is not the *Titanic*, there is no doubt about it.' She came and lay, at half past 11, alongside of us, until I suppose about a quarter past 1, within 4 miles of us. We could see everything on her distinctly; see her lights. We signaled her at half past 11, with the Morse lamp. She did not take the slightest notice of it. That was between half past 11 and 20 minutes to 12. We signaled her again at 10 minutes past 12, half past 12, a quarter to 1, and 1 o'clock. We have a very powerful Morse lamp. I suppose you can see that about 10 miles, and she was 4 miles off, and she did not take the slightest notice of it. When the second officer came on the bridge, at 12 o'clock, or 10 minutes past 12, I told him to watch that steamer, which was stopped, and I pointed out the ice to him; told him we were surrounded by ice; to watch the steamer that she did not get any closer to her. At 20 minutes to one I whistled up the speaking tube and asked him if she was getting any nearer. He said, 'No, she is not taking any notice of us.' So I said, 'I think I will go and lie down a bit.' At a quarter past one he said, 'I think she has fired a rocket.' He said, 'She did not answer the Morse lamp and she has commenced to go away from us.' I said, 'Call her up and let me know at once what her name is.' So, he put the whistle back, and apparently he was calling. I could hear him ticking over my head. Then I went to sleep."

Here Lord paused and Smith asked, "You heard nothing more about it?"

"Nothing more until about something between then and half past 4; I have a faint recollection of the apprentice opening my room door; opening it and shutting it. I said, 'What is it?' He did not answer and I went to sleep again. I believe the boy came down to deliver me the message that this steamer had steamed away from us to the southwest, showing several of these flashes or white rockets; steamed away to the southwest."

Smith then asked, "Captain, these Morse signals are a sort of language or method by which ships speak to one another?"

"Yes, sir; at night."

"The rockets that are used are for the same purpose and are understood, are they not, among mariners?"

"As being distress rockets?"

"Yes."

"Oh, yes; you never mistake a distress rocket."

It is particularly difficult to credit Lord's last answer, for it implied that there was only one specific type of rocket to be used as a distress signal, which simply wasn't true. That Smith was far more knowledgeable than Lord apparently believed him to be would be demonstrated when Smith introduced the contents of the British Board of Trade's signals regulations into the Investigation's official record, emphasizing that their legality was duly recognized by the United States government. Perhaps Lord took Smith's ignorance for granted, or smugly presumed he would not have access to the British Board of Trade regulations which outlined the use of signal rockets in the event of distress, and the procedures for responding to them. Or he may have simply assumed that he was more clever than Smith, and the blatant lies he had just told the Senator would never be found out. In light of what would subsequently be revealed about Lord's personality, the latter is the most likely.

What would assume a larger significance in the weeks and months ahead was Lord's willingness to distort and fabricate facts in order to put himself in the best possible light. At first he claimed that he had never actually seen the other ship, then later described how he had personally watched it come up "within 4 miles of us;" he admitted that he had never seen the *Titanic*, yet testified that he told Cyril Evans of the other ship, "This is not the *Titanic*, there is no doubt about it."

Most egregious of all, although Smith wasn't aware of it, Lord's account of the reports made to him by Stone and Gibson of the white rockets, as well as his own responses, was completely at variance with what had actually occurred.

Wireless operator Cyril Evans then took Stanley Lord's place on the witness stand, and Smith carefully drew from him a narrative of the exchanges between the *Californian* and the *Titanic* before Evans signed off for the night on April 14—including the infamous attempt by Evans to warn the *Titanic* that the *Californian* had been stopped by ice, which nearly deafened Phillips, who in turn cut off Evans in mid-signal. Smith then questioned Evans about the events of the morning of April 15, from the moment Evans was roused by Chief Officer Stewart, making a point of asking the wireless operator if he had any explanation for why he hadn't been awakened earlier, specifically when the ship to the south began firing rockets. Naturally, Evans was at a loss to provide a reason for this omission.

Evans' testimony closed the proceedings for the day, but Senator Smith was far from finished with Stanley Lord or the *Californian*. The New York and Boston newspapers were tenaciously clinging to the story of the *Californian*, and Smith was following them closely. What was disturbing was how dramatically and conveniently Stanley Lord's version of the night of April 14-15 changed—and how his public statements differed from his sworn testimony before the investigating committee.

On April 19, Lord had told the *Boston Traveler* that the *Californian* was "30 miles north of the scene of the frightful disaster," yet on April 22, he told the *Boston Post* his ship was only 20 miles from the *Titanic*, and later testified to the Senate committee that his ship was 19 miles away from the White Star liner's position. In that same report it was said that Lord "stoutly denied" that his ship had sighted "rockets or other signals of distress." He told the *Boston Globe* that the *Californian* spent "three hours . . . steaming about the spot, hoping to be able to pick up something, or recover some body. . . . At the end of three hours, our search having been without result, we put on steam and headed for Boston," but had told Senator Smith that his search lasted barely more than two. When asked by a number of reporters about the *Californian*'s actual position when she stopped for the night on April 14, Lord replied that such information was "state secrets," prompting the *Boston Evening Transcript* to remark on how different this was from the usual practice, where, "Ordinarily when a steamer reaches port and has anything to report, figures giving exact positions reckoned in latitude and longitude have always been obtainable from the ship's officers."

One newspaper report which apparently had a direct influence on Cyril Evans' appearance before the committee was found in the *New York Herald* on April 23, 1912, the same day the *Californian* story broke. Lord had told reporters questioning the veracity of Carpenter McGregor's allegations, as well as Ernest Gill's affidavit, that, "With the engines stopped, the wireless was of course not working, so we heard nothing of the *Titanic*'s plight until the next morning." To Smith, who had experience with railroad telegraphy and was at least conversant with wireless, this made no sense—as long as the Californian had steam up, there was power for the wireless; that her engines had stopped was irrelevant.

One curious remark made by Lord in the course of his conversations with the American press would not assume any significance until many years later, when its implications would suddenly loom huge. In the April 25, 1912, *Boston Journal*, appeared an account of a press conference Lord had held in his cabin aboard the *Californian* a few days after she docked in Boston. (It was in this interview that he made the infamous statement "*If* I go to Washington . . .") Lord continued to deny that anyone aboard the *Californian* had seen anything that might have been distress signals or rockets. At one point, however, for no apparent reason, Lord suddenly blurted out, "It is all foolishness for anybody to say that I, at the point of a revolver, took any man into this room and made him swear to tell any kind of a story. No member of the crew has ever been in this room, and none of them come near the place except to clean up." What made the remark so bizarre was that it came out of nowhere. No one, either among Lord's officers or members of the press, had even implied that such an incident, or anything remotely resembling it, had occurred. For some reason Lord was finding it necessary to deny any part in an incident which as far as anyone knew had never taken place.

Senator Smith, in the meantime, had contacted the U.S. Navy's

Hydrographer's Office, asking if it could supply the committee with all the information it had about the icefield the *Titanic* and the *Californian* had encountered, as well as about any ships in the vicinity of the *Titanic's* final position. The testimony of Captain John J. Knapp, US Navy, has frequently been overlooked in the argument over the *Californian* incident, and yet it is devastating.

Knapp, who clearly had carefully prepared his testimony in advance, began by explaining the responsibilities of the Hydrographic Office. "The duty of the Hydrographic Office, under the law, is to improve the means of safe navigation of the seas, for the benefit of the Navy and the maritime marine, by providing nautical charts, sailing directions, navigators, and manuals of instruction. . . . Whenever reports are made which have immediate effect upon the safety of navigation, they are given at once to the maritime community and the public generally, and are again flashed out to the sea by means of radiograms, the latter, as a rule, from the wireless stations under the control of the Navy Department."

He went on to explain how the Hydrographic Office of the Bureau of Navigation "has been publishing graphically from month to month a series of charts known as the Pilot Chart of the North Atlantic Ocean, depicting thereon the physical conditions of the ocean and of the atmosphere for the current month, as well as the location of dangers to navigation as reported by incoming ships." A more detailed description was "given from week to week on a printed sheet known as the Hydrographic Bulletin."

Just how valuable the Pilot Chart and Bulletins were was demonstrated, Knapp said, by the fact that "Practically all the captains in the trans-Atlantic trade cooperate in this work by handing in their information upon arrival in port to the branch hydrographic offices." Even more valuable, "the use of radio telegraphy and the Hydrographic Office is thereby enabled to publish daily in a so-called daily memorandum whatever important reports of dangers have been received. This sheet is prepared every afternoon and is mailed to the branch hydrographic offices and there given publicity to all concerned."

In response to Senator Smith's questions about the extent of the icefield encountered by both the *Titanic* and the *Californian*, Knapp introduced a series of three charts, the first two of which showed the icefield in the vicinity of the *Titanic*'s final position, as reported by the various ships which had passed through those waters during the day and evening of April 14. Representatives from the Hydrographers Office had, in the days following the loss of the *Titanic*, examined the logs and wireless records of scores of ships which had since arrived in American ports, making careful notes of any detail, however minute, which related to the loss of the White Star liner.

At Senator Smith request, Captain Knapp began correlating these snippets of information—weather reports, ice reports, sea conditions, position reports, ship sightings, notations of when various ships passed in and out of wireless range of each other, exchanges of signals—to produce a coherent picture of which ships were where on the night of April 14–15, 1912. Knapp's testimony was technical and somewhat long-winded, but it deserves to be presented verbatim, for it was so authoritative that it was damning. In short, Knapp introduced the evidence which would begin nailing down the lid on the coffin of Stanley Lord's career.

"I submit also another chart (Chart No. 3) and the following memorandum, marked '*Titanic*—Ice barrier—Near-by ships.'" What came next was so stunning that, because in the near-century that has passed since "The *Californian* Incident" no one who has approached the issue has possessed better professional credentials, practical experience and professional authority than Captain John Knapp, it deserves to be quoted in full:

"I invite especial attention to that part of the memorandum referring to the hypothetical position of the *Californian*, as shown on that chart, and, in connection therewith, it is desirable to explain that the arcs of circles drawn about the position of the steamship *Titanic* and about the position of the steamship *Californian* were drawn to graphically illustrate the testimony of certain witnesses before your committee."

"What do these arcs indicate?" asked Smith.

"The outer arc around each ship is drawn with a radius of 16 miles, which is approximately the farthest distance at which the curvature of the earth would have permitted the side lights of the *Titanic* to be seen by a person at the height of the side lights of the *Californian*, or at which the side lights of the *Californian* could have been seen by a person at the height of the side lights of the *Titanic*. The inner circle around each ship is drawn with a radius of 7 miles. This is approximately the distance after reaching which the curvature of the earth would have shut out the side lights of the *Californian* from the view of one in a lifeboat in the water. It appears, therefore, that if the *Titanic*'s position at the time of the accident was as fixed by the testimony, and if it was the side light of the *Californian* that was seen from the boat deck of the *Titanic*, the *Californian* was somewhere inside of the arc of the 16-mile circle drawn about the *Titanic*. It further appears that if the above hypothesis be correct and if the side light of the other steamer could not be seen, as is testified to, from one of the lifeboats of the *Titanic* after being lowered, the *Californian* was somewhere outside of the circle with the 7-mile radius drawn about the *Titanic*.

"In the case of the *Californian*, if the steamer which in the testimony given by members of the crew of the *Californian*, including the captain and the donkey engine-man and others, is said to have been seen by them, was the *Titanic*, she must have been somewhere inside of the circle with the 16-mile radius drawn around the *Californian*. If that be the case, as the *Californian*'s side light was shut out by the curvature of the earth from the view of anyone in a lifeboat of the *Titanic* after being lowered into the water, then the *Titanic* must have been outside of the circle drawn with the 7-mile radius around the *Californian*.

"Further reference to this chart will show plotted a hypothetical position of the *Californian*. On the hypothesis that the *Californian* was in this position, a dotted line is drawn on the chart on the bearing given by the captain of the *Californian* as that on which the steamer was sighted. This bearing is drawn on the chart to intersect the track of the *Titanic*. Another dotted line is drawn parallel thereto from a point on the course of the *Titanic* where she apparently was at 10:06 p.m., New York time, April 14, that being 11:56 p.m. of that date of the *Californian*'s time, at which Ernest Gill, a member of the crew of the *Californian*, in his testimony before your committee, stated that the large steamer was seen by him. If the *Californian* was in the hypothetical position shown on the chart, the *Titanic* could have been seen by the officers and crew of the *Californian* at the time mentioned."

At this, Smith, who had a comprehension of technical discussions which surpassed that of most people, invited Knapp to put his conclusion in terms even a layman could understand. "Captain, are you able to state to the committee whether there was any vessel between the position of the *Titanic* just preceding and following the accident and the position of the *Californian* at that time?"

"From being present at hearings before your committee and from reading the printed testimony of witnesses examined by the committee I am led to the conclusion that if there was any vessel between the *Californian* and the *Titanic* at the time referred to she does not seem to have been seen by any of the ships near there on the following morning, nor have there been any reports submitted to the Hydrographic Office which would indicate that there was any such steamer in that locality. The evidence does not indicate to me that there was any such third steamer in those waters, especially in view of the fact that no such steamer was seen by other steamers or by those in the lifeboats the following morning, and as the ice barrier, from all reports, between the reported position of the *Californian* and that of the *Titanic* was impassable to a vessel proceeding to the westward."

Smith had heard enough; such was the worldwide stature of the United States Navy's Hydrographic Office that there was no individual or institution possessed of the authority to convincingly gainsay it—even the Royal Naval Observatory in Greenwich, England had been known to defer to its American counterpart on questions of navigation. Knapp's personal and official credentials and the thoroughness of his work made as great an impression on the Senator as had Arthur Rostron's courage.

One of the most critical parts of Knapp's testimony was his determination of the *Californian*'s actual position (Knapp, conscious of the legal proprieties, called it her "hypothetical" position), as opposed to the patently false position entered in the *Californian*'s log. "Patently false" is strong language, yet it's the only appropriate description of the position Stanley Lord recorded in his log, for it was quite simply impossible for his ship to be where he said it was on the night of April 14–15, 1912. In the *Californian*'s log, her stated position when she stopped for the night at 10:20 p.m., April 14, 1912, was 42E5'N, 50E7'W. This would have put her 19 miles to the northeast of the position Boxhall had worked out for the *Titanic*, conveniently distant enough to support Lord's contention that the *Titanic* was not visible from his ship. Even when the *Titanic*'s correct position is taken into consideration, the *Californian* would still have been nearly twenty miles away. But the *Californian*'s logged position, which was calculated by dead reckoning in much the same manner as Boxhall had worked out that of the *Titanic*, was based on a sun-sighting taken almost six hours earlier.

When Cyril Evans relayed an ice warning to the *Titanic* at 7:30 p.m., he gave her position as 42E3'N., 49E9'W. At this time the *Californian* was on a west-by-south course (S 89E W true), yet when the *Californian* stopped three hours later, *the position recorded in the log put her well to the north of where that course would have taken her*, and there is no indication that Captain Lord ever ordered a course change. Even had he done so, it would have been to the south—changing course to the north would only have carried the *Californian* into even heavier ice than what had compelled her to stop.

Just as important, the logged position of the *Californian* did not allow for the 1½-knot current from the north-northwest that caused the ship to drift to the south-southeast as she was steaming, a drift which continued after she stopped at the edge of the icefield, which would in any case have pushed her nearly nine miles to the south of her "estimated" position. Factoring that drift into the *Californian*'s position leaves her less than eleven miles from the *Titanic*, a position where the sinking White Star liner would have been clearly visible.

There is also a nagging doubt—and a very strong one—about the truth of *any* of the entries in the *Californian*'s log for April 14 and 15, 1912. A ship's master is ultimately responsible for the contents of his vessel's log, and nothing is entered in it without his approval and permission. For this reason and to avoid errors in log entries, ships keep what is called a "scrap log." This is a record kept during a watch of everything that occurs on board relating to the handling of the ship, including helm and engine orders, signal and navigational information, and status of the crew and stores. It also records sea conditions and the presence of ice when it occurs, along with any sightings of other vessels, and a record of any signals observed being sent from those ships.

It is a captain's responsibility to review the contents of the scrap log daily and approve, amend, or correct the entries, after which they are entered into the ship's formal log. The scrap log is kept as a backup, though, and rarely disposed of during a voyage. It was noted with consternation by both the U.S. Senate Inquiry and the British Board of Trade Investigation that the *Californian*'s scrap log for the night of April 14–15, 1912 had vanished, and that the formal log contained no references whatsoever to the ship seen by three of Lord's officers, the rockets that ship fired, or Lord's order to attempt to contact the ship by Morse lamp—glaring omissions under any circumstances. The missing sections of the scrap log and the absence of any entries for the night in question would never be adequately explained by Captain Lord at either inquest.

With the last witness heard on May 9, Senator Smith began sifting through the testimony and trying to arrive at some conclusion about who was responsible for the *Titanic* disaster. To his utter astonishment, he found that despite the lax and almost reckless way most of the transatlantic liners were run, under the existing laws no one—not IMM, nor the White Star Line, nor the *Titanic*'s officers and crew—could be found negligent in a legal sense, so the whole tragedy fell into the category of an "Act of God." To William Alden Smith, it was unthinkable that 1,500 men, women, and children should lose their lives because of carelessness and bureaucratic inertia and no one could be called to account for it. Very well, then—it wouldn't happen again.

When Senator Smith presented his report to the full Senate on May 18, 1912, the gallery was packed and every Senator was present to hear his summation. Smith gave one of the best speeches of his career, reasoned yet filled with emotion. He outlined the events leading up to the collision, retold the tale of the sinking liner, and described how the *Carpathia* had rushed at her own peril to come to the survivors' rescue. Then he presented his conclusions.

As much as he admired the *Titanic*'s Captain Smith, the Senator could not hold him blameless. There had been no clear-cut procedure for handling wireless messages on the bridge, so that most of the warnings the *Titanic* had received on April 14 had gone unnoticed. Although Captain Smith was aware of some danger of ice ahead of his ship, he had no idea of the magnitude of the icefield stretching across the *Titanic*'s course, and so took only minimal precautions to avoid it.

The general attitude of "get on or get out" that prevailed in the North Atlantic steamship lines created an atmosphere that caused ships' masters to maintain high speeds in order to hold to their schedules in even the most dangerous conditions. That no serious accident or incident had yet happened caused a certain air of complacency to surround the navigational practices of the passenger liners. What Senator Smith discovered was that although Captain Smith had handled the *Titanic* no differently than he had every other ship under his command, and had followed the accepted practices on the North Atlantic, "standard operating procedure" had been a disaster waiting to happen.

The years of safe navigation had caused the captain to become complacent, Senator Smith said, just when he needed to be his most cautious. The *Titanic* had been going too fast, with inadequate precautions taken, when she entered the area where the ice was known to be waiting. While the Senator would not go very far in criticizing the man who had paid for his mistakes with his life, he hoped that the lesson was clear—accepted practice on the North Atlantic shipping lanes was no longer acceptable. Ships should be required to reduce speed and post extra lookouts when conditions became hazardous, and strict procedures for bringing wireless messages to the bridge and posting them properly once there would need to be implemented.

The question of lifeboats was dealt with summarily: there would be no more formulas or computations. The outdated Board of Trade regulations with its absurd methods of calculating and computing lifeboat requirements was hopelessly out of touch with the realities of shipping on the North Atlantic. The solution was painfully obvious, though no one had seen the necessity until now: ships would carry enough lifeboats to hold every passenger and crewman they were certified to carry.

Likewise, wireless couldn't be treated as just another business anymore, for there were now too many lives at stake. The instantaneous communications capability that wireless bestowed on ships at sea now meant that it could no longer be treated as a mere toy for the amusement of a handful of passengers or ignored by officers who didn't understand it. There would be a requirement for twenty-four-hour wireless watches to be maintained on all ships equipped with a wireless set. The need for a round-the-clock wireless watch had been driven home as no argument could have done by the public image of

Cyril Evans sleeping peacefully in his bunk while the *Titanic* sank just a few miles away, simply because his captain was too lazy—or too cowardly—to wake him up.

For all his supposed ineptitude, Senator Smith had correctly divined the causes of the disaster and suggested intelligent measures to prevent a similar tragedy in the future. His recommendations, including one to create an international patrol of the North Atlantic areas commonly threatened by ice hazards, were seen on both sides of the Atlantic as clear-headed and reasonable. Even the British press was generally approving in tone, although a few papers, refusing to moderate their hostility, suggested that the recommendations had actually come from other members of the committee, implying that the investigation had been productive only in spite of Senator Smith.

Congress and the assembled gallery held its collective breath when Smith addressed the subject of Captain Lord and the *Californian*. There was no hesitation on the Senator's part: after extensively reviewing all the testimony of Lord and Evans, of Assistant Engineer Gill, of the *Titanic*'s officers concerning the unknown ship they saw, and coupled with the expert findings of the U.S. Navy's Hydrographers' Office, Smith came to a devastating conclusion:

> "I am well aware from the testimony of the captain of the *Californian* that he deluded himself with the idea that there was a ship between the *Titanic* and the *Californian*, but there was no ship seen there at daybreak and no intervening rockets were seen by anyone on the *Titanic*—although they were looking longingly for such a sign—and saw only the white light of the *Californian*, which was flashed the moment the ship struck and taken down when the vessel sank. A ship . . . could not have gone west without passing the *Californian* on the north or the *Titanic* on the south. That ice floe held but two ships— the *Titanic* and the *Californian*."

Smith soundly condemned Captain Lord for failing to come to the *Titanic*'s assistance "in accordance with the dictates of humanity, international usage, and the requirements of law," and he called upon Great Britain to take action against the owners and master of the *Californian*. Then by way of emphasizing his point, he loudly praised

Captain Rostron of the *Carpathia* for his heroism, eventually introducing a resolution to award Rostron a Congressional Gold Medal, which Congress passed by acclamation.

But that was all that Senator William Alden Smith could do. He had shown to the world that there *was* a ship near the *Titanic* as the liner was sinking, and that this unknown ship had refused to answer the *Titanic's* signals of distress. That he was convinced beyond doubt that the other ship was the *Californian*, Smith would maintain to his death. But legally his hands were bound, and he could take no action against Captain Stanley Lord.

In part of his testimony to the Senate committee, Captain Knapp, the US Navy Hydrographer, had reminded Smith first of the International Rules of Seamanship and Navigation, commonly known as the "Rules of the Road," whereby a seaman was required "always to handle and navigate a ship in a seamanlike manner," and directly quoted Article 29: "Nothing in the rules shall exonerate any vessel, or the owner or master or crew thereof from the consequences of any neglect to carry lights or signals or of any neglect to keep a proper lookout, or of the neglect of any precaution which may be required by the ordinary practice of seamen, or by the special circumstances of the case."

This meant, Knapp explained, that "a captain must, in an emergency, handle or navigate his ship in a seamanlike manner." In essence, this meant that since a ship's master had the discretion to decide that if "special circumstances" made conditions too hazardous, he was absolved of any responsibility to respond to a distress call. To Stanley Lord, the scattering of ice in the ten miles of open water between the *Californian* and the *Titanic* were those "special circumstances"; no matter what his moral obligation, legally he was blameless.

The United States Senate investigation into the loss of the *Titanic* had run for four weeks, called eighty-two witnesses, including fifty-nine British subjects, and collected testimony, affidavits and exhibits totalling 1,198 pages. His work done, the committee's findings duly entered into the *Congressional Record*, and his recommendations codified in Senate Bill 6976 (which would quickly pass both Houses of Congress), Senator William Alden Smith faded from the scene. It was now up to the British Board of Trade to resolve the issue of the *Californian* and Stanley Lord.

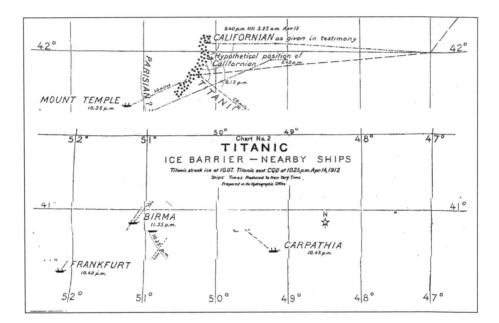

A copy of the U.S. Navy Hydrographer's Chart submitted by Captain
John Knapp at the U.S. Senate Inquiry.

Chapter 9

THE BRITISH INQUIRY

Despite its intense and probing nature—or perhaps because of it—the United States Senate Investigation into the loss of the *Titanic* was neither well regarded nor well received in Great Britain. Indeed, it is still regarded today with disdain within some circles of British maritime historians. Apparent gaffes like Senator Smith's questions about watertight compartments or the composition of icebergs quickly made him a laughingstock among the British press. At first furious over the sheer effrontery that the committee should think that it possessed the authority to subpoena and detain British subjects, the British newspapers soon began mocking Smith, lampooning him mercilessly, calling him "a born fool." Smith's naivete, his earnest manner, his persistence, and most of all the questions he asked, all provided a near-endless source of material for the British satirical press and comedians. The London Hippodrome publicly offered him $50,000 to appear there and give a one hour lecture on any subject he liked, while the music hall stages began to refer to him as Senator "Watertight" Smith.

More dignified but no less strident was the legitimate British press. That the *Titanic* had been the property of an American shipping combine was ignored by a majority of the editors of Britain's dailies—because she had been British-registered and British-crewed, she was, in their opinion, a British ship. Soon their editorial columns were running over with repetitious protests about Americans overstepping their authority, Smith's general or specific ignorance of things nautical, the affront to Britain's honor by the serving of subpoenas to the surviving crewmen, and so on. The magazine *Syren and Shipping* openly questioned the Senator's sanity, while the *Morning Post* declared that "A schoolboy would blush at Mr. Smith's ignorance." It was the position of the *Daily Mirror* that "Senator Smith has . . . made himself ridiculous in the eyes of British seamen. British seamen know something about ships. Senator Smith does not." The usually responsible *Daily Telegraph* summed up the British attitude best when it declared:

> The inquiry which has been in progress in America has effectively illustrated the inability of the lay mind to grasp the problem of marine navigation. It is a matter of congratulation that British custom provides a more satisfactory method of investigating the circumstances attending a wreck.

In other words, this inquiry was something best left to the British Board of Trade, and the Americans had no business conducting such an investigation. The Senator was accused of sullying the good name and reputation of the United States Senate, of political opportunism, and of hindering the process of discovering the truth about what happened to the *Titanic*. The outpouring of indignation was so self-righteous, so consistent, so loud, and so prolonged that it began to give the impression that the British press was actually afraid of what Smith's investigation might reveal about the British merchant marine that was better left unseen. But not all of the British press joined in the chorus of jeers and condemnation of Smith. G.K. Chesterton, writing in the *Illustrated London News*, was blunt in pointing out the differences:

> It is perfectly true, as the English papers are saying, that the American papers are both what we would call vulgar and vindictive; they set the pack in full cry upon a particular man; that they are impatient of delay and eager for savage decisions; that the flags under which they march are often the rags of a reckless and unscrupulous journalism. All this is true. But if these be the American faults, it is all the more necessary to emphasize the opposite English faults. Our national evil is exactly the other way: it is to hush everything up; it is to damp everything

down; it is to leave the great affair unfinished, to leave every enormous question unanswered.

The editor of *John Bull* agreed: "We need scarcely point out that the scope of such an inquiry [by the Board of Trade] is strictly limited by statute, and that its sole effect will be to shelve the scandal until public feeling has subsided. *What* a game it is!" The *Review of Reviews*, which had lost its founder on the *Titanic*, William Stead, issued the most stinging rebuke to the rest of the British papers: "We prefer the ignorance of Senator Smith to the knowledge of Mr. Ismay. Experts have told us the *Titanic* was unsinkable—we prefer ignorance to such knowledge!"

What the world was now anticipating was the inquiry by the British Board of Trade, which, as so many British papers had repeatedly pointed out during the Senate investigation, was to be a "more satisfactory method" of arriving at the truth of what had caused the *Titanic* to sink. The Inquiry would be conducted in a far more formal manner than the Senate investigation, and be constituted as a court of law under British jurisprudence.

The process began on April 29, when returning *Titanic* crewmen came down the gangway from the liner *Lapland*, which had brought them from New York to Plymouth, only to be put in a quarantine which was just short of imprisonment. They were not released until they were met by Board of Trade representatives who were waiting to take sworn statements from each of them. The Board of Trade then reviewed their statements, decided which crewmen would be called on to testify, and issued formal subpoenas to the ones chosen. The process took several days, during which the crewmen were allowed only limited contact with their families. Despite the bitterness this arrangement caused, not to mention its questionable legality, there were no confrontations between crew members and Board of Trade representatives.

The Board of Trade Court of Inquiry, as constituted by its Royal Warrant (the Crown document defining the scope of the Commission as well as its authority), was scheduled to begin sitting in session on May 3, in the London Scottish Drill Hall, near Buckingham Gate, and would consist of a President and five assessors. The assessors, all chosen for their distinguished credentials, were Captain A.W. Clarke, an Elder Brother of Trinity House; Rear Admiral the Honourable Sommerset Gough-Calthorpe, RN (Ret.); Commander Fitzhugh Lyon, RNR; J. H. Biles, Professor of Naval Architecture, University of Glasgow; and Mr. Edward Chaston, RNR, senior engineer assessor to the Admiralty. Presiding overall, indeed dominating the Court as thoroughly as William Alden Smith had dominated the Senate investigation, would be the fearsome Lord Mersey, Commissioner of Wrecks and formerly President of the Probate, Divorce and Admiralty Division of the High Court. Though Mersey would have the "assistance" of the five assessors, Mersey's authority over the Court would be absolute: the areas of investigation, the witnesses called, the admissibility of evidence, and the final findings of the Court would all be determined by him.

John Charles Bigham, who would eventually be raised to the peerage as the 1st Viscount Mersey, was born in 1840, in Liverpool, the son of a merchant. First studying law at London University, he completed his education in Berlin and Paris, and was called to the bar in 1870 by the Middle Temple. His early practice was centered in Liverpool and consisted mostly of commercial law; in 1883, Bigham was named a Queen's Counsel.

In 1885 Bigham turned his attention to a political career, when he ran—and lost—in a bid for Parliament as the Liberal candidate for Toxteth. A second candidacy also met with defeat in 1892, but in 1895, running as a Liberal Unionist, he was finally elected, taking his seat as the Member for the Liverpool Exchange. His political career never came to much, however, as in that same year he was appointed a judge to the Queen's Bench; he also continued his work in business law. During the Boer War he reviewed court-martial cases, and by 1904 was presiding over the railway and canal commission. He worked in the bankruptcy courts, and reviewed courts-martial sentences handed down during the Second Boer War. In the next six years he worked in probate, divorce, and Admiralty courts, but by 1910 he had grown dissatisfied with the entire legal profession and chose to retire at the age of 70. That same year Bigham was raised to the peerage as Baron Mersey of Toxteth.

It was Lord Loreburn, the Lord Chancellor of the Asquith government, which summoned Lord Mersey out of retirement to preside over the Board of Trade inquiry into the loss of the *Titanic*. Mersey had first come to prominence as a public figure in Great Britain in 1896 when he headed an inquiry into the notorious Jameson Raid, a madcap adventure inspired by Cecil Rhodes which tried—and failed— to seize the diamond and gold fields of the Rand in South Africa. From the first, Mersey exhibited those characteristics which would come to be the hallmarks of any inquest he would conduct: he was autocratic, impatient, and not a little testy. Above all, he did not suffer fools gladly, and he was famous for the barbed rebukes he issued from the bench to witnesses or council that he considered were wasting the Court's time. (The transcript of the *Titanic* Inquiry would record how at one point Alexander Carlisle, who had helped design the *Titanic*, related that he and an official of the White Star Line often merely rubberstamped decisions made by their superiors with the words, "Mr. Sanderson and I were more or less dummies." Mersey replied dryly, "That has a certain verisimilitude.")

Lord Mersey would become as closely associated with the British Inquiry into the loss of the *Titanic* as Senator Smith would be with the American investigation. Yet there was little the two men shared in common. Mersey's roots were in the ambitious middle class, while Smith came from the working class. Mersey was very much part of the "Establishment," while Smith took pains to stand apart from it. While Mersey was very much aware of issues roiling the different social classes, he was not driven by them in the way that Smith was. Both men, however, were deeply committed to discovering the truth, and on the bench, Mersey could be formidable in this pursuit. Off the bench, he was a complete contrast to his in-chambers persona: a soft-spoken, mild-mannered man of good taste, he readily showed himself to be well-educated and thoroughly urbane. Politically, he remained a Liberal, and his company and conversation were much appreciated in London social circles.

A widely held opinion among professional seaman in Great Britain was that a whitewash brush would be liberally wielded, the "more satisfactory manner" of a British investigation notwithstanding. This suspicion grew out of the fact that the Inquiry was being carried out by the Board of Trade, which was viewed in some circles to be in part responsible, if not for the *Titanic* disaster itself, then certainly for the lack of sufficient lifeboats aboard the liner. Not unexpectedly or unrealistically perhaps, the idea of the Board of Trade conducting an investigation of itself created consternation in quite a number of people.

The *Titanic*'s Second Officer Lightoller homed in on the inconsistency with unerring accuracy: "The B.O.T. had passed that ship [the *Titanic*] as in all respects fit for sea, in every sense of the word, with sufficient margin of safety for everyone on board. Now the B.O.T. was holding an inquiry into the loss of that ship—hence the whitewash brush."

What was to surprise many observers, but not those who knew Lord Mersey well, was the surprising objectivity that the Court was to display during the next five weeks. Despite the anticipation of many that the findings would be a whitewash, when the Inquiry was completed, the Board of Trade would not escape Mersey's keen eye or sharp tongue. Some observers would later suggest that the findings of the U. S. Senate investigation exerted an unexpected influence on how Lord Mersey conducted the Court of Inquiry, but save for one specific subject, on close examination that doesn't seem likely. The Court began hearing testimony two weeks before Senator Smith released his committee's findings; furthermore, the emphasis of the two investigations were quite different, though strikingly complementary. The Senate subcommittee had emphasized asking *how* the disaster happened, while the Mersey Commission asked *why*. Some twenty-one passengers were called to testify before the Senate investigation; Lord Mersey would call only three. The majority of witnesses appearing before the Court would be officers and crewmen from the *Titanic*, *Carpathia*, and *Californian*; various experts in the field of ship construction; and representatives of Harland and Wolff and the White Star Line. In fact, of the three passengers who would testify, none of them would be as "material" witnesses.

The Court sat for a total of thirty-six days over a span of eight weeks, from May 2 to July 3, 1912, called ninety-six witnesses, and asked more than 25,600 questions, the longest and most detailed Court of Inquiry ever held in Great Britain up to that time. The transcript ran to over a thousand pages, supplemented by exhibits and depositions, and the Report of the Commissioner added another forty-five pages. The entire cost of the Inquiry came to nearly £20,000.

Just as everyone expected, the first great sensation of the Inquiry was the question of the *Californian*. The one area of the British Inquiry which *was* unquestionably influenced by the American investigation was the issue of the *Californian*'s inactivity on that fateful night. Had the story not been broken by the American press and pursued with such determination by Senator Smith, it is entirely possible that it would have never come to light in the Board of Trade Inquiry.

That this might have been so was due to the rather curious nature of a British Court of Inquiry. Included in the Royal Warrant that granted the Court its authority was a list of questions to which the Court was charged with finding answers. In the case of the *Titanic* inquiry, these included questions about the design and construction of the ship, her compliance with existing safety regulations, her handling and navigation, the nature of the collision and the damage done, etc. None of the questions of the original Royal Warrant were pertinent to the presence of another ship in the vicinity of the *Titanic* as she sank; consequently it would have been a legal impossibility to introduce the issue under those circumstances. Instead, the questions raised in the Senate investigation would lead Lord Mersey to seek a modification to the Warrant's original list of questions. He would then preside over some of the most intense cross-examinations ever to take place in a British board of inquiry, as Captain Lord and the officers of the *Californian* would all be called upon to testify about the events of April 14 and 15.

The process began on the seventh day of the Inquiry, May 14, when Captain Lord, Apprentice Officer Gibson, and Second Officer Stone gave testimony to the Inquiry. Chief Officer Stewart and Third Officer Groves would appear the next day. The most devastating exchange of the day took place, predictably, between Lord and the Attorney-General, as more than seven hundred questions were put to him variously by Lord Mersey and Sir Rufus, as well as Butler Aspinall, KC, for the Solicitor General.

The Attorney-General, Sir Rufus Isaacs, was particularly relentless in his questioning of Lord, pressing over and over again on points in his testimony that Isaacs found unsatisfactory. From the outset Sir Rufus seemed to harbor some suspicion about Stanley Lord that went beyond the simple issue of whether or not the *Californian* had been near to the *Titanic* when the White Star liner went down. It was as if he sensed that there was something fundamentally wrong about the relationship between Lord and his officers. The first indication came early in the questioning, when Lord's version of the events of the night was being established.

"Did you know that she [the other ship] had fired a number of rockets?" Isaacs asked.

"I did not."

"According to you, did she fire only one rocket?"

"Only one rocket."

"Have you never heard from the other officers that she fired a number of rockets?"

"Since."

"When did you hear that?"

"The next day."

"Who told you?"

"The second officer first."

"What did he say?"

"He said she had fired several rockets in his watch—no, the chief officer told me, about 5 o'clock, that she had fired several rockets."

Abruptly Sir Rufus broke off his questioning and turned toward the Commissioner, Lord Mersey, saying, "My lord, I think it very desirable that the other witnesses from the *Californian* should be out of court while this witness is giving evidence." Mersey agreed, and Chief Officer Stewart, Second Officer Stone, Third Officer Groves, Apprentice Officer Gibson, and Cyril Evans, the wireless operator, were all ushered from the hall. Apparently something in Lord's tone of voice, his general demeanor, had caused the Attorney-General to suspect that the captain of the *Californian* was, by the way he delivered his testimony, attempting to tell his officers what story they should repeat once they were in the witness box. Whether the rumors about Lord's overbearing, intimidating nature had reached—and influenced—Sir Rufus remains unknown; it is interesting to note, however, that Lord Mersey did not require Sir Rufus to offer any explanation for his request.

From that point on in his questioning, Stanley Lord was very much on the defensive, even more so than would be expected of a man who was the master of a vessel some believed had refused to answer a distress call. It was if he sensed that because he could no longer exert an influence over what his officers might say to the court, he would choose to say as little as possible himself, determined to offer up only the minimum of information. Gone was the glib Stanley Lord who had faced William Alden Smith, certain he could outwit the rube American Senator. Gone were the elaborate, loquacious answers, the smug self-confidence. Lord was suddenly reduced to answering most of the questions with monosyllables, while those few times when he did expand his answers, he was almost visibly squirming in an effort to shift responsibility onto his subordinates.

At first Lord tried to convince the court that the ship to the south was nothing more than a small tramp steamer, hardly larger than the *Californian* herself, that he had only been told of a single rocket being fired, and that he had only the vaguest recollection of the night of April 14–15 as he had been asleep in the chartroom at the time. This satisfied neither Sir Rufus nor Lord Mersey, especially when later that day and the next, Lord's officers independently contradicted him on nearly every important point in their testimony, most significantly about the number of times Lord had been told about the rockets and how many there were. Mersey drew particular attention to discrepancies in Captain Lord's defense, notably the suspicious lack of any entries about rockets in the *Californian*'s log and the disappearance of the relevant pages of the scrap log.

The most damning moments for Lord came in the middle of his testimony. Sir Rufus opened his line of questioning innocently enough by asking, "Did you remain in the chart room when you were told that a vessel was firing a rocket?"

"I remained in the chart room when he [Stone] told me that this vessel had fired a rocket," Lord parroted.

"I do not understand you. You knew, of course, that there was danger in this field of ice to steamers?"

"To a steamer steaming, yes."

"You knew there was danger?"

"Yes."

"That is why you stopped?"

"Yes."

"And you knew also that it was desirable, at any rate, to communicate with the *Titanic* to tell that ice was there?"

"Yes."

"You had done that?"

"I had done that."

"And you knew that this vessel, whatever it was, that you say had stopped . . ."

"Had stopped, yes."

At this point, it's almost possible to see Sir Rufus frowning in feigned bewilderment, just as he was preparing to strike home. "I do not understand you, it may be my fault. Shall I explain it to you? *What do you think this vessel is firing a rocket for?*"

"I asked the Second Officer. I said, 'Is that a company's signal?' and he said he did not know."

"That did not satisfy you?"

"No, it did not."

"I mean, whatever it was, it did not satisfy you that it was a company's signal?"

"It did not, but I had no reason to think it was anything else."

At this point Lord Mersey stepped in. Clearly there was something wrong here: Lord's answers were making no logical sense, he was contradicting himself. How could he be saying that he didn't believe the rockets sighted by Stone were company signals yet didn't believe them to be anything else?

"That seems odd," Mersey said. "You knew that the vessel that was sending up this rocket was in a position of danger?"

"No, my Lord, I did not."

"Well, danger if she moved." The annoyance in Mersey's voice is almost audible in the transcript.

"If she moved, yes."

"What do you think the rocket was sent up for?"

"Well, we had been trying to communicate with this steamer by Morse lamp from half past 11, and he would not reply." Now Lord was attempting to evade directly answering Mersey's questions.

"This was a quarter past one?"

"Yes, we had tried at intervals from half past eleven."

Again Mersey put the question: "What do you think he was sending up a rocket for?"

"I thought it was acknowledging our signals, our Morse lamp. A good many steamers do not use the Morse lamp."

"Have you ever said that before?"

"That has been my story right through—my impression right along." It is entirely possible, almost certain in fact, that at this point both Lord Mersey and Sir Rufus knew that Captain Lord was an accomplished liar. In Boston he had repeatedly told the tale that the officers of the *Californian* "had sighted no rockets," that "no signals of distress or anything else had been seen." Later he told Senator Smith that he had received only one report of a white rocket being seen to the south of the *Californian*. This was the first time anyone had heard the idea put forward that the rockets were being fired as some sort of acknowledgment of the *Californian*'s signals by Morse lamp.

The Attorney-General now tried a slightly different tack, gradually pressing Lord harder and harder: "Just let me put this to you. When you asked him whether it was a company's signal he said he did not know. That would not satisfy you?"

"No."

"Was it then you told him to Morse her and find out what ship it was?"

"Yes."

"After the white rocket had been sent up?"

"After the white rocket had been sent up." Here Lord was contradicting himself again, saying that he'd instructed Stone to try using the Morse lamp *after* the first rocket went up, when just moments earlier he had tried to suggest that the rockets were being fired to acknowledge the Morse lamp signal. What is also intriguing about these exchanges is that at no time does Lord ever dispute that the signals his officers saw and reported were *white rockets*. Later generations of revisionists would conveniently refer to them as "lights" or "flares" in an effort to reduce their significance, yet Lord repeatedly affirmed that the signals were "white rockets."

"If it was not a company's signal, must it not have been a distress signal?"

"If it had been a distress signal, the officer on watch would have told me." This blatant attempt by Lord to shift the responsibility onto Stone was so jarring that the Attorney-General felt compelled to repeat the question, blurting out, "I say, if it was not a company's signal, must it not have been a distress signal?"

"Well, I do not know of any other signal but distress signals that are used at sea." It's unfortunate that the official transcript makes no allowance for recording the reactions of the Board members, for their consternation at this point must have been considerable. First, here was the master of a vessel in the British Merchant Marine admitting that neither he nor the officer of the watch had any idea of the meaning of signals sighted by that officer, yet the captain declares that it is the sole responsibility of his subordinate to decide if the signal is of any importance! It was almost as if Lord had completely forgotten—or never read—the Board of Trade regulations. Now Sir Rufus, exasperated, pressed Lord hard; Lord, in turn, did his best to avoid giving the Attorney-General the direct answer he was seeking. In the end, though, Lord would find himself cornered.

"You have already told us that you were not satisfied it was a company's signal. You have told us that."

"I asked the officer, was it a company's signal?"

"And he did not know?"

"He did not know."

"You have already told me some time ago . . ."

"Very well, sir."

". . . that you were not satisfied it was a company's signal. You did not think it was a company's signal?"

"I inquired, was it a company's signal?"

"But you had been told that he did not know?"

"He said he did not know."

"Very well, that did not satisfy you?"

"It did not satisfy me."

"*Then if it was not that, it might have been a distress signal?*"

"It might have been."

"And you remained in the chart room?"

"I remained in the chart room."

With those words, Stanley Lord effectively wrote "Finis" to his career as a merchant captain on the North Atlantic run, though it would be his officers who actually turned the screws on his professional coffin. As the questioning continued, Lord attempted to convince the court that, according to his officers, the unknown ship to the south of the *Californian* had slowly steamed away some time around half-past two in the morning. If she had done so, then clearly she had never been in any danger and so the rockets she had fired could *not* have been distress signals. Both the Attorney-General and the Commissioner were skeptical, but as Lord himself never claimed to have seen the other ship steam away, neither man pressed the point with Lord.

That did not mean they accepted that explanation, however. When Second Officer Stone, who in retrospect seems to be the one officer most heavily under Lord's influence, attempted to repeat this story in an effort to come to his captain's rescue, Sir Rufus would have none of it. As Stone tried to explain it, the other ship, which had been presenting its red sidelight to the *Californian* for more than two hours, suddenly steamed off to the southwest at about 2:20 a.m., and did so without presenting her green sidelight at all. In other words, according to Stone, the ship had been showing her port (left) side to the *Californian*, then abruptly turned about 180 degrees and somehow did so without ever showing her starboard (right) side.

Sir Rufus was not fooled, and would have none of it. "How did she do it," he asked incredulously, "without showing her green light?"

"I did not see her green light at all. She ported. She shut in her red side light and showed her stern light.... I did not see the green light."

Sir Rufus knew enough of ships to know that this was simply not possible. "She must have shown her green light, you know?"

"We are heading west-southwest and the steamer's stern was southwest ahead of us. All we would see is her stern light. I did not see any side lights at all after she started to steam away." Isaacs did not pursue the subject any further with Stone, but he didn't let it go either. Stone's testimony was, of course, nonsense. He knew from the position of the stranger's masthead light and red sidelight that her bow was facing the *Californian*, so his assertion that he had been looking at the stranger's stern was simply untrue—and he knew it. Likewise was his assertion that he had seen the stranger's stern light: she had never shown her stern to the *Californian*. Equally absurd was his statement that a ship to the *southeast* of the *Californian* could steam away from her to the *southwest* without showing a green sidelight, regardless of the bearing of the *Californian* herself. Isaacs made this point when he questioned Apprentice Officer Gibson the next day.

"Did you ever see her green [light]?" he asked.

"No."

"To show you her red light, she must have been heading to the northward of NNW on your story?"

"Yes."

"You told us you never saw the green light of this vessel?"

"No."

"Was the glare of light which you saw on the afterpart of this vessel forward or aft of the masthead light?"

"Abaft the mast head light."

"So that you would be seeing her starboard side?"

"No, her port side . . ."

"Did you see her turn around?"

"No."

Gibson then began to add details, saying that he saw, "A white masthead light and a red sidelight," and "a glare of white lights on her after-deck." Realizing the significance of what Gibson was saying, the Attorney-General began to draw him out, asking next about the glare of lights Gibson saw on the other ship: "Now tell me, when you first saw that glare of lights in the after part, could you see a line of lights?"

"No."

"It was more than a single light, was it not?"

"Yes."

Sir Rufus then established exactly where on the other ship these lights seemed to come from: "Did the glare of light that you saw on the after part of this boat seem to be a pretty considerable distance from the masthead light?"

"Yes."

The significance of Gibson's answer, which was immediately obvious to every member of the Commission, though Gibson did not seem to appreciate it, was that "a considerable distance" between the ship's masthead light and the deck lights was a direct indication that she was significantly larger than a tramp steamer, where the deck lights would be positioned just aft of the masthead light. The Attorney-General decided that the time had come to ask Gibson specifically about what sort of ship he thought it was. "What was it made you think it was a tramp steamer? You saw nothing but the lights?"

"Well, I have seen nearly all the large passenger boats out at sea and there was nothing at all about it to resemble a passenger boat."

"What is it you expected to see?"

"A passenger boat is generally lit up from the water's edge." At first glance this seemed to confirm Stanley Lord's account that the strange ship had been a small tramp steamer. Stone's recollection seemed to do the same, when he said that all he could see of her was "One masthead light and a red sidelight and two or three small indistinct lights." It would be a member of the *Titanic*'s crew, Trimmer Samuel Hemming, who would unexpectedly provide an explanation for how a ship as large as the *Titanic* could offer so little light to a distant observer. When examined by Sir Rufus and Butler Aspinall, Hemming recounted how First Officer Murdoch had instructed him to turn down the lights in the forward part of the ship, making sure that "everything [was] dark before the bridge" in order to avoid dazzling the lookouts up in the crow's nest. This included closing the scuttles over the forward end of B Deck, leaving the only light showing from the forward end of the *Titanic*'s superstructure coming from a handful of windows on A Deck. When the *Titanic* turned sharply to the north in her effort to avoid the iceberg, she suddenly presented only her darkened bow toward the *Californian*, creating the confusion.

But it was the rockets, along with Captain Lord's insistence that they could not have been distress signals, which so greatly disturbed the Attorney-General, and which have been the bane of those who would attempt to exonerate Stanley Lord ever since. Returning to Stone's observation that the ship to the south was firing white rockets, Sir Rufus asked, "What had the Captain told you which would force your mind to the conclusion that that is a vessel which is not in distress?"

"He emphasized the fact about company's signals."

"But you knew they were not company's signals, did you not?"

"I said I did not think so."

Mersey stepped in again at this point. "You did not believe they were company's signals?"

"I had never seen company's signals like them before."

"Then what did you think they were?"

"I did not think what they were intended for; white rockets is what I saw them as." Mersey began losing his patience again, and his acerbic nature took over, offering one of history's most memorable courtroom exchanges.

"Wait. You did not think they were company's signals?"

"No."

"You did not think they were being sent up for fun?"

"No."

"What did you think?"

"I just thought they were white rockets, that is all."

Again the Counsel for the Solicitor General, Butler Aspinall headed off another of Mersey's biting retorts. Clearly not satisfied with Stone's answers, it seemed inconceivable to him that neither Stone nor Gibson would ever mention the possibility that what they were seeing was, indeed, a distress signal. Rising to his feet, he began his own line of questions to Stone. "I want to take you back. You remember those 20 minutes you told me you were talking to Gibson—not all the time, but you and he were from time to time having a conversation about the ship, after the eight rockets. That was between 1.40 and 2 o'clock; it was 20 minutes?"

"Yes."

"Did anything of that sort pass? Did you say something of this sort to Gibson: 'A ship is not going to fire rockets at sea for nothing'?"

"Yes," Stone replied, with an ambiguity worthy of his captain, "I may possibly have passed that expression to him."

"Well, do you think you did?"

"Yes, I think I did do so—it is quite possible."

"And were you talking about the ship all the time until she disappeared?"

"No."

"Are you sure?"

"Yes."

"Did you say this to Gibson, 'Have a look at her now; it looks queer. She looks to have a big side out of the water'?"

"No, I did not say she had a big side out of the water; he remarked it to me."

"Did you say, 'Have a look at her now; she looks queer'?"

"That is at the time when I told him the lights appeared to be altering their position with regard to one another. Yes."

"Did you think she looked queer?"

"I merely thought it was a funny change of her lights, that was all. That was before I had looked at her through the binoculars."

"In view of the fact that this vessel had been sending up rockets, and in view of the fact that you said it looks queer, did not you think at the time that that ship was in distress?"

"No."

"Are you sure?"

"I did not think the ship was in distress at the time."

"It never occurred to you?"

"It did not occur to me because if there had been any grounds for supposing the ship would have been in distress *the Captain would have expressed it to me.*" The consternation in the London Drill Hall was complete: Stanley Lord earlier testified that he had expected Second Officer Stone to inform him if the rockets he was reporting were a distress signal, and here was Stone emphatically declaring that he expected *Lord* to tell *him.* Just what was going on aboard the *Californian* that night?

Lord Mersey, for one, had had enough of this nonsense. Turning to Stone, he said bluntly, "Never mind about the Captain. You are being asked about what you thought yourself. Do you mean to tell us that neither you nor Gibson expressed an opinion that there was something wrong with that ship?"

"No, not wrong with the ship, but merely with this changing of her lights."

"Well, about this changing of her lights?"

"That is when I remarked that the lights looked queer. The lights, I said, not the ship."

Mersey was completely out of patience with such semantic pedantry: "The lights are what I call part of the ship. The whole thing, lights and all, make up the ship. You want me to believe, do you, that notwithstanding these rockets, neither you nor Gibson thought there was anything wrong on board that ship; you want me to understand that?"

"Yes."

Aspinall, perhaps sensing Mersey's rising impatience, interceded, again addressing Stone. "I went back for a moment, but I want now to take you to the later period, when you spoke to the Captain and told him that the steamer had disappeared?"

"Yes."

"Will you tell me whether the Captain made any reply to that, and, if so, what?"

"He again asked me if I was certain there were no colors in those lights whatsoever. I again assured him that they were all white, just white rockets."

Now Aspinall began to delve into the heart of issue: "Can you explain why it was that the captain should again ask you if you were sure there were no colors in the lights?"

"No."

"Have you no idea?" Aspinall was clearly disbelieving, casting a thinly-veiled aspersion on Stone's professionalism, "You *are* a sailor?"

"Yes."

"You were an onlooker paying careful attention, keeping those lights under observation, and then this question again comes from the Master. What did you think he meant by such a question?"

"I did not know, except that he had the thought in his mind that they may have been company signals of some sort."

"But do you really mean that?" In other words, do you really believe that? Aspinall was asking.

"That thought may have been in his mind; I did not say it was in his mind."

"Was it in yours?"

"That they were company's signals?"

"Yes."

"No, not that they were. They may possibly have been."

Here Mersey asked for a clarification, "Would there be any significance in the lights if they were colored as distinct from white, Mr. Aspinall?"

"As I understand it, white lights are distress signals; company's lights are very often colored."

"Would distress signals be colored?"

Aspinall was momentarily at a loss for the appropriate regulation, but a colleague came to his rescue, handing Lord Mersey a copy of the Board of Trade pamphlet covering the use of nighttime signals. Thumbing through it, Mersey quickly discovered the appropriate passage, reading it aloud to the court: "Rockets or shells throwing stars of any color or description, fired one at a time at short intervals."

Aspinall turned back to Stone. "Do you mean to tell his Lordship that you did not know that the throwing up of 'rocket, or shells, throwing stars of any color or description fired one at a time at short intervals' is the proper method for signaling distress at night?"

"Yes, that is the way it is always done as far as I know."

"And you knew that perfectly well on the night of the 14th of April?"

"Yes."

Mersey looked straight at Stone and asked simply, "And is not that exactly what was happening?" Stone made no reply, and Mersey repeated the question: "The very thing was happening that you knew indicated distress?"

"If that steamer had stayed on the same bearing after showing these rockets . . ."

"No, do not give a long answer of that kind. Is it not the fact that the very thing was happening which you had been taught indicated distress?"

"Yes."

There it was. Earlier that day Stanley Lord had admitted that the rockets reported by Stone could well have been distress signals, but attempted to absolve himself by blaming Stone for not informing him of such. Stone in turn had attempted to shift the responsibility to Lord, then admitted that the rockets he had seen were indeed a distress signal, according to the Board of Trade regulations. As if to drive the point home, Mersey once more asked Stone, this time admonishing him to have care with his answer.

"Now do think about what you are saying. You have just told me that what you saw from that steamer was exactly what you had been taught to understand were signals of distress. You told me so?"

"Yes."

With that, what would become known as the "*Californian* incident," which would evolve into a bitter controversy that would not be settled for more than nine decades, should have ended. Stone admitted that the rockets he saw fulfilled the definition of a distress signal, which he was legally obligated to report to his captain. Stanley Lord admitted that the rockets as reported to him might have been a distress signal, which he was under both a legal and moral obligation to verify, and that he refused to do so. Ultimately, nothing more need ever be said by, for, or against either man, for they had both admitted their culpability.

The testimony of the *Carpathia*'s Captain Arthur Rostron was in some ways a reprise of his appearance before the American inquiry, but there were also some surprises. As did Senator Smith, the Attorney-General and Lord Mersey both offered their thanks to Rostron on behalf of a grateful nation for his prompt and selfless actions in his rescue of the *Titanic*'s survivors.

And just as had happened at the American Inquiry, his innate self-effacing nature, combined with the unquestionable demonstration of seamanship he had shown on the morning of April 15, impressed everyone who heard his testimony.

Much as had been done in New York and Washington, Rostron was asked to recount how the *Carpathia* had received the *Titanic*'s wireless signals and responded, although this time there was a much greater degree of technical questioning. One surprising revelation that came out of this round of questioning was exactly how dangerous were the waters into which Rostron took the *Carpathia*. Once more Rostron told how he had relentlessly pushed his ship, approaching the icefield, dodging icebergs, relying on the sharp eyes of his officers, his own skill as a seaman, and his faith in Divine Intervention.

One curious passage in Rostron's testimony would subsequently be seized upon by partisans of Stanley Lord in his defense. The attorney representing the Leyland Line, Mr. Bucknill, had Rostron confirm the text of an affidavit Rostron had made in New York a few days earlier. It read, "I approached the position of the *Titanic* 41.46 N. L.,

50.14 W. L. on a course substantially N. 52 W. (true), reaching the first boat shortly after 4 a.m. It was daylight at about 4.20 a.m. At 5 o'clock it was light enough to see all round the horizon. We then saw two steamships to the northwards, perhaps seven or eight miles distant. Neither of them was the *Californian*. One of them was a four-masted steamer with one funnel, and the other a two-masted steamer with one funnel. I never saw the *Mount Temple* to identify her. The first time that I saw the *Californian* was at about eight o'clock on the morning of 15th April. She was then about five to six miles distant, bearing W.S.W. true, and steaming towards the *Carpathia*. The *Carpathia* was then in substantially the position of the *Titanic* at the time of the disaster as given to us by wireless. I consider the position of the *Titanic*, as given to us by her Officers, to be correct."

To those who would then and later come to Stanley Lord's defense, this statement by Rostron that the *Californian* was not one of the ships he saw, and that he only became aware of her that morning when she drew alongside the *Carpathia,* was proof that the *Californian* had been far distant from the site of the sinking. But Rostron himself eventually disabused anyone so inclined to believe that notion, saying, "Dean and others, and some passengers, said they saw the *Californian* and watched her approaching. Well, I was mistaken. I had so much to do I wasn't thinking of the *Californian* and didn't recognize her." And while Lord's defenders would be quick to seize on Rostron's distraction and case of mistaken identity (and ignore his subsequent rebuttal), they were equally quick to overlook a line of questions which followed just moments later. Referring to the same affidavit, Sir Rufus asked Rostron, "Does that state all the vessels that you saw? I think it stated two steamers?"

"No; I saw one more, but it was during the night previous to getting out of the *Titanic*'s position. We saw masthead lights quite distinctly of another steamer between us and the *Titanic*. That was about quarter-past three."

"The masthead lights?"

"Yes, of another steamer, and one of the Officers swore he also saw one of the sidelights."

"Which one?"

"The port sidelight."

"Do you know of any identification of that steamer at all?"

"No; we saw nothing but the lights. I did not see the sidelights; I merely saw the masthead lights."

Here a Mr. Bucknill, an attorney for Harland and Wolff, suddenly leaped up, asking, "May we have the distance and bearing of these lights that he saw, as far as he can remember?" Mersey, annoyed at the interruption, and at the same time apparently having had enough of the *Californian* and Lord, ignored Bucknill and instead asked Rostron, "You did not see the additional lights yourself, the sidelight?"

"I saw the masthead lights."

"Did you see the lights your Officer spoke of?"

"I saw the masthead lights myself, but not the sidelight."

"What time was it?"

"About a quarter-past three."

"And how was the light bearing?"

"About 2 points on the starboard bow."

"On your starboard bow?"

"On my starboard bow; that would be about N. 30, W. true."

It was obvious to everyone in the London Scottish Drill Hall what these times, ship's bearings, and compass directions meant. There was another vessel, within sight of the *Carpathia*, facing to the west, north of where the *Titanic*'s lifeboats waited, but clearly within visual distance of the spot where the *Titanic* sank: it was the *Californian*.

Inadvertantly, Rostron caused new doubts about Stanley Lord's truthfulness as a witness to surface, which shook Lord's credibility to its foundations. It was immediately clear to everyone in the court that for the *Californian*'s lights to have been visible to the north of the *Carpathia* when the Cunard ship arrived among the *Titanic*'s lifeboats, the *Californian* would have been visible from the sinking *Titanic* as well. Captain Lord had claimed, and the *Californian*'s logbook apparently bore him out, that his ship's position put her at least twenty miles, and possibly as much as thirty miles, from the *Titanic*'s last position. Yet now Rostron's testimony deepened an already growing pall of suspicion not only over Lord but over the logbook as well. These suspicions had already been aroused when it came out in Lord's earlier testimony that no mention of the ship to the south of the *Californian*, nor any reference to the rockets that ship fired, appeared anywhere in the *Californian*'s log for the whole of the morning of April 15, 1912. They continued to grow when Chief Officer Stewart and Third Officer Groves gave widely differing—and mutually exclusive—explanations for the missing "scrap log."

As described earlier, in order to prevent errors and omissions, a ship at sea normally kept what was called a "scrap log," a bound book of blank pages in which a record was kept during each watch of everything that occurs on board relating to the handling of the ship, including any sightings of other vessels as well as visual signals received. The scrap log is kept as a back-up to the final log, and that of the *Californian*, for the morning of April 15, was missing. Chief Officer Stewart claimed that once the entries were made in the formal log, the corresponding pages of the scrap log were then torn out and thrown away, while Third Officer Groves maintained that the entire book would be disposed of, but only when all the pages in it were used. Taken together, the absence of the scrap log, the conflicting explanations, and the inexplicable silence of the log entries for early April 15 raised very grave doubts about the truthfulness of the Californian's log—and her captain.

Meanwhile, as the succession of revelations was taking place within the London Scottish Drill Hall, another drama was being played out beyond the courtroom. Sylvia Lightoller, the wife of the Titanic's Second Officer, faithfully attended every session of the Board of Trade Inquiry. To her it was a question of keeping faith with her husband's colleagues, living and dead. On the eighth day of the inquiry, after they had given testimony, a handful of the *Californian*'s officers, including Groves and Stone, were approached by this petite but formidable lady, and stood near-mute when she reproached them for such a sorry performance of their duties. Abashed, the *Californian*'s officers openly admitted that they had seen signals that night which they fully believed were distress signals, but had not been able to rouse Captain Lord to take any action. More importantly, it became readily apparent that they tried none too hard, for fear of their captain's temper. The normally feisty Lightoller, who only was beginning to have his own doubts about Stanley Lord's integrity, attempted to be a peacemaker, taking his wife by the arm and leading her over to Lord himself, nudging her to shake the man's hand, with the gentle admonition,

"My dear, you can't kick a man when he's down!"

The truth, as it so often does, finally, gradually, came out. Captain Lord was a virtual tyrant, sharp-tongued and quick with disparaging remarks, and his officers were utterly cowed by him, to the point that they were bereft of any initiative, leaving all decisions to the captain. Stone in particular was vulnerable to this sort of treatment. Despite his apparent air of confidence, he was shy, insecure, and fearful of his job security. Like every one of his contemporaries, he knew there were more qualified officers seeking postings than there were berths available, and a malign word from his captain could well ruin his career, not something that a newly-wed man of 25 wants to contemplate. It was only when the threat of retribution at the hands of Stanley Lord was removed that Stone felt he could tell the truth. The image created in the mind of the public ever since—and rightly so—has been of the *Californian*'s officers standing idly on the bridge, so thoroughly intimidated by their captain that they would rather watch another ship sink than run the risk of facing his wrath. Even Stone, who had been so obviously overawed and intimidated by Lord, finally confessed that he and Gibson did indeed think the rockets they saw were distress signals, but they "couldn't get the old man out of the chartroom."

It was on June 30, 1912 that the Board of Trade Inquiry issued its Final Report. Written by Lord Mersey himself, it was detailed sometimes to the point of tediousness, yet no one could deny that the Inquiry had been thorough. He concluded that the loss of the *Titanic* was due solely to the damage caused by the collision with the iceberg and not to any inherent design flaw in the ship, and that collision was the direct result of the ship steaming into an area known to be hazardous with ice at an excessively high speed. There was an insufficient lookout kept, given the danger of the sea conditions, and an overall sense of complacency among the ship's officers had contributed to this oversight.

The *Titanic*'s lifeboats, while fulfilling the Board of Trade requirements, were insufficient in number, and a change in the regulations was necessary. The boats themselves had been properly lowered but not properly filled, and had been insufficiently manned with trained seamen. Finally, the Board of Trade received a fair amount criticism, despite the earlier misgivings in some quarters that its self-investigation would be a whitewash. In addition to condemning the outdated lifeboat regulations, the Court found the Board of Trade's required "boat drill" procedures were laughable—usually one or two boats filled with picked crewmen who would go through the motions of rigging and lowering a lifeboat while the ship was in port. Nothing had been done to acquaint the passengers with their boat assignments or any of the life-saving equipment on board. That too would have to change.

On the subject of Captain Lord and the *Californian*, Lord Mersey was merciless. The evidence, he said, made it abundantly clear to him that the ship the *Californian*'s officers saw from their bridge, and watched as she fired rocket after rocket, was the *Titanic*. Captain Lord's excuse that he was sound asleep in the chartroom and couldn't recall having been told about the rockets didn't wash with Lord Mersey, and he believed that Captain Lord had acted most improperly in failing to ascertain what was the matter with that ship and go to the stricken liner's aid. The language of his conclusion was uncompromising:

> There are contradictions and inconsistencies in the story as told by the different witnesses. But the truth of the matter is plain. The *Titanic* collided with the berg 11.40. The vessel seen by the *Californian* stopped at this time. The rockets sent up from the *Titanic* were distress signals. The *Californian* saw distress signals. The number sent up by the *Titanic* was about eight. The *Californian* saw eight. The time over which the rockets from the *Titanic* were sent up was from about 12.45 to 1.45 o'clock. It was about this time that the *Californian* saw the rockets. At 2.40 Mr. Stone called to the Master that the ship from which he'd seen the rockets had disappeared.
>
> At 2.20 a.m. the *Titanic* had foundered. It was suggested that the rockets seen by the *Californian* were from some other ship, not the *Titanic*. But no other ship to fit this theory has ever been heard of.
>
> These circumstances convince me that the ship seen by the *Californian* was the *Titanic*, and if so, according to Captain Lord, the two vessels were about five miles apart at the time

of the disaster. The evidence from the *Titanic* corroborates this estimate, but I am advised that the distance was probably greater, though not more than eight to ten miles. The ice by which the *Californian* was surrounded was loose ice extending for a distance of not more than two or three miles in the direction of the *Titanic*. The night was clear and the sea was smooth. When she first saw the rockets the *Californian* could have pushed through the ice to the open water without any serious risk and so have come to the assistance of the *Titanic*. Had she done so she might have saved many if not all of the lives that were lost.

Chapter 10

THE UNDELIVERED VERDICT

So what really happened that night in April 1912, on that mirror-smooth patch of the North Atlantic at the edge of that icefield? Did the officers of the *Californian* indeed watch as the *Titanic* fired off her distress rockets in the vain hope of attracting their attention, and stand idly by as she sank? Did the *Californian*'s captain actually ignore those signals when they were reported to him? Or was the ship that Stone and Gibson saw in truth only a small tramp steamer just a few miles away, the rockets nothing more than simple company signals? Was Stanley Lord in fact justified in not moving his ship during the same hours that the *Carpathia* was racing to the northwest, toward the icefield?

One myth that has been needlessly perpetuated since the disaster and deserves to be dispelled is that *had* the *Californian* immediately responded to the white rockets her officers saw, she would have arrived alongside the *Titanic* in time to save everyone aboard. This simply isn't true, and in fairness to Lord and his ship it deserves to be put to rest. Time was everyone's enemy that night, from the men and women aboard the *Titanic*, desperately hoping some ship would appear before the liner sank, to Arthur Rostron on the *Carpathia*, knifing through the darkness in the hope of reaching the *Titanic* before it was too late, and even for the *Californian*, who, though she could have performed a legendary feat of mercy that night had she responded to the *Titanic*'s distress signals, still would have been unable

191

to rescue all of the *Titanic*'s passengers and crew.

In the most ideal scenario, when the *Titanic* fired her first rocket at 12:50, Second Officer Stone, standing on the *Californian*'s bridge, would have spotted it, but taken only passing notice—after all, a single rocket does not a distress signal make. But when a second one went up ten minutes later, Stone would have called down to Captain Lord with the news that there is a ship to the south firing white rockets. Lord would be concerned, but not unduly so at this point, and take the easiest and most practical action at the moment, advising Stone to awaken Cyril Evans, the wireless operator. Evans, after setting up his equipment, would have heard the *Titanic*'s CQD and rushed to the bridge with the news. Stone in turn would instantly inform Lord, who orders the ship to get underway while he returns to the bridge to work out the course to the sinking *Titanic*.

By now the time would have been somewhere between 1:15 and 1:20; Lord would likely have been confused by the position given in the *Titanic*'s wireless calls, knowing that 41.46 N, 50.14 W is ten to twelve miles distant, on the other side of the ice field that had stopped him for the night. But the rockets Stone saw—and by now Chief Officer Stewart most likely would have reached the bridge in time to see one or two more go up—came from the south-southeast. Did this mean the *Titanic* had steamed through the icefield, only to come to grief on the other side? Deciding that this was hardly likely, and that the officer on the *Titanic* who had worked out the position had made a mistake somewhere, Lord would have ordered the *Californian* to steam toward the ship to the south, and rang down to the engine room for "Slow Ahead," cautiously taking the ship away from the ice until he was confident he was in open water, where he would gradually increase speed.

Meanwhile Evans and Phillips would continue to exchange signals, as Evans tries to get more information for Captain Lord. After a few minutes, Phillips sends Bride to the bridge to ask Captain Smith to come back to the wireless office; once Phillips explained the situation, Smith instructs him to signal the *Californian* to assume that the ship she saw to the south firing rockets is indeed the *Titanic*. Phillips sends this to Evans, who in turn passes it up to the Californian's bridge.

When the *Californian* stopped for the night, Captain Lord had instructed the chief engineer to keep up steam in her boilers, in case it would become necessary to move the ship during the night. Now, in this hypothetical scenario, Lord's caution pays an unexpected dividend, allowing the *Californian* to get underway almost immediately. Working her way clear of the scattered drift ice nearby, it still takes time for the ship to begin to build up to her full speed, and now the iron constraints of time begin their work against the *Titanic* and the *Californian*. Nothing can done to alter how rapidly the *Titanic* is sinking, while the *Californian* has to cross ten miles of open water to reach her—it will take her almost forty minutes to travel that distance. As the smaller ship approaches the doomed liner, the *Californian*'s officers and crew see that she is sharply down by the head, her bow entirely submerged, her stern beginning to rise out of the water. It is 2:10 a.m., the last lifeboat had been launched, and clearly the end is only minutes away for the *Titanic*.

The *Californian*'s crew have worked hard to get their ship ready for a rescue at sea: her lifeboats are uncovered and swung out, cargo nets slung along the ship's sides, rope ladders and slings at the ready. But Captain Lord sees the panic sweeping over the *Titanic*'s decks, and as the *Californian* stands off a few hundred yards from the White Star ship, he orders his boats lowered with the instructions to stay well clear of the wreck. There is no way of telling what sort of suction or disturbance the *Titanic* would create when she goes under, and he doesn't want his boats to be swamped or capsized by frenzied swimmers trying to escape the sinking ship. The *Titanic*'s lifeboats begin converging on the *Californian*, while her own boats are plucking people out of the water as best they can. For those left aboard the *Titanic*, there is little hope: for most, her decks are too far above the water for them to safely jump. Some slide down the empty lifeboat falls, while a few near the bow are able to leap into the water, only to be sucked under by the sinking ship. The *Titanic*'s lights grow red, while the din is tremendous as her stern suddenly begins to rear into the sky. It settles back slightly after a few moments, the lights flash brightly for a second, then go out forever, and at 2:20 a.m. the hull quickly slips under. The *Titanic* is gone.

Now, those who are in the water began swimming desperately for the lifeboats. This too is a race against time, as hypothermia begins its insidious work, numbing arms and legs, sucking away the swimmers' breath, sapping their strength. Within ten minutes most of them are unconscious. After another ten minutes have passed, most of them have died. The *Californian*'s boats do their best, plucking possibly as many as three hundred of the *Titanic*'s passengers and crew from the water. Added to the more than seven hundred men, women, and children in the *Titanic*'s lifeboats, over a thousand lives have been saved. But tragedy hasn't been averted, only somewhat diminished. Twelve hundred people still have lost their lives.

But none of that would have been the fault of the *Californian*, had she responded. By making the effort to come to the aid of the stricken liner, Captain Lord and his crew would have fulfilled every moral and legal obligation to which they might have been held accountable. They could not have saved everyone, but they would have saved some—and even one life would have been worth the effort. But in reality, Stanley Lord never made the effort. And so hundreds needlessly died.

But was the *Californian* truly so close to the *Titanic* that she could see the White Star liner as she was sinking? That has been the crux of the "*Californian* incident" for almost a hundred years. For every argument put forward by those who would condemn Stanley Lord which places the *Titanic* in sight of the *Californian*—and vice-versa—there is a counter-argument made by his defenders which moves the two ships far apart, beyond the range of either's vision. The issue could only be decided if there was one set of facts, one chain of events or incidents which conclusively separates the two ships—or ties them together.

Fortunately for historians, and unfortunately for Stanley Lord, just such a framework of incidents exists, one which irrefutably places the sinking *Titanic* and the *Californian* within plain sight of each other. Certain bits of information gathered by Senator Smith began to lead in this direction at the US Senate investigation, but it wasn't until Sir Rufus Isaacs had thoroughly examined Lord, Gibson, Stone, Groves, Boxhall, and Rowe that it became clear there were four distinct incidents which were independently corroborated by witnesses aboard both ships, and which inseparably tied them together.

The first incident was when the *Titanic*'s Fourth Officer Boxhall, while working with the crew uncovering the lifeboats, saw the lights of a ship about "two points off the port bow," that is, about thirty degrees to the left. This meant that the *Titanic* was showing her red (port) sidelight to any ship along that bearing, including the ship Boxhall spotted. The Fourth Officer could clearly see the green (starboard) sidelight of the stranger; he was convinced that the other ship carried three or four masts, and was quite certain that she was "not a two-master." He pointed her out to Quartermaster Rowe, who had just arrived from the auxiliary bridge at the stern with a box of rockets under his arm. Rowe immediately began fitting one of the rockets into the firing socket on the starboard bridge wing, and sometime around 12:50, he estimated, he lit off the first one.

Aboard the *Californian*, Second Officer Stone had been keeping an eye on the ship to the south. She was abaft the starboard beam; that is, she was sitting slightly behind the *Californian*, and her red sidelight was clearly visible. Together with the position of her masthead light, this showed that she was pointing north, toward the *Californian*. The *Californian*, in turn, was bearing to the east-northeast, drifting on the current, her bow slowly swinging to the south, toward the other ship. At the moment she was showing her green light to this stranger. It was sometime between 12:45 and 12:50 a.m. when Stone saw a white rocket burst over the stranger, followed by four more sent up over the next thirty minutes. Unsure of what to do, Stone notified Captain Lord.

The second incident came when Fourth Officer Boxhall, who was working with Rowe in firing the distress rockets, took a long look at the strange ship to the north, certain now that she was a "four-mast steamer." It was then that he noticed two details: the first was her green sidelight, the second was a shift in her masthead lights. It appeared to Boxhall that she was turning "very, very slowly," as if her bows were swinging around toward the *Titanic*.

At 1:15 a.m., Apprentice Officer Gibson joined Second Officer Stone on the bridge of the *Californian*. Stone immediately told Gibson about the ship to the south and the rockets she was firing, five having gone up so far. While Stone was speaking, Gibson noticed that the *Californian*'s bow was slowly swinging southward. She was still displaying a green sidelight, but to any observer on the other ship, the *Californian*'s masthead lights would have been visibly shifting. While

Stone and Gibson were talking, two more rockets went up over the strange ship, making a total of seven. By pure luck, Gibson had his glasses to his eyes as one of the rockets was fired, and he could clearly see the flash of the detonator on her deck. It would prove to be a crucial detail, for it would prove that the other ship was well short of the horizon, unquestionably less than eleven miles from the *Californian*. Gibson would never forget those rockets, always recalling how each of them "burst into white stars."

Back aboard the *Titanic*, Boxhall and Rowe have fired off seven rockets between them. The shortage of qualified seamen on the Boat Deck meant that both men were harried, working at multiple tasks. Boxhall would tell Senator Smith that during this time he was "manning them [the lifeboats] . . . firing off distress rockets, and trying to signal a steamer that was almost ahead of us." Rowe was doing much the same. Once more peering to the north, Boxhall now noticed a distinct change in the other ship's lights. She seemed to continue her slow turn toward the sinking liner, and for the first time, in addition to her green light, Boxhall could see her red light. The other ship was now squarely bows-on to the *Titanic*—she must be coming toward her.

Up on the bridge of the *Californian*, Gibson took note that the slow swing of the ship on the current had brought her bow around to where it was pointing directly at the stranger to the south, so that the *Californian* would be showing both her red and green lights. Stone apparently sensed something wrong about the stranger, for he suddenly blurted out, "Look at her now Gibson, her lights look queer." Gibson agreed; raising his glasses to his eyes once again, he took a long look at the other ship, then remarked, "She seems to have a big side out of the water."

The fourth incident came just moments later. Standing on the *Titanic*'s starboard bridge wing, Boxhall watched as the other ship's green light disappeared; only the red light was visible now. Boxhall would remember that. "I thought maybe she had got stuck in the ice and so had turned around." He fired off his last rocket, the eighth, and then on orders from Captain Smith, took command of Lifeboat No. 2. The time was approximately 1:30 a.m.

Stone and Gibson, meanwhile, watched as the stranger fired an eighth rocket, the last one they would see from her. Stone was convinced that the rockets came from the ship, while Gibson, who clearly saw the detonator flash of at least one of the rockets, was certain of it. At the same time, Gibson noticed that the *Californian* continued to swing with the current: her bow now pointed to the west, the ship having swung through nearly 180 degrees. Only her red sidelight would have been visible to the other ship; the only sidelight ever seen on the stranger was her own red light. The time, according to the clock on the *Californian's* bridge, was 1:30 a.m.

Both Senator Smith and Lord Mersey would notice the strange congruence of rockets, lights, ship movements, and times in these four incidents, and quickly recognized the truth: the only explanation which reconciled what was seen from each ship and the circumstances was that the two ships could only have been the *Titanic* and the *Californian*. It was this conclusion which led Senator Smith to declare in his address to Congress, "The failure of Captain Lord to arouse the wireless operator on his ship . . . places a tremendous responsibility upon this officer from which it will be very difficult to escape." It led Lord Mersey to announce, without qualification, that "These circumstances convince me that the ship seen by the *Californian* was the *Titanic*."

Stanley Lord would stand condemned by American and British inquiries, a condemnation which has stood for nearly a century, despite determined efforts then and since by Lord's defenders to prove it wrong. To the end of his life, Stanley Lord would steadfastly maintain that the rockets seen by the officers of the *Californian* were not from the *Titanic*, but some other ship. In the months and years immediately following the disaster, it could readily be believed that those people who rallied to Lord's cause felt—as did Lord himself, of course—that he had been unjustly accused, then tried and convicted in a court of public opinion. Now, however, more than nine decades later, those who still seek to exonerate Stanley Lord give off a distinct aroma of having more of an interest in making a name for themselves than any genuine desire to see justice done. Exculpating Lord has practically become a cottage industry for some of them, especially in the "now-you-see-it-now-you-don't" world of publication on the internet.

What is disturbing is how those who choose to defend Stanley

Lord will demand the most exacting execution of duty from people aboard the *Titanic*, who were working under conditions of fear and strain that few of them had ever encountered, yet those same critics will allow Lord, who was under no duress whatsoever, the most astonishing leeway in fulfilling his responsibilities. One critic, writing no doubt from the safety of his armchair, has gone so far as to condemn for ineptitude the crewmen of the *Titanic* for not firing off the distress rockets in precisely the prescribed manner outlined in the Board of Trade regulations, yet offers no word of criticism for Lord's refusal to make even the simplest effort to follow the injunction of those same regulations to investigate unusual or ambiguous signals, particularly rockets. Some have gone so far as to commend Lord for his prudence in refusing to steam southward toward the unknown steamer, as doing so might have exposed the *Californian* to damage by the floating ice around her, and at the same time condemn Arthur Rostron for recklessness in driving the *Carpathia* at high speed toward the icefield which sank the *Titanic*.

Others have condemned Rostron, going so far as to call him "silly" and deride him as "a company man," for his repeated requests for guidance from the Cunard office on how to handle the glare of publicity following the *Carpathia*'s rescue of the *Titanic*'s survivors. Yet the same carping voices offer no word of approbation to Stanley Lord and the representative of the Leyland Line for closeting themselves in Lord's cabin as soon as the *Californian* docked in Boston, seeking to contain the damage that might be done should word leak out of the *Californian*'s proximity to the *Titanic*. Such a double-standard is beyond question a form of hypocrisy. Not surprisingly, C.H. Lightoller, onetime Second Officer of the *Titanic*, offered perhaps the most pungent observation on this despicable practice: in his book *Titanic and Other Ships*, he wrote with almost audible acidity, "The armchair complaint is a very common disease, and generally accepted as one of the necessary evils from which the seafarer is condemned to suffer."

Beyond all other considerations, though, what is completely inexplicable is the callous selectiveness which the champions of Stanley Lord use in his defense. No matter what form their efforts take, in the end they center exclusively on proving that the ship seen by the

Californian was not the *Titanic*—and vice versa—and that even if the rockets seen by Stone and Gibson were those fired by the *Titanic*, the *Californian* was in any case too far away to have been any help. Therefore, they reason, since their efforts "prove" that the *Californian* and the *Titanic* were never were in sight of each other, Stanley Lord can hardly be held responsible for failing to go to the assistance of the sinking White Star liner. Like Lord himself, they conclude that since he is innocent of this charge, he is then blameless on any account, and those who condemn him are guilty of falsely accusing an innocent man.

Yet there is a blindness to this stance. For the simple truth is that on the night of April 14–15, 1912, somewhere on the North Atlantic, within sight of the steamship *Californian*, someone was firing white rockets into the night sky, in a desperate hope that some ship—any ship—would respond in time. The crime of Stanley Lord was not that he may have ignored the *Titanic*'s signals, but that he unquestionably ignored *someone's* cry for help. This is a cold, hard truth that, no matter how much the partisans of Stanley Lord might wish to deny it, they are unable to do so. Nothing can make those eight white rockets go away; nothing can make Lord's frank acknowledgment—then and subsequently—that the signals *were* white rockets go away; and nothing can make Lord's refusal to respond to them go away. The chilling reality is that Lord's inaction probably cost those unfortunate people, whoever they were, their lives.

At this point comes the final denouement of the story of Stanley Lord and the *Californian*. What has remained unexplained for more than nine decades is *why* Lord would so callously choose to disregard such a cry for help. The answer to that question will not be found in any testimony or transcript, nor in any set of regulations or traditions of the sea; it is not an issue of navigation or seamanship, or any body of maritime law. The answer lies instead in the realm of medical science, for Stanley Lord was a man with a deep-seated flaw in his character, one which may never have revealed itself had the *Californian* not been in that particular expanse of the North Atlantic on the night of April 14–15, 1912. Instead, circumstances unconsciously conspired to reveal that Stanley Lord was a man without conscience: Stanley Lord was a sociopath.

A sociopath is defined as someone who displays a certain set of distinguishing characteristics, among them deceit, a tendency to be manipulative, a failure to plan ahead or anticipate consequences, aggressiveness, and—particularly relevant in the case of Stanley Lord—a reckless disregard for the safety of others, and a lack of remorse for any injury to others which might result from their actions or inactions. Surprisingly, such people can often be quite charming, but they will ruthlessly use that charm in order to achieve their ends. At the same time they seem to have an innate ability to find weaknesses in people, and are ready to exploit these weaknesses to their own ends through deceit, manipulation, or intimidation. While they can appear to establish conventional social relationships, even marriages, to them these exist in name only, and can be ended whenever their usefulness ceases. Ultimately sociopaths are interested only in their personal safety, needs, and desires, without concern for the effect of their behavior on others.

Fundamentally, sociopaths are people with defective consciences. They either lack one entirely, or it is in some way dysfunctional, or they have the ability to completely neutralize or compartmentalize any sense of moral or ethical responsibility. Bluntly, they are incapable of ever conceiving themselves to be wrong, let alone doing something wrong. They are their own moral compass, recognizing no ethical or moral standard other than whatever will advance their ends. Consequently, what sets a sociopath apart from the rest of humanity is that they lack the capacity for any true emotions, from love to shame to guilt.

The nature of Stanley Lord's sociopathic behavior revealed itself in a number of subtle but distinct ways. The first clue was his reaction when Stone reported seeing white rockets being fired by the ship to the south. Captain Lord knew full well, as did any qualified master of the British merchant marine, the meaning of white rockets at sea, as well as the Board of Trade regulations requiring him to investigate in the event of an ambiguous signal. He also knew that Stone was a weak reed, hesitant and unsure of himself, lacking initiative, instead relying on his captain to make decisions. Yet rather than rouse himself, Lord's response was to ask some fatuous questions, then go back to dozing in the chartroom. What was most remarkable, then as now, was his failure to even suggest that Cyril Evans, the wireless operator, be awakened to see if he could learn anything. If the wireless gave no news, nothing had been risked, nothing was lost, save an hour or two of sleep for Evans. However, should Evans have been awakened, he would have immediately learned of the *Titanic*'s plight, and Captain Lord would have been compelled to act.

Action was something Stanley Lord most definitely wanted to avoid. The only genuine reality for a sociopath is their own self-preservation; at no time will such a person ever place themselves in a position of real or perceived danger. This is the key to Lord's refusal to entertain the idea that the rockets sighted by Stone were distress signals, as well as his failure to awaken Evans. If the possibility that a ship nearby might be in peril was never raised, Lord and the *Californian* would not be compelled to respond, and in responding steam into what Lord believed were dangerous waters.

Therein lies the explanation for Lord's inaction: he had already stopped, because, as Sir Rufus Isaacs had said, "the Captain of the vessel was in ice for the first time and would not take the risk of going to the rescue of another vessel which might have got into trouble, as he thought, from proceeding through the ice when he himself had stopped." Lord, in his mind, had done the wise and prudent thing by stopping; anyone else who failed to exhibit such sagacity should be left to suffer the consequences of their rashness. Nor would he risk his own personal safety. He had stopped because of the ice, and in his judgment the waters around the *Californian* were dangerous. To attempt to answer the distress call of some unknown ship foolish enough to run onto the ice would have required him to expose the *Californian*—and himself—to danger. He would refuse to take such action as long as it could be plausibly avoided. It should not be forgotten that it was Chief Officer Stewart, not Captain Lord, who roused Cyril Evans to "see what he could learn" about the ship that had fired rockets in the night. This was, in its coldest and most cynical form, genuinely "reckless disregard for the safety of others."

Demonstrations of the other major characteristics of a sociopath, duplicity coupled with a lack of remorse, quickly followed. Even when Lord was confronted with unavoidable proof that the *Titanic* had sunk, his actions were carefully qualified and orchestrated. The infamous gaffe about the *Titanic*'s position—"This won't do, you must get me a better position"—was followed by a carefully crafted series of maneuvers calculated not to bring the *Californian* to the *Titanic*'s position as quickly as possible, but rather to create the impression that the ship had traveled much farther and with considerably greater difficulty than she actually did.

The duplicity went even further, of course, including the inexplicable disappearance of the *Californian*'s scrap log, for example, or the impossibly innocuous entries in the formal log for the morning of April 15, 1912. Falsifying a log entry is one of the most egregious offenses which any captain can commit, yet only someone truly credulous would believe that Stanley Lord was not responsible for the alterations and omissions found in the logbook of the *Californian*.

Lord's demand for signed affidavits from his officers, Stone and Gibson, is particularly revealing, as were his words in Boston, when he said, "It is all foolishness for anybody to say that I, at the point of a revolver, took any man into this room and made him swear to tell any kind of a story." Lord quite clearly knew that awkward questions would almost certainly be asked when the *Californian* docked in Boston, and the statements from the two officers were an early attempt to make certain that Lord's version—and only his version—of the events of the night would be published. The "point of a revolver" remark is fraught with implications: no one had ever suggested that Lord *had* coerced his officers to say anything. When Lord made the remark, the existence of the affidavits was still completely unknown; yet here he was, defending himself against non-existent allegations.

But it was in front of Senator Smith, and later Lord Mersey, that Lord's duplicity would be given free rein. His story would change substantially between Boston and Washington, and again between Washington and London. First he claimed that he had never actually seen the other ship, but then later recounted how he had personally watched it come up "within 4 miles of us." Initially he would say that he had never seen the *Titanic*, yet a few days later he testified that he told Cyril Evans of the other ship, "This is not the *Titanic*, there is no doubt about it."

Most damning of all was how Lord's account of the white rockets seen by Stone and Gibson, as well as his own responses, was altered with the passage of time and changing of venues. From not having seen any rockets or signals of any kind on the night of April 15, 1912, as he told the Boston press, he then told Senator Smith that Second Officer Stone had indeed reported seeing rockets fired by the distant ship to the south. While at that point he carefully avoided offering any explanation of what he believed those rockets were, by the time he was sitting before the Board of Trade Inquiry, Lord's story had evolved into his expressing the opinion that they were only company signals, and claiming that this had been his openly stated belief all along. What set Lord apart from all of the other witnesses at both investigations was that he was the only one to substantially change his story. Others would remember details differently, but only Lord would attempt to present fundamentally different—and contradictory—accounts of his actions.

(His remark to the Boston press the day prior to his appearance before the Senate subcommittee is also revealing, when he said, "*If* I go to Washington . . ." Lord had been served with a Congressional subpoena and there was no "if" about his appearance; had he ignored the subpoena, he would have been arrested by U.S. Marshals and brought to Washington in shackles. Yet another symptom of a sociopath is a disdain for authority when its requirements seem inconvenient.)

The manipulative and intimidating side of Lord's character showed itself even before the *Titanic* disaster, as evidenced by his autocratic style of command. He was not a captain who inspired loyalty, rather he was a superior who motivated through fear. He was not given to towering rages, but rather a quieter, more subtle anger, one that created a brooding undercurrent of tension among his officers and crew. It is telling to note that it was members of his own crew who first came out against him. Lord's treatment of Second Officer Stone and Apprentice Officer Gibson, on the other hand, went even further than simple intimidation. Both men were vulnerable—Gibson as a consequence of his youth and inexperience, and Stone by dint of his insecurity. Lord drew a bead on both of these weaknesses, knowing that an unfavorable report to the Leyland offices could do significant damage to Gibson's career prospects, an unspoken threat which Lord could hold over the young apprentice whenever it was useful. At the same time he knew that he could depend on Herbert Stone's loyalty, which stemmed from a compound of the young officer's respect for the father-figure of Lord and fear of his position as captain. Lord literally held the careers of both men in his hands, and if that loyalty were tested too sorely, he would have the man's affidavit on hand to assure it.

At the same time it is worth noting that Lord made no similar attempt to coerce Third Officer Charles Groves into giving testimony that supported Lord's version of the events in question. Groves was a much different kettle of fish from Stone and Gibson, possessing far more self-confidence than either, and with a broader range of experience at sea. It was Groves' assertion that the ship to the south of the *Californian* was a large passenger liner that undermined Captain Lord's contention that she was just a small tramp steamer. Despite his relatively junior grade, Groves' experience with large passenger ships was considerably greater than Lord's, and made his testimony difficult to credibly refute.

The final and most compelling evidence of Lord's sociopathy, though, comes from one glaring omission that spanned the remainder of his life. At no time did Lord ever express the slightest remorse or regret for his inaction in the early hours of April 15, 1912. Not one word of condolence for the families of those lost on the *Titanic* ever passed his lips. Never once was there the recognition, however belated, that he might have—should have, could have—done things differently that night. Instead he only sought unqualified validation of his actions. There was never the slightest expression of doubt on his part that he was absolutely right in what he did and did not do; not even a passing recognition that others might see the circumstances differently and draw different conclusions. It was not simply a case where Stanley Lord did not believe himself to be guilty of the actions of which he was accused: to him, it was simply inconceivable that he could have done anything wrong.

The question would arise many times in the years since 1912, as to why, if he were so clearly guilty of criminal negligence at the very least, Captain Lord was not prosecuted. That he wasn't is often seized upon by his defenders as proof that Lord was a scapegoat for the Board of Trade. The Board, they claim, was right to blame for the loss of life on the *Titanic*, even though it was never suggested at the time that Lord was at fault for failing to save everyone aboard the doomed White Star liner, but rather that he had failed to come to her aid. A conspiracy existed then and still exists, they claim, to prevent certain facts from emerging which would clear Lord's name.

Yet here again the very selectiveness they employ in presenting the facts of their case betrays them. In point of fact, the opposite is true: in the Board of Trade files can be found a series of memorandums and legal opinions which reveal just how seriously the Board was considering bringing charges against Stanley Lord. Lord Mersey was far from alone in his judgment of Captain Lord's culpability; even among professional seamen there were serious questions raised about the master of the *Californian*. At one point, after the proceedings were closed but before Lord Mersey drew up his report, Captain A.H.F. Young, the Professional Member of the Marine Department for the Board of Trade, went so far as to press Lord Mersey for a formal inquiry into Lord's "competency to continue as Master of a British ship." After a few weeks debate—some of it rather heated—the decision was made to not pursue a criminal case.

"Captain Lord's fault carries its own punishment," and "his punishment is already real and very heavy" were among the comments made, though this was not a universally held opinion. Captain Young would write of the decision, "From the point of view of 'gross misdemeanour' I think an Inquiry should have been held, but as I gather . . . that it has been decided by the President not to do so, I cannot well offer any further observation." In an unspoken but obvious rebuke of Lord, however, the Board of Trade circulated a pamphlet to all British merchant marine officers carrying Master's and Extra Master's certificates, which reiterated the proper use of rockets as distress signals, as well as emphasizing the responsibility of all watch-keeping officers to take swift action to confirm the meaning of any signals sighted that they did not immediately understand. Never again would hundreds die needlessly while Herbert Stone ineptly paced his bridge, Cyril Evans slept peacefully in his bunk, and Stanley Lord napped uncaring in his chartroom, barely eleven miles away from a tragedy.

So, in the end, a formal verdict on Stanley Lord was never delivered. Yet under the weight of the evidence, and despite the workings and machinations of those who supported him, it was unnecessary, for the undelivered verdict bore punishment enough—the condemnation of generations, and the example of Stanley Lord as the model of that to which no merchant marine officer must ever aspire. In the decades that followed, the conclusions of both the American and British Inquiries, echoing each other with devastating precision, have withstood all the legal maneuvering, political posturing, and forensic legerdemain that has been employed in the attempt to refute them, and so Lord continues to stand condemned.

It has often been maintained and it may be true, at least superficially, that Stanley Lord in person was charming, warm, kindhearted, and a devoted family man; but in a moment of crisis which would bring out the very best in the character of other officers, the deadly flaw in his own would be revealed for all the world to see. Arthur Rostron was a man who would risk everything in the hope that he could reach the *Titanic* in time to save as many lives as he could. Stanley Lord was a man who simply didn't care enough to awaken his own wireless operator in an effort to learn why a ship nearby was firing distress rockets into the night sky.

It was the Attorney General, Sir Rufus Isaacs, who at the time came closest to understanding what compelled Stanley Lord to do nothing in response to those white rockets. It was there, lurking in the dry, almost detached language of British jurisprudence that the truth about Stanley Lord has abided since that day in May 1912 when these words were uttered by Sir Rufus: "I am unable to find any possible explanation of what happened, except it may be the Captain of the vessel was in ice for the first time and would not take the risk of going to the rescue of another vessel." It was with those five words, "*would not take the risk*," that Sir Rufus struck what for Stanley Lord's reputation and career was a mortal blow. The man who "would not take the risk" was a coward.

Epilogue

FLOTSAM AND JETSAM

The *Titanic* disaster was the beginning of the end for the White Star Line. When she vanished into the depths of the North Atlantic, the *Titanic* took with her the company's hopes and dreams for a new ascendancy on the North Atlantic. Gone were the plans for a weekly express service between New York and Southampton which would rival Cunard's service from Liverpool. There were to have been three sister ships: the *Olympic*, the *Titanic*, and the still-building *Gigantic*. The loss of the *Titanic* crippled the plan, while delays in completing the *Gigantic* put paid to it.

One of the consequences of the *Titanic* disaster was a decision by the company's directors that *Gigantic* was too pretentious a name, and changed it to the more subdued but still dignified *Britannic*. It wasn't until July 1914, after expensive and time-consuming modifications to her inner hull and watertight bulkheads, that the *Britannic* was finished, and hardly had she completed her sea trials than the Great War exploded across Europe. The Royal Navy quickly requisitioned her to serve as a hospital ship. In November 1916, while steaming off the coast of Greece in the Aegean Sea, she struck a mine and sank in an hour and a half. Only plenty of lifeboats and a warm sea kept the death toll down to thirty-five.

Once the guns fell silent, only the *Olympic* was left of what was to have been that grand trio of ships to carry on for the White Star Line. Her career as a troopship in the First World War was distinguished, and even turned heroic when she rammed and sank the *U-103* in May 1918. She returned to passenger service in 1919, becoming one of the best-loved ships on the North Atlantic. But the effect of losing both her sisters could never be undone—even with the addition of two liners seized from Germany as war reparations (they became the *Homeric* and the *Majestic*), the planned express service never materialized. Although by the mid-1920s the numbers of passengers crossing the North Atlantic began to approach those of the pre-war years, the line suffered. Revenues fell and costs rose as the 1920s progressed, and the White Star Line began a dangerous decline as profits shriveled, then vanished. In 1928, work was begun on a 1,000-foot, 80,000-ton superliner, to be called the *Oceanic*, that would, it was hoped, be the salvation of the line, but when the Great Depression struck in 1929, it devastated White Star's finances so that the money to complete the new ship was never found.

By 1932, crippled and impotent, the White Star Line was merged with Cunard, which was in dire straits of its own, at the instigation of the British government. Very much the junior partner in the new Cunard-White Star Line, the company saw most of its aging fleet sent to the breakers during the 1930s. The *Olympic* was taken out of service in 1934, after she rammed and sank the Nantucket lightship, killing all seven crewmen aboard that hapless vessel. She was broken up in 1935, many of her interior fixtures and decorations finding their way into houses and pubs in Liverpool, Southampton, and London. By 1950, the last of the line's assets were dissolved; after eighty years of service on the North Atlantic, the White Star Line had ceased to exist.

Second Officer Lightoller never received a command of his own—nor did any of the surviving officers of the *Titanic*. He retired from the sea in the early 1920s, but never lost his lust for adventure. In 1940 he took his sixty-foot yacht, the *Sundowner*, to Dunkirk, and despite being bombed and strafed by the Luftwaffe, managed to bring back 131 British soldiers. After an adventure-filled life he died peacefully in 1952.

Fourth Officer Joseph Boxhall would spend another twenty years at sea, but like Lightoller, would never command his own ship. Over the years the accuracy of the final position he had worked out for the

Titanic would be questioned by critics, but he defended his position of 41.40 N 50.14 W until the end of his days. His last posting was as First Officer of Cunard's *Aquitania* in the 1930s. After his death in 1963, in compliance with his last wishes, his ashes were scattered over the North Atlantic, at the spot that marks the *Titanic*'s grave.

The story of the Cunard line after the *Titanic* disaster would be far, far different from that of the White Star Line.

Even before the Great War, Cunard had established a pre-eminence on the North Atlantic that it would never relinquish. The *Lusitania* and *Mauretania* proved to be so much faster than any of their rivals that the company's grip on the Blue Ribband seemed unbreakable. Passengers flocked to the Cunard ticketing offices. A new ship, the *Aquitania*, was introduced in 1913, and many people felt that her interiors were the most beautiful ever installed on an ocean-going vessel. The First World War took a severe toll on the Cunard fleet, but despite the loss of nearly a dozen ships to German U-boats—most terribly the *Lusitania* on May 7, 1915—when the war ended Cunard was still in a stronger position than any other passenger line on the North Atlantic.

When the merger with the White Star Line came in 1932, Cunard was able to complete its own superliner, known up to the moment of her launching only as Hull 532, but beloved forever after as the *Queen Mary*. Prosperity gradually returned to the North Atlantic trade in the 1930s, and a second superliner, the *Queen Elizabeth*, was launched in 1938. Yet in 1939, war once more swept across Europe, and the two liners, soon to become revered as the "Warrior Queens," began carrying troops across the Atlantic from the United States to Great Britain in such huge numbers that they ultimately provided the margin of victory for the Allies over Nazi Germany.

The 1940s and 1950s were a Golden Age for Cunard, as the company utterly dominated the transatlantic trade. The rise of air travel in the 1960s, however, saw a corresponding decline in Cunard's fortunes, despite the introduction of a new liner, the *Queen Elizabeth 2*, in 1965. By the end of the decade, both the *Queen Mary* and *Queen Elizabeth* had been retired, while the Cunard fleet, which had once boasted more than fifty ships, was now reduced to the *QE 2* and a handful of lesser vessels. By the end of the 1970s, the very existence of the line was in jeopardy.

Cunard staggered through the last two decades of the 20th century, going though a series of owners who never quite seemed to be able to find a niche for the line to return it to profitability. In 1996, however, a white knight appeared in the form of Carnival Corporation, which bought Cunard with the avowed purpose of returning the line to its former prestige. The *Queen Elizabeth 2* was completely refurbished and in 2004, the *Queen Mary 2*, the largest passenger liner ever built, was introduced to the North Atlantic run. Fittingly, Cunard, which was the first company to introduce regular transatlantic passenger service, has become the last company to offer it.

One of the last losses suffered by Cunard during the Great War was the *Carpathia*. When World War I broke out she remained on the Mediterranean run, at one point being the source of a minor *contretemps* for the company. On September 5th, 1914 the Italian government levied a fine against her for carrying immigrants without a license. In early 1915 she was requisitioned by the British government and converted to a troopship. Refitted, the *Carpathia* could now carry more than 3,000 officers and other ranks, or alternatively, a thousand cavalry mounts and troopers, along with a thousand tons of supplies.

On July 17, 1918 as part of a convoy bound for Boston, she was 120 miles west of Fastnet when two torpedoes fired by a German submarine slammed into her starboard side, and she immediately began to sink. Five crewmen were killed in the explosions, while the rest of the crew immediately saw to the safety of the fifty-seven military personnel aboard, getting them away in lifeboats. A third torpedo struck the ship, but despite the severe damage she had taken, the *Carpathia* remained afloat long enough for the rest of her officers and crewmen to escape. She went down at 12:40 a.m. and her survivors were picked up a few hours later by the destroyer H.M.S. *Snowdrop* and taken to Liverpool. For the most part, the world soon forgot about the *Carpathia*, save for her part in rescuing the *Titanic*'s survivors. Few people knew her ultimate fate, and even fewer had any idea where she lay.

All that changed on September 22, 2002, when an American by the name of Clive Cussler brought the *Carpathia* back to the front pages of the world's newspapers. At a press conference held at the

Bedford Institute of Oceanography in Halifax, Nova Scotia, video footage was first shown to the world's press which confirmed that a wreck discovered by Cussler and his associates a year before was in fact the remains of the *Carpathia*. Using side-scan sonar and surveying the wreck with remote operating vehicles, Cussler and his team methodically combed the area where the *Carpathia* was believed to have gone down, and were finally able to pinpoint the wreck's location. They found her, as expected, lying in just over 500 feet of water, not far from the east coast of Ireland.

Searching for shipwrecks was at first just a hobby for Cussler, who was best known as a phenomenally successful novelist whose fictional adventures take place on or below the sea. His interest began with what he unashamedly admits were fairly amateurish efforts in 1979, but as his searches grew in scope and sophistication, he was persuaded to form a non-profit, volunteer foundation "dedicated to preserving our maritime heritage through the discovery, archaeological survey and conservation of shipwreck artifacts." Over Cussler's objections, the board of directors, in a sly nod to the fictional government agency which features prominently in all of Cussler's novels, promptly named the foundation NUMA, the National Underwater and Marine Agency.

While the name of the foundation may have been a bit tongue in cheek, the quality of the work done by NUMA has become serious and professional. The foundation's greatest success came in 1995, when it discovered the wreck of the Confederate submarine *Hunley*, whose location had eluded similar efforts for a century and a quarter, just outside the harbor of Charleston, South Carolina. Over the years, Cussler and NUMA have searched for—and usually found—more than eighty crashed aircraft or sunken ships of historical significance (as well as one locomotive, but that's a different story). Yet for all of NUMA's accomplishments, Cussler regarded finding the wreck of the *Carpathia* as one of the most fulfilling. At the news conference he would remark, the intensity in his voice unmistakable, that "we have footage of the RMS *Carpathia* in her watery grave at the bottom of the ocean off the coast of Ireland. It humbles me. My goal in founding NUMA was to increase awareness of maritime history. We have been succeeding beyond my wildest dreams. I did not think this would happen in my life time."

While the *Carpathia* may have soon faded from the public's consciousness, not so Captain Arthur Rostron. In recognition of his efforts on the morning of April 15, 1912, he was presented with a silver cup and gold medal by a group of the survivors. Presented to President William Howard Taft at the White House, Rostron was given a formal letter of thanks signed by the President, and a few months later he was presented with a Congressional Gold Medal (not, as is sometimes asserted, the Medal of Honor) unanimously voted him by the United States Congress. In Great Britain he would be given the Shipwreck and Humane Society's medal by Lord Derby; yet another gold medal was awarded him by the Shipwreck Society of New York.

Remaining on the bridge of the *Carpathia* for a year, he then was transferred to the *Caronia*, a larger and more glamorous command. In the next two years he would be named master of the *Carmania*, the *Campania*, and the *Lusitania*. When the *Lusitania* was briefly taken out of service in August 1914, Rostron was given the *Aulania*, and continued as her captain after she was turned into a troopship later that autumn, carrying the first Canadian troops sent from Halifax to Plymouth, then later spending time on the passage from India. The spring and summer of 1915 saw Rostron, who was now known as Commander Arthur Rostron, RNR (Royal Naval Reserve), and the *Aulania* carrying troops to Gallipoli. In September 1915, Rostron was given command of the *Mauretania*, and six months later the Royal Navy transferred him to the *Ivernia*, on which he continued his service in the Mediterranean Sea. It must have been something like a homecoming for him, as the *Ivernia* was the Carpathia's sister ship. He returned to the bridge of the *Mauretania* in 1917, and then in the last year of the war, variously commanded the *Andania*, *Saxonia*, and *Carmania* before returning to the *Mauretania* yet again. His name was posted on the Acting list of the Royal Navy Reserve as a captain in December 1918, and in the following year, in recognition of his wartime service, Rostron was made a Commander of the Order of the British Empire.

Now properly styled Arthur Rostron, CBE, RNR, he remained in command of the *Mauretania* after she was returned to Cunard and went back into passenger service in June, 1919. The *Mauretania* was always his favorite ship, and he remained her master until July 1928, when he was given the *Berengaria*, then the largest ship in the Cunard fleet, one of the trio of German-built giants awarded to the Allies as reparations. In the meantime, in 1926, he had been made a Knight Commander of the Order of the British Empire (KCBE), and was appointed the commodore of the Cunard fleet. The same day that his KCBE was announced, he was awarded the Freedom of New York, "For his splendid services to humanity, to the City of New York and to the people of the United States over many years." An appointment as aide-de-camp to King George V soon followed, and he was even invested by the Admiral in Command at Cherbourg with the French *Legion d'Honneur*.

Retirement eventually came Arthur Rostron's way in May 1931. His was not sedentary, however, for he was an enthusiastic member of the Southampton Master Mariner's Club, at one point serving as its Captain. He was also active in the British Legion. In his closing years he wrote his autobiography, *Home from the Sea*, which today is eagerly sought by *Titanic* enthusiasts. When the Second World War erupted in 1939, Rostron was seventy years of age and his health allowed him to take no part in the war effort. He developed pneumonia in the autumn of 1940, and died in Chippenham on November 4 of that year. He is buried at the West End Church in Southampton. There he lies next to his wife, Ethel Minnie Rostron, who died three years later.

Although International Mercantile Marine would survive as a corporate entity well into the 1940s, it would ultimately prove a gargantuan failure. Far from dominating the passenger and shipping trade on the Atlantic, the combine never secured more than 40 percent of the business on that route—a far cry from the monopoly that J.P. Morgan had envisaged when he spawned the concept. In his eagerness to acquire as many of the transatlantic lines as possible, and at the same time overestimating the potential profits of such a monopoly, Morgan had overreached himself, dramatically overpaying for much of the stock he acquired, and when a proposed subsidy was turned down by the U.S. Congress, the company began to flounder in its search for profitability. In fact it was rarely a money maker, and more than once the combine went into technical bankruptcy, while reorganizations of its component shipping lines, disguised as "rationalizations" of their fleets, as well as their rates and schedules, left many of the companies in disarray.

The *Baltimore Sun* was simply stating the obvious when it wrote in late 1918 that "the great results originally looked for in this merger did not materialize," and that "IMM was one of the few financial mistakes that the older Morgan made, and one of the very few ventures in which he engaged that did not turn out successfully." The blunt truth was that Morgan got himself too deeply involved in a business which was complex beyond his comprehension, and the shareholders paid the price for his ambition. IMM never paid stock dividends, and by the early 1930s the corporate deficit had soared to $27,000,000. A series of liquidations followed until by the end of the decade International Mercantile Marine existed in name only. Before the Second World War ended, the company would be dissolved.

Probably because of its obscurity outside the shipping world, the Leyland Line did not suffer adversely from the *Californian*'s sudden notoriety, but remained one of the few bright stars in the IMM constellation. After the Great War, Leyland went through one of Morgan's "rationalizations," when IMM purchased all of the Line's outstanding common shares of stock. The Red Star and Dominion Lines were folded into Leyland, although for purposes of prestige their names were retained. The 1920s proved to be profitable for the new company, but only marginally so, and when the economic collapse of 1929 hit, Leyland found itself in the same position as White Star—its ships were aging and wearing out, while there was no money for new construction. The result was inevitable: by 1935 the last of Leyland's assets were sold off, and the company's house flag was hauled down for the last time.

The *Californian* was not part of that decline, however. She continued to ply her trade between New Orleans, Boston, and Liverpool, returning to obscurity. She remained on her transatlantic run when the Great War erupted in the autumn of 1914, finally being transferred to the Mediterranean in the summer of 1915, where she carried supplies to the Aegean Sea in support of the Allied landings at Gallipoli.

About 7:45 a.m. on November 9, 1915, the *Californian* was steaming off Cape Matapan, near the Greek coast, on her way from Saloniki and Marseilles. Serving at this time as a troopship carrying

British soldiers to Gallipoli, there was no way for her officers or crew to know that she was being stalked by a German U-boat. Luckily, there were no troops aboard her this particular morning. Without any warning a torpedo struck her starboard side, but the damage seemed manageable, and a French torpedo boat that had been escorting the *Californian* took her in tow. The U-boat was not to be denied, however, and continued to shadow the *Californian*. When, after a few hours, the tow line parted, and while the two crews were working to make fast a second line, another torpedo hit the ship. This time she began taking on water fast, and the crew was forced to abandon ship, which then quickly sank. Two stokers were scalded by escaping steam, the only injuries suffered in the attack. Her wreck has never been found, and given that it lies in more than 5,000 feet of water, it most likely never will be.

Cyril Evans would rise far above the humble station he held as a wireless operator on April 15, 1912. His somewhat erratic behavior during that morning—which can be excused in no small part by his youth and inexperience—would give way to a mature, conscientious operator in the years to come. His professional status and the recognition of his skills were rightly unaffected by the events of that morning. He spent his entire working life with the Marconi Company, with the exception of his military service in *both* World Wars, eventually becoming one of the firm's Managing Engineers. He died suddenly and unexpectedly of a heart attack in June 1959 at age 67.

Apprentice James Gibson eventually left the Leyland line to join Cunard, serving aboard the *Carmania* and the *Scythia*. He ultimately earned his Master's Certificate, and reached the rank of Second Mate with the Holt Line, sailing along the West African coast. A veteran of the Second World War, Gibson died in 1963.

Third Officer Charles Groves had a varied and colorful career after his stint on the *Californian*. Coming through the British Inquiry untainted by association with Stanley Lord, he went on to earn his Master's and Extra Master's tickets. Always an adventurous soul, Groves volunteered for the Royal Navy's submarine service during the First World War. After the Armistice he joined the Sheaf Line, and eventually became their Marine Superintendent, based at Newcastle upon Tyne.

In 1925, thirteen years after the *Titanic* disaster, Groves had an extraordinary encounter. A captain himself by this time, master of the SS *Mount Sheaf*, Groves came face to face with Stanley Lord in Rose Bay, Australia. Lord, who was with the firm Lawther Latta at the time, had just brought in his ship, and hailed the harbor launch which was already carrying Groves. Apparently, as Groves told the story (Lord never made mention of it), neither man immediately recognized the other, and it wasn't until the next day that Groves realized who he had encountered. While walking through the town with a friend, Groves happened upon Lord again, and when Groves' companion remarked, "Are you Lord, of the *Californian*?" Lord snapped back, "Well, what of it?" In the awkward silence that inevitably ensued, the three men parted ways and no further mention was made of the incident. After the Second World War, Groves frequently served as an assessor on Board of Trade Inquiries, much like the one he had sat before in 1912. He became noted for his fairness and objectivity; among the twenty-five cases he oversaw, his most famous case was the inquiry into the loss of the *Princess Victoria* in 1953. He died in September 1961.

The second-greatest personal enigma of the early morning hours of April 15, 1912, Second Officer Herbert Stone all but vanished into obscurity after the Board of Trade inquiry. He never attained a command of his own, as far as is known, and poor health forced him to retire from the sea in 1933. He took a position as a storeman in Liverpool, where he continued to work for the remainder of his life. While it's said that he never mentioned the "*Californian* incident" to his son, his widow would later say he once confided to her that he was sure that what he had seen that night in 1912 were distress rockets, but that he was too fearful of Captain Lord to press the issue with him. There would be no happy ending for Herbert Stone, as he died of a brain hemorrhage in September 1959 on his way to work. Apparently there was some foundation for the insecurity he felt during the Board of Trade investigation; managing money was never his strong point, and he left his wife and son penniless.

Not the enigma Stone was, Chief Officer George Stewart achieved some professional success at sea following the events of 1912. Remaining with Leyland, he was promoted to captain and given ships of his own to command after the First World War. He retired when the line was dissolved in 1935. When war again came to Great Britain in the autumn of 1940, the shortage of qualified officers and men for the merchant marine was critical, and Stewart answered a call to return to service. In March, 1940, at the age of 62, he was the Third Officer on the cargo steamer *Barnhill*. On March 20, just off the Isle of Wight in the English Channel, the *Barnhill* was caught up in a swift and skillful attack by the German Luftwaffe. Within minutes the Nazi fighters and bombers had left the ship a flaming wreck, yet only five of the *Barnhill*'s crew were killed. Among them, though, was George Frederick Stewart; his body was never found.

Captain Stanley Lord had his appointment as master of the *Californian* suspended by the Leyland Line within days of his appearance before the Board of Trade Inquiry. On August 13, 1912, he received a letter from Leyland's board of directors, informing him that he would not be given another ship from Leyland. A second letter a few days later informed him that his services were no longer required in any capacity by the Leyland Line. Within the formal and somewhat stylized language of the day, he had been sacked.

Nearly a year would pass before Lord would find another berth as master; it can readily be imagined how awkward the applications and interviews must have been. In the summer of 1913, Lord was taken on as captain by the shipping firm of Lawther Latta, which specialized in supplying nitrates to fertilizer and munitions manufacturers. He remained with them until his retirement in 1927 at the age of 50. Though Lord's supporters would make much of his long tenure with Lawther, hailing it as proof of his competence and an implicit endorsement of his innocence of any wrongdoing the night of April 14–15, 1912, the truth is a good deal more prosaic. "Nitrates" is a polite euphemism for the reality of the cargoes carried by Lawther Latta vessels. Stanley Lord spent the last fifteen years of his career commanding ships hauling cargoes of nitrogen-rich bird droppings collected on the islands off the coast of Chile to various ports in the British Empire. It was honest, honorable, and even necessary work, to be sure; nevertheless, in terms of professional prestige, it was the very bottom of the ladder, a far, sad comedown for a man who had once aspired to the most prestigious commands on the North Atlantic.

Not much is known about Lord's experiences during those years, aside from his awkward encounter with Groves in 1925. Certainly he never again did anything to come to the attention of the British or American public. He made a few half-hearted attempts during his retirement to have his case reopened, but they came to nothing. It wasn't until four years before his death that his protests of innocence finally received some attention. In 1955, an American author named Walter Lord (no relation to Stanley Lord) published a book called *A Night to Remember,* which introduced a whole new generation to the *Titanic* disaster, and in it portrayed Captain Lord as being deliberately detached and uncaring when told by his officers about the ship nearby firing white rockets.

When the book was made into a movie of the same name in 1957, Stanley Lord concluded that he was being publicly maligned, and decided once more to attempt to clear his name. So it was that one morning in early 1958 he walked into the offices of the Mercantile Marine Service Association in Liverpool and thunderously announced, "I am Lord of the *Californian* and I have come to clear my name!" Not surprisingly perhaps, no one in the office knew who he was or had the least idea of what he meant, but eventually the association's general secretary, Leslie Harrison, took up the case, more for political reasons than for any genuine belief that the Board of Trade's forty-five year old report would be overturned.

Harrison petitioned the Board of Trade on Lord's behalf, asking that the case be reopened, but more than seven years would go by before the Board responded, rejecting his petition. In 1965, Peter Padfield, a professional maritime historian of enviable reputation, published a book defending Lord, *The Titanic and the Californian.* While it seemed to demonstrate that the two ships had been as much as thirty miles apart on April 15, 1912, Padfield's work suffered from two handicaps: he apparently never realized that Stanley Lord had altered the *Californian*'s logbook, and so accepted everything in it, as well as everything Lord himself said in his defense, as truthful; and he lacked the mass of information which would gradually come to light over the next three decades.

In the meantime, Leslie Harrison had taken a personal affront to the Board of Trade's rejection of his petition, and filed another, which was likewise rejected in 1968. Believing that his own credibility was at stake, Harrison then became even more determined to clear Lord's name. The daughter of one *Titanic* survivor once described him as "a fanatical person" for the way he pressured her father to recant his account of the sinking in 1912, which contained recollections damaging to Lord. In 1986, Harrison published *A Titanic Myth: The Californian Incident*, in which he attempted to show that the whole controversy had been manufactured by the Board of Trade to hide its own culpability for the loss of life on the *Titanic*, and trotted out all of the old arguments which supposedly exonerated Stanley Lord. Unfortunately for his work and his reputation (Harrison himself died in 1996), he found it necessary to resort to fabricating certain "facts" while selectively suppressing other, contradictory evidence, in order to make his case.

In 1992, the British government's Marine Accident Investigation Branch (MAIB), under pressure from Harrison, who was capitalizing on the recent discovery of the wreck of the *Titanic* by loudly claiming that it offered proof that the *Californian* was even father from the Titanic than earlier claimed, opened what it termed the "Reappraisal of Evidence Relating to the SS *Californian*." Despite the fact that the Board seemed favorably inclined toward Lord when it convened, the conclusions of the report were a devastating blow to Harrison and Lord's supporters. The only area of contention within the report was when the two leading investigators disagreed over the distance which separated the *Californian* and the *Titanic*. Deputy Chief Inspector James De Coverly believed the two ships were 17 to 20 miles apart, while Master Mariner Thomas Barnett, whose professional qualifications were superior to De Coverly's, maintained that only 5 to 7 miles separated the Titanic from the Californian. For political reasons, De Coverly's figure was used in the final report.

Most critically, however, the Board concluded unanimously that the *Titanic*'s rockets were seen from the *Californian*, that they should have been interpreted as distress signals, and that further action should have been taken by the *Californian*'s officers as soon as multiple rockets had been sighted. While a certain emphasis was placed on Second Officer Stone's actions and inactions, the report strongly emphasized the point that the ship's master bore the ultimate responsibility for what happened aboard his vessel, and that Lord had failed to fulfill his obligations as the *Californian*'s captain. Eighty years after both the American and British inquiries had come to the same conclusion, an inquest constituted for the sole purpose of exonerating Stanley Lord had condemned him anew.

The thirty-five years Lord spent in retirement were far from uncomfortable, his family's finances and his own investments providing well for him during those years. Lord appears to have put the sea well behind him when he retired; there is no record of him ever again seeking a berth after he left Lawther Latta. Perhaps not surprisingly, during the Second World War, when Great Britain's shortage of qualified merchant marine officers and masters was approaching critical proportions, and despite the fact that many of his contemporaries answered the call to the colors and voluntarily came out of retirement to serve, Stanley Lord remained safely ashore. He died of kidney disease in 1962 at the age of eighty-five, at last safely beyond the reach of his critics as well as the solace of his supporters.

Of all the incredible events of that incredible night, April 14–15, 1912, the most startling must be the contrast in conduct between Captains Rostron and Lord, found in their reactions the moment each of them was informed that a ship nearby was signaling distress. When told of the *Titanic*'s distress call, Rostron acted immediately and decisively. Even though he knew he might be taking his ship into peril, he believed that he did not have the luxury of remaining in relative safety and security while hundreds or even thousands of others might be in danger of losing their lives. In short, he was the best possible kind of man to have in command of the *Carpathia* in the early morning hours of April 15, 1912.

Stanley Lord's reaction upon being informed of a ship nearby firing white rockets, on the other hand, suddenly revealed the sociopath that had long been lurking beneath his apparently urbane and civilized exterior, as he manipulated the ambiguities of the circumstances to allow him to avoid taking any decisive action until such a time as the danger to himself was minimal. Lord was indeed the worst possible sort of individual to be the master of the *Californian* at precisely the time when that person would be faced with the greatest moral and professional challenge of his life.

For when all is said and done, at issue when deciding the question of Stanley Lord's responsibility—and whether or not he abandoned that responsibility—in the early morning of April 15, 1912, is not whether Lord refused to go to the aid of the stricken *Titanic*, but rather why did he refuse to go to the aid of people who were so clearly in distress? It was in exactly these terms that Lord himself would define the debate over his conduct: to his dying day he maintained that he was innocent of abandoning the passengers and crew of the *Titanic* to their fate, for his ship was too far away to even see the sinking liner, let alone reach her in time to be of any help. And yet that carefully crafted position never acknowledged—and indeed seemed to dodge as effectively as Lord did the decision to wake Cyril Evans in the crucial hours of April 15, 1912—that there was an even deeper, more fundamental moral and legal obligation which Lord abandoned: the obligation to go to the assistance of *whomever* was signalling distress. Stanley Lord consciously, callously chose to let people die rather than run even the slightest risk to his ship and himself.

No amount of manipulation of ships' positions, questions of visibility, curvature of the earth, "hyper-refraction," numbers of rockets fired, navigational errors, "mystery ships," nor any tricks of verbal legerdemain or legalistic obscurantism, can alter that one simple fact. *Stanley Lord chose to do nothing*. Precisely why has been a riddle for more than nine decades; only now can the underlying flaw in his character, the defect of his personality, be fully explained, even if it can never be fully understood.

It was the great tragedy of his life that Stanley Lord was the man on the bridge of the *Californian* on April 15, 1912. In contrast, it was literally salvation for those hundreds of people in a score of lifeboats bobbing about on an open sea that Arthur Rostron stood on the bridge of the *Carpathia* during those same hours. Ultimately the final story of the "night to remember," is the story of "the other side of the night," the story of these two men, one who refused to hesitate in answering the call for help, and the other who pretended he never heard it.

Appendix I

The Resolution Authorizing the Senate Investigation into the Loss of RMS *Titanic*

IN THE SENATE OF THE UNITED STATES,

April 17, 1912

Resolved, That the Committee on Commerce, or a subcommittee thereof, is hereby authorized and directed to investigate the causes leading to the wreck of the White Star liner Titanic, with its attendant loss of life so shocking to the civilized world.

Resolved further, That said committee or a subcommittee thereof is hereby empowered to summon witnesses, send for persons and papers, to administer oaths, and to take such testimony as may be necessary to determine the responsibility therefor, with a view to such legislation as may be necessary to prevent, as far as possible, any repetition of such a disaster.

Resolved further, That the committee shall inquire particularly into the number of lifeboats, rafts, and life preservers, and other equipment for the protection of the passengers and crew; the number of persons aboard the Titanic, whether passenger or crew, and whether adequate inspections were made of such vessel, in view of the large number of American passengers travelling over a route commonly regarded as dangerous from icebergs; and whether it is feasible for Congress to take steps looking to an international agreement to secure the protection of sea traffic, including regulation of the size of ships and designation of routes.

Resolved further, That in the report of said committee it shall recommend such legislation as it shall deem expedient; and the expenses incurred by this investigation shall be paid from the contingent fund of the Senate upon vouchers to be approved by the chairman of said committee.

Attest: CHARLES C. BENNETT,
Secretary.
By: H. M. ROSE,
Assistant Secretary.

Appendix II

The Order for the Board of Trade Inquiry and the Questions to be Investigated

ORDER FOR FORMAL INVESTIGATION.

Whereas, on or about the 14th day of April, 1912, the British Steamship 'Titanic', of Liverpool, Official Number 131,482, struck ice in or near latitude 41° 46' N., longitude 50° 14' W., North Atlantic Ocean, and on the following day foundered, and loss of life thereby ensued or occurred. And whereas a shipping casualty has occurred, and the Board of Trade have requested a Wreck Commissioner appointed under this Act to hold a Formal Investigation into the said shipping casualty, and he has consented to do so.

Now the Board of Trade, in pursuance of the powers vested in them by Section 466 of the Merchant Shipping Act, 1894, do hereby direct that the Formal Investigation shall be held into the said shipping casualty in the Scottish Hall, Buckingham Gate, London, S.W.

Annexed hereto is a Statement of the Case upon which the said Formal Investigation has been ordered.

Dated this 30th day of April, 1912.

Walter J. Howell.

An Assistant Secretary to the Board of Trade.

The British Steamship "Titanic," of the port of Liverpool, Official Number 131,428.

STATEMENT OF CASE.

The following is a Statement of the Case on which a Formal Investigation is ordered:

The above named ship left Queenstown for New York on or about the 11ᵗʰ day of April, 1912, with a crew of about 892 hands all told, and about 1,316 passengers.

On the night of Sunday the 14th day of April, 1912, the vessel struck ice in or near latitude 41° 46' N., longitude 50° 14' W., North Atlantic Ocean, and at about 2 a.m. on the following day foundered in about the same locality, and loss of life thereby ensued or occurred.

Dated this 30ᵗʰ day of April, 1912.

> Walter J. Howell
> An Assistant Secretary to the Board of Trade.

S. S. "TITANIC."

1. When the "Titanic" left Queenstown on or about 11th April last: -
   (*a.*) What was the total number of persons employed in any capacity on board her, and what were their respective ratings?
   (*b.*) What was the total number of her passengers, distinguishing sexes and classes, and discriminating between adults and children?

2. Before leaving Queenstown on or about 11th April last did the "Titanic" comply with the requirements of the Merchant Shipping Acts, 1894-1906, and the Rules and Regulations made thereunder with regard to the safety and otherwise of passenger steamers and emigrant ships.

3. In the actual design and construction of the "Titanic" what special provisions were made for the safety of the vessel and the lives of those on board in the event of collisions and other casualties?

4. Was the "Titanic" sufficiently and efficiently officered and manned? Were the watches of the officers usual and proper? Was the Titanic supplied with proper charts?

5. What was the number of boats of any kind on board the "Titanic"? Were the arrangements for manning and launching the boats on board the "Titanic" in case of emergency proper and sufficient? Had a boat drill been held on board, and, if so, when? What was the carrying capacity of the respective boats?

6. What installations for receiving and transmitting messages by wireless telegraphy were on board the "Titanic"? How many operators were employed on working such installations? Were the installations in good and effective working order, and were the number of operators sufficient to enable messages to be received and transmitted continuously by day and night?

7. At or prior to the sailing of the "Titanic" what, if any, instructions as to navigation were given to the Master or known by him to apply to her voyage? Were such instructions, if any, safe, proper and adequate, having regard to the time of year and dangers likely to be encountered during the voyage?

8. What was in fact the track taken by the "Titanic" in crossing the Atlantic Ocean? Did she keep to the track usually followed by liners on voyages from the United Kingdom to New York in the month of April? Are such tracks safe tracks at that time of year? Had the Master any, and, if so, what discretion as regards the track to be taken?

9. After leaving Queenstown on or about the 11ᵗʰ April last, did information reach the "Titanic" by wireless messages or otherwise by signals, of the existence of ice in certain latitudes? If so, what were such messages or signals and when were they received, and in what position or positions was the ice reported to be, and was the ice reported in or near the track actually being followed by the "Titanic"? Was her course altered in consequence of receiving such information, and, if so, in what way? What replies to such messages or signals did the "Titanic" send and at what times?

10. If at the times referred to in the last preceding question or later the "Titanic" was warned of or had reason to suppose she would encounter ice, at what time might she have reasonably expected to encounter it? Was a good and proper look-out for ice kept on board? Were any, and,

if so, what directions given to vary the speed - if so, were they carried out?

11. Were binoculars provided for and used by the look-out men? Is the use of them necessary or usual in such circumstances? Had the "Titanic" the means of throwing searchlights around her? If so, did she make use of them to discover ice? Should searchlights have been provided and used?

12. What other precautions were taken by the "Titanic" in anticipation of meeting ice? Were they such as are usually adopted by vessels being navigated in waters where ice may be expected to be encountered?

13. Was ice seen and reported by anybody on board the "Titanic" before the casualty occurred? If so, what measures were taken by the officer on watch to avoid it? Were they proper measures and were they promptly taken?

14. What was the speed of the "Titanic" shortly before and at the moment of the casualty? Was such speed excessive under the circumstances?

15. What was the nature of the casualty which happened to the "Titanic" at or about 11.45 p.m. on the 14th April last? In what latitude and longitude did the casualty occur?

16. What steps were taken immediately on the happening of the casualty? How long after the casualty was its seriousness realised by those in charge of the vessel? What steps were then taken? What endeavours were made to save the lives of those on board and to prevent the vessel from sinking?

17. Was proper discipline maintained on board after the casualty occurred?

18. What messages for assistance were sent by the "Titanic" after the casualty and at what times respectively? What messages were received by her in response and at what times respectively? By what vessels were the messages that were sent by the "Titanic" received, and from what

vessels did she receive answers? What vessels other than the "Titanic" sent or received the messages at or shortly after the casualty in connection with such casualty? What were the vessels that sent or received such messages? Were any vessels prevented from going to the assistance of the "Titanic" or her boats owing to messages received from the "Titanic" or owing to any erroneous messages being sent or received? In regard to such erroneous messages, from what vessels were they sent and by what vessels were they received and at what times respectively?

19. Was the apparatus for lowering the boats on the "Titanic" at the time of the casualty in good working order? Were the boats swung out, filled, lowered, or otherwise put into the water and got away under proper superintendence? Were the boats sent away in seaworthy condition and properly manned, equipped and provisioned? Did the boats, whether those under davits or otherwise, prove to be efficient and serviceable for the purpose of saving life?

20. What was the number of (a.) passengers, (b.) crew taken away in each boat on leaving the vessel? How was this number made up having regard to:
  1. Sex.
  2. Class.
  3. Rating?
How many were children and how many adults? Did each boat carry its full load and, if not, why not?

21. How many persons on board the "Titanic" at the time of the casualty were ultimately rescued, and by what means? How many lost their lives? Of those rescued how many have since died? What was the number of passengers, distinguishing between men and women and adults and children of the 1st, 2nd, and 3rd classes respectively who were saved? What was the number of the crew, discriminating their ratings and sex, that were saved? What is the proportion which each of these numbers bears to the corresponding total number on board immediately before the casualty? What reason is there for the disproportion, if any?

22. What happened to the vessel from the happening of the casualty until she foundered?

23. Where and at what time did the "Titanic" founder?

24. What was the cause of the loss of the "Titanic," and of the loss of life which thereby ensued or occurred? Was the construction of the vessel and its arrangements such as to make it difficult for any class of passenger or any portion of the crew to take full advantage of any the existing provisions for safety?

25. When the "Titanic" left Queenstown on or about 11ᵗʰ April last was she properly constructed and adequately equipped as a passenger steamer and emigrant ship for the Atlantic service?

26. The Court is invited to report upon the Rules and Regulations made under the Merchant Shipping Acts, 1894 -1906, and the administration of those Acts, and of such Rules and Regulations, so far as the consideration thereof is material to this casualty, and to make any recommendations or suggestions that it may think fit, having regard to the circumstances of the casualty with a view to promoting the safety of vessels and persons at sea.

Appendix III

Extract from the
British Wreck Commissioner's
Inquiry Report

(Note: numbers in parentheses in the text cite specific questions from the full transcript.)

CIRCUMSTANCES IN CONNECTION WITH THE
SS CALIFORNIAN

It is here necessary to consider the circumstances relating to the s.s. "Californian."

On the 14th of April, the s.s. "Californian" of the Leyland line, Mr. Stanley Lord, Master, was on her passage from London, which port she left on April 5th, to Boston, U.S., were she subsequently arrived on April 19th. She was a vessel of 6,223 tons gross and 4,038 net. Her full speed was 12 1/2 to 13 knots. She had a passenger certificate, but was not carrying any passengers at the time. She belonged to the International Mercantile Marine Company, the owners of the "Titanic."

At 7.30 p.m., ship's time, on 14th April, a wireless message was sent from this ship to the "Antillian." (Evans, 8941, 8943)

"To Captain, 'Antillian,' 6.30 p.m., apparent ship's time, lat. 42° 3' N., long. 49° 9' W. Three large bergs, 5 miles to southward of us. Regards.—Lord."

The message was intercepted by the "Titanic," and when the Marconi operator (Evans) of the "Californian" offered this ice report to the Marconi operator of the "Titanic," shortly after 7.30 p.m., the latter replied, "It is all right. I heard you sending it to the 'Antillian,' and I have got it." (8972) (Lord, 6710)

The "Californian" proceeded on her course S. 89° W. true until 10.20 p.m. ship's time, when she was obliged to stop and reverse engines because she was running into field ice, which stretched as far as could then be seen to the northward and southward.

The Master told the Court that he made her position at that time to be 42E 5' N., 57E 7' W. (6704) This position is recorded in the log book, which was written up from the scrap log book by the Chief Officer. The scrap log is destroyed. It is a position about 19 miles N. by E. of the position of the "Titanic" when she foundered, and is said to have been fixed by dead reckoning and verified by observations. I am satisfied that this position is not accurate. The Master "twisted her head" to E.N.E. by the compass and she remained approximately stationary until 5.15 a.m. on the following morning. The ship was slowly swinging round to starboard during the night. (6713) (Groves, 8249)

At about 11 p.m. a steamer's light was seen approaching from the eastward. The Master went to Evans' room and asked, "What ships he had." The latter replied: "I think the 'Titanic' is near us. I have got her." (Evans, 8962, 8988) The Master said: "You had better advise the 'Titanic' we are stopped and surrounded by ice." This Evans did, calling up the "Titanic" and sending: "We are stopped and surrounded by ice." (8993) The "Titanic" replied: "Keep out." The "Titanic" was in communication with Cape Race, which station was then sending messages to her. (8994) The reason why the "Titanic" answered, "Keep out," (9004) was that her Marconi operator could not hear what Cape Race was saying, as from her proximity, the message from the "Californian" was much stronger than any message being taken in by the "Titanic" from Cape Race, which was much further off. (9022) Evans heard the "Titanic" continuing to communicate with Cape Race up to the time he turned in at 11.30 p.m.

The Master of the "Californian" states that when observing the approaching steamer as she got nearer, he saw more lights, a few deck lights, and also her green side light. He considered that at 11 o'clock she was approximately six or seven miles away, and at some time between 11 and 11.30, he first saw her green light, she was then about 5 miles off. (Lord, 6761) He noticed then about 11.30 she stopped. In his opinion this steamer was of about the same size as the "Californian"; a medium-sized steamer, "something like ourselves." (6752)

From the evidence of Mr. Groves, third officer of the "Californian," who was the officer of the first watch, it would appear that the Master wasnot actually on the bridge when the steamer was sighted.

Mr. Groves made out two masthead lights; the steamer was changing her bearing slowly as she got closer, (Groves, 8147) and as she approached he went to the chart room and reported this to the Master; he added, "she is evidently a passenger steamer." (8174) In fact, Mr. Groves never appears to have had any doubt on this subject: In answer to a question during his examination, "Had she much light?" he said, "Yes, a lot of light. There was absolutely no doubt of her being a passenger steamer, at least in my mind." (8178)

Gill, the assistant donkeyman of the "Californian," who was on deck at midnight said, referring to this steamer: "It could not have been anything but a passenger boat, she was to large." (Gill, 18136)

By the evidence Mr. Groves, the Master, in reply to his report, said: "Call her up on the Morse lamp, and see if you can get any answer." This he proceeded to do. The Master came up and joined him on the bridge and remarked: "That does not look like a passenger steamer." (Groves, 8197) Mr. Groves replied "It is, sir. When she stopped, her lights seemed to go out, and I suppose they have been put out for the night." (8203) Mr. Groves states that these lights went out at 11.40, and remembers that time because "one bell was struck to call the middle watch." (8217) The Master did not join him on the bridge until shortly afterwards, and consequently after the steamer had stopped.

In his examination Mr. Groves admitted that if this steamer's head was turning to port after she stopped, it might account for the diminution of lights, by many of them being shut out. Her steaming lights were still visible and also her port side light. (8228)

The Captain only remained upon the bridge for a few minutes. (8241) In his evidence he stated that Mr. Groves had made no observations to him about the steamer's deck lights going out. (Lord, 6866) Mr. Groves' Morse signalling appears to have been ineffectual (although at one moment he thought he was being answered), and he gave it up. He remained on the bridge until relieved by Mr. Stone, the second officer, just after midnight. In turning the "Californian" over to him, he pointed out the steamer and said: "she has been stopped since 11.40; she is a passenger steamer. At about the moment she stopped she put her lights out." (Stone, 7810) When Mr. Groves was in the witness-box the following questions were put to him by me: -

"Speaking as an experienced seaman and knowing what you do know now, do you think that steamer that you know was throwing up rockets, and that you say was a passenger steamer, was the 'Titanic'? - Do I think it? Yes? - From what I have heard subsequently? Yes? - Most decidedly I do, but I do not put myself as being an experienced man. But that is your opinion as far as your experience goes? - Yes, it is, my Lord." (Groves, 8441)

Mr. Stone states that the Master, who was also up (but apparently not on the bridge), pointed out the steamer to him with instructions to tell him if her bearings altered or if she got any closer; he also stated that Mr. Groves had called her up on the Morse lamp and had received no reply. (Stone, 7815)

Mr. Stone had with him during the middle watch an apprentice named Gibson, whose attention was first drawn to the steamer's lights at about 12.20 a.m. (Gibson, 7424) He could see a masthead light, her red light (with glasses) and a "glare of white lights on her after deck." He first thought her masthead light was flickering and next thought it was a Morse light, "calling us up." (7443) He replied, but could not get into communication, and finally came to the conclusion that it was, as he had first supposed, the masthead light flickering. Some time after 12.30 a.m., Gill, the donkeyman, states that he saw two rockets fired from the ship which he had been observing, (Gill, 18156-61) and about 1.10 a.m., Mr. Stone reported to the Captain by voice pipe, they he had seen five white rockets from the direction of the steamer. (Stone, 7870) He states that the Master answered, "Are they Company's signals?" and that he replied, "I do not know, but they appear to me to be white rockets." The Master told him to "go on Morsing," and, when he received any information, to send the apprentice down to him with it. (7879) Gibson states that Mr. Stone informed him that he had reported to the Master, and that the Master had said the steamer was to be called up by Morse light. (Gibson, 7479) This witness thinks the time was 12.55; he at once proceeded again to call the steamer up by Morse. He got no reply, but the vessel fired three more white rockets; these rockets were also seen by Mr. Stone.

Both Mr. Stone and the apprentice kept the steamer under observation, looking at her from time to time with their glasses. Between 1 o'clock and 1.40 some conversation passed between them. Mr. Stone remarked to Gibson: "Look at her now, she looks very queer out of water, her lights look queer." (7515) He also is said by Gibson to have remarked, "A ship is not going to fire rockets at sea for nothing;" (7529) and admits himself that he may possibly have used that expression. (Stone, 7894)

Mr. Stone states that he saw the last of the rockets fired at about 1.40, and after watching the steamer for some twenty minutes more he sent Gibson down to the Master.

"I told Gibson to go down to the Master, and be sure to wake him, and tell him that altogether we had seen eight of these white lights like white rockets in the direction of this other steamer; that this steamer was disappearing in the southwest, that we had called her up repeatedly on the Morse lamp and received no information whatsoever."

Gibson states that he went down to the chart room and told the Master; that the Master asked him if all the rockets were white, and also asked him the time. (Gibson, 7553) Gibson stated that at this time the Master was awake. It was five minutes past two, and Gibson returned to the bridge to Mr. Stone and reported. They both continued to keep the ship under observation until she disappeared. Mr. Stone describes this as "A gradual disappearing of all her lights, which would be perfectly natural with a ship steaming away from us."

At about 2.40 a.m. Mr. Stone again called up the Master by voice pipe and told him that the ship from which he had seen the rockets come had disappeared bearing SW. 1/2 W., (Stone, 7976) the last he had seen of the light; and the Master again asked him if he was certain there was no colour in the lights. "I again assured him they were all white, just white rockets." (7999) There is considerable discrepancy between the evidence of Mr. Stone and that of the Master. The latter states that he went to the voice pipe at about 1.15, but was told then of a white rocket (not five white rockets). (Lord, 6790) Moreover, between 1.30 and 4.30, when he was called by the chief officer (Mr. Stewart), he had no recollection of anything being reported to him at all, although he remembered Gibson opening and closing the chart room door. (6859)

Mr. Stewart relieved Mr. Stone at 4 a.m. (Stewart, 8571) The latter told him he had seen a ship four or five miles off when he went on deck at 12 o'clock, and 1 o'clock he had seen some white rockets, and that the moment the ship started firing them she started to steam away. (8582) Just at this time (about 4 a.m.) a steamer came into sight with two white masthead lights and a few lights amidships. He asked Mr. Stone whether he thought this was the steamer which had fired rockets, and Mr. Stone said he did not think it was. At 4.30 he called the Master and informed him that Mr. Stone had told him he had seen rockets in the middle watch. (8615) The Master said, "Yes, I know, he has been telling me." (8619) The Master came at once on to the bridge, and apparently took the fresh steamer for the one which had fired rockets, (8632) and said, "She looks all right; she is not making any signals now." This mistake was not corrected. He, however, had the wireless operator called.

At about 6 a.m. Captain Lord heard from the "Virginian" that the "'Titanic' had struck a berg, passengers in boats, ship sinking"; and he at once started through the field ice at full speed for the position given. (Lord, 7002)

Captain Lord stated that about 7.30 a.m. he passed the "Mount Temple," (7014) stopped, and that she was in the vicinity of the position given him as where the "Titanic" had collided (lat. 41° 46' N.; long. 50° 14' W.). (7026) He saw no wreckage there, but did later on near the "Carpathia," which ship he closed soon afterwards, and he stated that the position where he subsequently left this wreckage was 41° 33' N.; 50° 1' W. It is said in the evidence of Mr. Stewart that the position of the "Californian" was verified by stellar observations at 7.30 p.m. on the Sunday evening, and that he verified the Captain's position given when the ship stopped (42° 5' N.; 50° 7' W.) as accurate on the next day. The position in which the wreckage was said to have been seen on the Monday morning was verified by sights taken on that morning.

All the officers are stated to have taken sights, and Mr. Stewart in his evidence remarks that they all agreed. (Stewart, 8820) If it is admitted that these positions were correct, then it follows that the "Titanic's" position as given by that ship when making the C.Q.D. signal was approximately S. 16° W. (true), 19 miles from the "Californian"; and further that the position in which the "Californian" was stopped during the night, was thirty miles away from where the wreckage was seen by her in the morning, or that the wreckage had drifted 11 miles in a little more than five hours.

There are contradictions and inconsistencies in the story as told by the different witnesses. But the truth of the matter is plain. (7020) The "Titanic" collided with the berg 11.40. The vessel seen by the "Californian" stopped at this time. The rockets sent up from the "Titanic" were distress signals. The "Californian" saw distress signals. The number sent up by the "Titanic" was about eight. The "Californian" saw eight. The time over which the rockets from the "Titanic" were sent up was from about 12.45 to 1.45 o'clock. It was about this time that the "Californian" saw the rockets. At 2.40 Mr. Stone called to the Master that the ship from which he'd seen the rockets had disappeared.

At 2.20 a.m. the "Titanic" had foundered. It was suggested that the rockets seen by the "Californian" were from some other ship, not the "Titanic." But no other ship to fit this theory has ever been heard of.

These circumstances convince me that the ship seen by the "Californian" was the "Titanic," and if so, according to Captain Lord, the two vessels were about five miles apart at the time of the disaster. The evidence from the "Titanic" corroborates this estimate, but I am advised that the distance was probably greater, though not more than eight to ten miles. The ice by which the "Californian" was surrounded was loose ice extending for a distance of not more than two or three miles in the direction of the "Titanic." The night was clear and the sea was smooth. When she first saw the rockets the "Californian" could have pushed through the ice to the open water without any serious risk and so have come to the assistance of the "Titanic." Had she done so she might have saved many if not all of the lives that were lost.

AUTHOR'S NOTE

It has become something of a cliché for an author to acknowledge in some form that while it's his or her name alone which appears on the cover of a book, the writing process is a far from solitary undertaking. Well, count me in the ranks of those who are guilty of doing so—unashamedly so, for although such a sentiment is indeed a cliché, that doesn't make it any less true. Nor does it diminish in the least degree the efforts of those who provided me with assistance, support, resources or encouragement while I was writing *The Other Side of the Night*. And so I mean to offer my most profound thanks to all of them as best I can.

First and foremost, I have to acknowledge my undying gratitude to the late Walter Lord, author of *A Night to Remember*, the book that has introduced the *Titanic* story to so many millions of people over the past half-century, myself among them. He became known—and rightly so—as "the dean of *Titanic* historians;" there are few, if any, people who could match his knowledge not only of the ship and the disaster, but also of the humanity involved. I'm willing to submit that while there may be some who may possess a more intimate technical knowledge of the *Titanic*, no one has matched his understanding of the men and women who built her, crewed her, sailed in her.

It was this genuine affection for people that most impressed me when I first became acquainted with Walter Lord, more than two decades ago. I was just beginning work on my own book about the *Titanic*, "Unsinkable," and Walter was particularly gracious in his readiness to make his own resource material available to me. As time passed and our acquaintance grew into a more of a friendship—albeit a long-distance one, as I lived in Florida and he in New York—he began to take a closer interest in my work, offering his encouragement as often as he did his knowledge. I was at once humbled yet immensely proud when he reviewed *"Unsinkable"* as it went to press and declared it "A masterful retelling of the *Titanic* story."

The pinnacle of our relationship came on a Wednesday afternoon in April 1998, as I sat in the living room of his New York apartment, and described to him how I had begun receiving letters and emails from children ten, eleven, twelve years old, telling me how excited they were to read about the *Titanic* in *"Unsinkable."* A huge grin spread across his face as I recounted that I had been in that same age group when I first read *A Night to Remember*, and discovered the *Titanic* story for myself, triggering a life-long fascination. "Well, Dan," he said, with a pleased tone in his voice, "that just makes you my successor." Few words spoken to me have ever meant so much.

Within another year, Walter's health began to fail, and as it did, hope faded for one last *Titanic* project that he had envisioned. In 1986 he had published a second book about the *Titanic*, *The Night Lives On*, in which he explored aspects of the disaster which were originally outside the scope or the knowledge of *A Night to Remember*. It was Walter's hope to combine them both, along with a considerable amount of new material, into a sort of *"Titanic* Omnibus," meant to be a near-definitive work on the subject, as far as such a thing was possible. (Walter readily acknowledged that no one would ever have the last word on the *Titanic*.) Alas, it was not to be, and Walter Lord died in May 2002.

But he had left me with a glimmering of an idea. I was not egotistical enough to believe that I could—or should—attempt the *"Titanic* Omnibus" project. But in one of our last conversations, Walter and I discussed how he had created a story arc in *A Night to Remember* and *The Night Lives On*. In the first book he had focused almost exclusively on the *Titanic*, shifting occasionally to the *Carpathia*, with only brief detours aboard the *Californian*. In the second book, he devoted considerably more attention to both the latter ships, though the primary focus was still the *Titanic*. Was it his intent, I wondered, to produce a third volume, where the emphasis was on the *Carpathia* and the *Californian*, with the *Titanic* providing the link between them? No, he said, he never had such an idea in mind, but there was some merit to it. We left it at that, and there the concept lay for more than five years.

Finally, in the autumn of 2004, I picked up the threads of the story again and began writing. It was never my intention to try to produce a "sequel" to *A Night to Remember* and *The Night Lives On*. What I wanted to tell this time was not another recounting of the disaster—I had already written about the *Titanic* herself in *"Unsinkable"*—but rather to focus on the rescue of the survivors and the aftermath: the two investigations and the consequences of the actions and inactions of the *Carpathia* and the *Californian*. I wanted to tell the story of that "night to remember" from an entirely new perspective—I wanted to tell the tale that was *The Other Side of the Night*.

It should come as no surprise then that many of the same people and institutions which made significant contributions to *"Unsinkable"* also played a part in the writing of *The Other Side of the Night*. The first place any United States citizen researching the *Titanic* should start is the Library of Congress. It not only holds the original transcript of the Senate Investigation, but there are literally hundreds of Titanic-related references in its collection, including the only surviving original copy of the ship's manifest. Other libraries where I did work and research include the Van Wylen Library, Hope College, Holland, Michigan; the libraries of the Grand Valley State University, Allendale, Michigan; the Public Library of Grand Rapids, Michigan; and the Broward County Library System, Fort Lauderdale, Florida.

Museums played a major part in my research, beginning with the Grand Rapids Public Museum, Grand Rapids, Michigan, which was a fountain of information on Senator Smith, as Grand Rapids was his hometown. The Mariners Museum of Newport News, Virginia, and the National Maritime Museum in Philadelphia, Pennsylvania, in the United States, and the National Maritime Museum in Greenwich, England, are repositories of excellent archival collections; also worth particular mention is the Maritime Museum of the Atlantic in Halifax, Nova Scotia, Canada. Also well worthy of note and mention are the Public Archives of Nova Scotia, also located in Halifax, where the staff is always ready to assist anyone who wants to learn more about the *Titanic*. Because many of the *Titanic*'s dead rest in Halifax cemeteries, the city has always held her memory in a special place.

The Ulster Folk and Transport Museum of Belfast, Northern Ireland, possesses a unique institutional knowledge of the men who designed and built the *Titanic*, of their times and their world, and can make those lives and times very, very real to a dedicated researcher. I want to make specific mention of the curator of maritime history, Mr. Michael McCaughan, who went out of his way to be helpful to me.

The city of Southampton has never entirely forgotten the grief caused by the terrible death toll among the crew. As a result, the Southampton City Heritage Centre has kept the legacy and memory of the crew and their families alive, and the community history manager, Mr. Donald Hyslop, never hesitated to assist me, whenever it was possible, in my efforts to tell their story.

The glory days of the great British shipyards have gone the way of the glory days of British shipbuilding, now just a thing of memory. That sadly includes Harland and Wolff in Belfast, where the *Titanic* and her sisters were built. The slipways where they were constructed, the vast Thompson Graving Dock where they fitted out, and the old Administration Building are about all that is left of the yard from 1912, when Harland and Wolff was the largest shipbuilder in the world. The shipyard itself is now an engineering firm, and it is very much in doubt if any ships will ever be built there again, despite the fact that the yard possesses the largest drydock in the United Kingdom. But the sense of the firm's history—along with a pride in it—is growing in Belfast, and much that might have been lost is now being preserved. What is priceless for an historian is the friendliness of the people of Belfast, and their willingness to share the stories of the fathers and grandfathers who built the great ships for the White Star Line. Whenever I'm in Belfast, I never feel as though I'm a visitor—it feels more like I've come home.

And an especial word of thanks to the British Public Records Office. It is there that the transcript of the Board of Trade Inquiry is held, along with those of the Parliamentary debates which followed it. I was a source of endless amusement to the staff there, as my late 20th Century "American English" was not up to the demands of early 20th Century "English English," particularly when it had been contorted by lawyers. Not to fear, the staff at the PRO were always willing to help out "the fellow from the colonies."

Where maritime issues were involved I relied very heavily on the advice and guidance of men who knew ships and the sea first hand, as a profession. First among them is Capt. Ronald Warwick, retired commodore of the Cunard Line, one time master of the *Queen Elizabeth 2* and the first captain of the *Queen Mary 2*. He was more than generous in sharing his insights and experiences in the pleasures, perils, and burdens of commanding a passenger liner on the North Atlantic. He has both my thanks and my admiration.

Another source of practical experience and advice was my father, Harold E. Butler, who passed away in 2002; as a young man he had served as a quartermaster with the United States Merchant Marine during the Second World War. As a consequence of his experience, he was able to provide me with a wealth of knowledge and insights into the details, technicalities, and, above all, the realities of the life of a sailor at sea. My debt to him, for a multitude of reasons, is boundless.

I'm also deeply grateful to Matthew McLean, a retired bosun from the British Merchant Marine. His intimate knowledge of life in the fo'c's'le of a British merchantman has been priceless, not in the least for his insights into the sometimes complex relationships between officers and crew aboard British ships.

Worth particular attention—and mention—are four individuals and their websites. They are: Dave Billnitzer, who maintains the site http://home.earthlink.net/~dnitzer/Titanic.html; William "Bill" Wormstedt, whose website can be found at http://home.att.net/~wormstedt/titanic; Dave Gittins, whose site URL is http://users.senet.com.au/~gittins/; and George Behe, whose site, "Titanic Tidbits," can be found at http://ourworld.compuserve.com/ homepages/Carpathia. If these four gentlemen are considered "amateurs," it is only because they don't make their living as historians. Their work is, collectively and individually, sterling and well worth taking the time to examine in detail.

In understanding and explaining the character of Stanley Lord, and in particular the nature of his personality, I'm deeply indebted to the clinical psychologists with whom I consulted and who, independently of each other, returned identical verdicts about Captain Lord's sociopathy. They are Dr. Dorothy Mihalyfi of Boca Raton, Florida; Dr. Marilyn Wyndham of Sacramento, California; Dr. Julian Edney, Dr. Jeffrey Hirsch, and J. Lee Brubaker, PhD., all of Los Angeles, California. I'm also indebted to Dr. Martha Stout, of Cape Ann, Massachusetts, and Dr. Robert D. Hare, of Vancouver, British Columbia, whose work added confirmation their colleagues' conclusions.

There were other individuals who gave of their time and expertise and deserve recognition. There are few experiences more gratifying to an author than to have an editor whose excitement about a project matches their own. My editor at Casemate, Steven Smith, is just such an individual: he was enthusiastic about this book from the time that the idea first came up in conversation. I want to thank him for his determination and effort in seeing it go into print. Likewise, my gratitude goes out to David Farnsworth, the publisher at Casemate, who came to share Steven's enthusiasm, and to Tara Lichterman, who, I believe, actually keeps Casemate up and running—at the very least, she kept me on track.

Thanks also to James and Denise Carlisle, of Belfast, Northern Ireland, not only for their hospitality, but also for Jim's reminiscences of his grandfather, Alexander Carlisle, who as a young man had worked on the *Titanic* at Harland and Wolff. A special word of acknowledgment is due to Captain Tony Crompton, retired Master Mariner, and Ilya McVey, an officer in the British Merchant Marine. These two gentlemen, in a correspondence that stretched out over a period of more than four years, offered many insights and real-life examples of how the realities of life at sea differ from the ideals cherished by regulators and academics. It was an eye-opening experience, to say the least.

Trish Eachus came through once again in her stalwart role as proofreader and advance editor—and as determined as ever to cure me of my run-on sentences, however hopeless a task that may be. Leonard Crabtree was tireless as a researcher, always ready, willing and available to help. Chris Dickerson, a playwright, director, and author in his own right, deserves a nod and a tip of the hat for his service as one of my First Readers; also deserving mention is his help with creating the concept for the cover.

For so much assistance from so many people and institutions, "gratitude" seems to be a somewhat inadequate word; however, mine is deep and abiding, and very genuine. If this book has become greater than the sum of its parts—and I fervently hope it has—it is because of the selflessness with which so many of those parts were provided by the people mentioned here. Whatever information, support, or encouragement they offered me, they did so without any qualification whatsoever. So while it is my name only which appears on the cover, I can never hope to claim sole credit for this work. All to which I will selfishly lay claim is that if there have been any errors, the blame is mine and mine alone. As always, I wouldn't have it any other way.

—Daniel Allen Butler
Los Angeles, California
January 2009

SOURCES AND BIBLIOGRAPHY

GOVERNMENT DOCUMENTS

Great Britain, *Parliamentary Debates* (Commons), 5th series, 37–42, April 15–October 25, 1912.

Great Britain, *Proceedings on a Formal Investigation ordered by the Board of Trade into the loss of the S. S. "Titanic."* HMSO, 1912.

Great Britain, *Report on the Loss of the "Titanic (S.S.),"* HMSO, 1912.

U.S. Congress, Senate, *Hearings of a Subcommittee of the Senate Commerce Committee pursuant to S. Res. 283, to Investigate the Causes leading to the Wreck of the White Star liner "Titanic."* 62nd Congress, 2nd session, 1912, S. Doc. 726 (#6167).

U.S. Congress, Senate, International Conference on Safety of Life at Sea, 63rd Congress, 2nd session 1914, S. Doc. 463 (#6594)

U.S. Congress, Senate, *Report of the Senate Commerce Committee pursuant to S. Res. 283, to Investigate the Causes leading to the Wreck of the White Star liner "Titanic," with speeches by William Alden Smith and Isidor Rayner*, 62nd Congress, 2nd session, May 28, 1912, S. Rept. 806 (#6127)

U.S. Navy Department, "Report of the Hydrographer." *Annual Reports of the Navy Department*, Appendix 3, 193–208. Washington, D.C.: Government Printing Office, 1913.

ARCHIVES

United Kingdom
Harland and Wolff Shipyards, Belfast, Northern Ireland. Historical

Section, *Titanic* Collection (now in the possession of the Ulster Folk and Transport Museum).

National Maritime Museum, Greenwich, London, England. *Titanic* Collection.

Public Records Office, London, England. Documents #BT100/259 (Cargo Manifests); #BT100/260 (Ship's Articles0; #M12266/12 (Order for Formal Investigation); #MT9/920/4 M23780 (Sailing Clearances); #MT9/920/5 M23448 (Request for Hearing by Captain Stanley Lord); #MT15/142 M13505 (Crew Muster).

Southampton Maritime Museum (Wool House), Southampton, Surrey, England. William Burroughs Hill Collection, Stuart Collection, Titanic Archive.

Ulster Folk and Transport Museum, Belfast, Northern Ireland. Department of Archival Collections. R.C.W. Courtney Collection.

United States

Grand Rapids Public Museum, Grand Rapids, Michigan. William Alden Smith Collection.

Library of Congress, Washington, D.C. Manuscript Division. The Presidential Papers of William Howard Taft: Case File # 3175 (*Titanic*).

Mariners Museum, Newport News, Virginia. *Titanic* Collection.

Port Authority of New York, New York City. Collector of Customs Office, Immigration Records, April 1912.

Canada

Public Archives of Nova Scotia, Halifax, Nova Scotia. *Titanic* Collection.

BOOKS

Baarslag, Karl. *SOS to the Rescue.* New York: Oxford University Press, 1935.

Beesley, Lawrence. *The Loss of the SS Titanic.* Boston: Houghton Mifflin, 1912.

Behe, George. *Titanic: Speed, Safety and Sacrifice.* Polo: Transportation Trails, 1997.

Bisset, Sir James. *Ladies and Tramps.* Glasgow: Brown and Ferguson, 1955.

Brinnin, John Malcolm. *The Sway of the Grand Saloon.* New York: Delacorte, 1971.

Bullock, Shan. *Thomas Andrews, Shipbuilder.* Baltimore: Norman, Remington, 1913.

Butler, Daniel Allen. *The Age of Cunard.* Culver City, Lighthouse Press, 2004

_____. *"Unsinkable"–the Full Story of RMS Titanic,* Mechanicsburg, Stackpole Books, 1998.

Davie, Michael. *Titanic: the Death and Life of a Legend.* London: Bodley Head, 1986.

Eaton, John P. and Charles Haas. *Titanic: Triumph and Tragedy.* New York: W. W. Norton, 1988.

Hyslop, Donald, Alistair Forsyth, and Sheila Jemima. *Titanic Voices: Memories of the Fatal Voyage.* New York: St. Martin's Press, 1997.

Jolly, W.P. *Marconi.* New York: Stein & Day, 1972.

Lightoller, C.II. *Titanic and Other Ships.* London: Ivor Nicholson and Watson, 1935.

Lord, Walter. *A Night to Remember.* New York: Holt, Rinehart and Winston, 1955.

_____. *The Good Years.* New York: Harper, 1960.

_____. *The Night Lives On.* New York: William Morrow, 1986.

Marcus, Geoffrey. *The Maiden Voyage.* New York: Viking Press, 1969.

Merideth, Lee. *1912 Facts About the Titanic* (rev. ed.). Sunnyvale, CA: Historical Indexes, 2003.

Padfield, Peter. *The Titanic and the Californian.* New York: John Day, 1965.

Reade, Leslie. *The Ship the Stood Still.* New York: Ingraham Book Company, 1994.

Rostron, Sir Arthur. *Home from the Sea.* London: Hodder and Stoughton, 1937.

Shaw, David W. *The Sea Shall Embrace Them: the Tragic Story of the Steamship Arctic.* New York, The Free Press, 2002.

Wade, Wynn Craig. *Titanic–The End of a Dream.* New York: Penguin books, 1986.

NEWSPAPERS

Boston American
Boston Globe

Boston Post
Detroit Free Press
Detroit News
Glasgow Herald
Grand Rapids Evening Press
Grand Rapids Herald
Grand Rapids News
Illustrated London News
London Daily Express
London Daily Mail
London Daily Telegraph
London Globe
London Morning Post
London Standard
London Times
New York American
New York Evening Mail
New York Herald
New York Sun
New York Times
New York World
Philadelphia North American
Philadelphia Press
Providence Evening Bulletin
Wall Street Journal
Washington Evening Star
Washington Post

INDEX